S0-DUW-380

2006
Moon Sign
Book

Interior Illustrations:
Photographs © IndexOpen
Photographs p. 34, 101 © Getty
Photographs p. 9 © BrandX
Stock photography model(s) used for illustrative purposes only and may
not endorse or represent the book's subject.

Copyright 2005 Llewellyn Worldwide. All rights reserved. Printed in the
U.S.A. Typography owned by Llewellyn Worldwide.
Editor/Designer: Sharon Leah
Cover Design & Art: Kevin R. Brown
Cover Photos © Digital Stock
Special thanks to Aina Allen for astrological proofreading.
ISBN 0-7387-0148-3

Llewellyn is a registered trademark of Llewellyn Worldwide, Ltd.
P.O. Box 64383 Dept. 0148-3
St. Paul, MN 55164-0383 U.S.A.
Printed in the U.S.A.

2006

JANUARY

S	M	T	W	T	F	S
1	2	3	4	5	6	7
8	9	10	11	12	13	14
15	16	17	18	19	20	21
22	23	24	25	26	27	28
29	30	31				

FEBRUARY

S	M	T	W	T	F	S
			1	2	3	4
5	6	7	8	9	10	11
12	13	14	15	16	17	18
19	20	21	22	23	24	25
26	27	28				

MARCH

S	M	T	W	T	F	S
			1	2	3	4
5	6	7	8	9	10	11
12	13	14	15	16	17	18
19	20	21	22	23	24	25
26	27	28	29	30	31	

APRIL

S	M	T	W	T	F	S
						1
2	3	4	5	6	7	8
9	10	11	12	13	14	15
16	17	18	19	20	21	22
23	24	25	26	27	28	29
30						

MAY

S	M	T	W	T	F	S
	1	2	3	4	5	6
7	8	9	10	11	12	13
14	15	16	17	18	19	20
21	22	23	24	25	26	27
28	29	30	31			

JUNE

S	M	T	W	T	F	S
				1	2	3
4	5	6	7	8	9	10
11	12	13	14	15	16	17
18	19	20	21	22	23	24
25	26	27	28	29	30	

JULY

S	M	T	W	T	F	S
						1
2	3	4	5	6	7	8
9	10	11	12	13	14	15
16	17	18	19	20	21	22
23	24	25	26	27	28	29
30	31					

AUGUST

S	M	T	W	T	F	S
		1	2	3	4	5
6	7	8	9	10	11	12
13	14	15	16	17	18	19
20	21	22	23	24	25	26
27	28	29	30	31		

SEPTEMBER

S	M	T	W	T	F	S
					1	2
3	4	5	6	7	8	9
10	11	12	13	14	15	16
17	18	19	20	21	22	23
24	25	26	27	28	29	30

OCTOBER

S	M	T	W	T	F	S
1	2	3	4	5	6	7
8	9	10	11	12	13	14
15	16	17	18	19	20	21
22	23	24	25	26	27	28
29	30	31				

NOVEMBER

S	M	T	W	T	F	S
			1	2	3	4
5	6	7	8	9	10	11
12	13	14	15	16	17	18
19	20	21	22	23	24	25
26	27	28	29	30		

DECEMBER

S	M	T	W	T	F	S
					1	2
3	4	5	6	7	8	9
10	11	12	13	14	15	16
17	18	19	20	21	22	23
24	25	26	27	28	29	30
31						

Table of Contents

Advertise (Internet) • Advertise (Print) • Automobiles •
Animals • Animals (Breed) • Animals (Declaw) •
Animals (Neuter or spay) • Animals (Sell or buy) •
Animals (Train) • Animals (Train dogs to hunt) • Baking
Cakes • Beauty Treatments (Massage, etc.) • Borrow
(Money or goods) • Brewing • Build (Start foundation)
• Business (Start new) • Buy Goods • Canning • Clothing
• Collections • Concrete • Construction (Begin new) •
Consultants (Work with) • Contracts (Bid on) • Copy-
rights/Patents • Coronations and Installations • Culti-
vate • Cut Timber • Decorating or Home Repairs •
Demolition • Dental and Dentists • Dressmaking •
Egg-setting • Electronics (Repair) • Electronics (Buy-
ing) • Electricity and Gas (Install) • Entertain Friends •
Eyes and Eyeglasses • Fence Posts • Fertilize and Com-
post • Find Hidden Treasure • Find Lost Articles •
Fishing • Friendship • Grafting or Budding • Habit
(Breaking) • Haircuts • Harvest Crops • Health •
Home Furnishings (Buy new) • Home (Buy new) •

Home (Make repairs) • Home (Sell) • Job (Start new) •
Legal Matters • Loan (Ask for) • Machinery, Appliances,
or Tools (Buy) • Make a Will • Marriage • Medical
Treatment for the Head • Medical Treatment for the
Eyes • Medical Treatment for the Nose • Mining •
Mow Lawn • Move to New Home • Negotiate • Occupa-
tional Training • Paint • Party (Host or attend) • Pawn •
Pick Mushrooms • Plant • Promotion (Ask for) • Prune
• Reconcile People • Roof a Building • Romance •
Sauerkraut • Select a Child's Sex • Sell or Canvas • Sign
Papers • Spray and Weed • Staff (Fire) • Staff (Hire) •
Stocks (Buy) • Surgical Procedures • Travel (Air) • Travel
(Automobile) • Visit • Wean Children • Weight (Reduce)
• Wine and Drink Other Than Beer • Write

Home, Health, and Leisure Section

To Readers

Llewellyn Worldwide is growing and changing to meet the needs of our readers, as well as the company's need for more space that will allow us to continue providing you with the best known selection of titles in alternative health and healing, astrology, earth-based religions, shamanism, Gnostic Christianity, and Kabbalah. In the summer of 2005, we moved all of our operations into a new building in Woodbury, a nearby suburb, where we will continue with our commitment to provide books and tools for exploring new worlds of mind and spirit to help expand our human potential and spiritual consciousness.

The *Moon Sign Book* has been continuously published since 1905, and we're beginning our second century in print with an updated look that we hope you'll enjoy. We have filled each section with timely, entertaining, and informative articles on a range of subjects from how to increase potential for personal income in Natori Moore's "Finding Money by the Moon," to April Elliott Kent's "New Moon Beginnings," that is a guide to planting "seeds" for new things you may want to include in your own life. And Leeda Alleyn Pacotti's "Here Comes the Bride!" provides new insight into the "marrying man," while Maggie Anderson has some excellent suggestions for low-budget gardening in "The Thrifty Gardener." And back again with his delightful humor is Daniel Brawner, who coaches the guys in his "Quickie Gourmet Cooking Guide for Men." In addition to the many great articles, we are pleased to have Dorothy Kovach writing her economic outlook forecasts for 2006, and to have Kris Brandt Riske's 2006 weather forecasts again this year.

For those of you who want to incorporate the advantages of lunar timing in your lives, we offer the Moon void-of-course tables, retrograde tables, the monthly Moon Tables and Lunar Aspectarian, the Favorable and Unfavorable Days tables; and the best dates for hunting and fishing, setting eggs, planting, and for doing other garden-related activities.

You'll find the various elected activities, which help you decide on the best times to begin things, such as buying a home, signing contracts, entertaining, starting a business, etc., beginning on page 40. And beginning on page 24, you'll find an expanded list of things ruled by the different planets to help you with your important decisions.

If this is the first time you've used the *Moon Sign Book*, you may be wondering how and why it is different from other almanacs. Well, read on.

Our Almanac Is Different from Some Almanacs

Readers have asked why the *Moon Sign Book* says that the Moon is in Taurus, when some almanacs indicate that the Moon is in Aries. It's because there are two different zodiac systems in use today: the tropical and the sidereal. The *Moon Sign Book* is based on the tropical zodiac.

The tropical zodiac takes 0 degrees of Aries to be the Spring Equinox in the Northern Hemisphere. This is the time and date when the Sun is directly overhead at noon along the equator, usually about March 20–21. The rest of the signs are positioned at 30 degree intervals from this point.

The sidereal zodiac, which is based on the location of fixed stars, uses the positions of the fixed stars to determine the starting point of 0 degrees of Aries. In the sidereal system, 0 degrees of Aries always begins at the same point. This does create a problem though, because the positions of the fixed stars, as seen from Earth, have changed since the constellations were named. The term "precession of the equinoxes" is used to describe the change.

Precession of the equinoxes describes an astronomical phenomenon brought about by the Earth's wobble as it rotates and orbits the Sun. The Earth's axis is inclined toward the Sun at an angle of about 23½ degrees, which creates our seasonal weather changes. Although the change is slight, because one complete circle of the Earth's axis takes 25,800 years to complete, we can actually see that the positions of the fixed stars seem to shift. The result is that each year, in the tropical system, the Spring Equinox occurs at a slightly different time.

Does Precession Matter?

There is an accumulative difference of about 23 degrees between the Spring Equinox (0 degrees Aries in the tropical zodiac and 0 degrees Aries in the sidereal zodiac) so that 0 degrees Aries at Spring Equinox in the tropical zodiac actually occurs at about 7 degrees Pisces in the sidereal zodiac system. You can readily see that those who use the other almanacs may be planting seeds (in the garden and in their individual lives) based on the belief that it is occurring in a fruitful sign, such as Taurus, when in fact it would be occurring in Gemini, one of the most barren signs of the zodiac. So, if you wish to plant and plan activities by the Moon, it is helpful to follow the *Moon Sign Book*. Before we go on, there are important things to understand about the Moon, her cycles, and their correlation with everyday living. We'll start by looking at some basic astrological principles.

How Important Is the Moon?

Before we move on, there are other important things to understand about the Moon, her cycles, and their correlation with everyday living. We'll start by looking at some basic astrological principles.

Everyone has seen the Moon wax (increase) and wane (decrease) over a period of approximately twenty-nine days. This succession from New Moon to New Moon is called the lunation cycle. The cycle is divided into parts, called quarters or phases. The astrological system of naming the lunar phases does not always correspond to systems used in other almanacs and calendars. (See explanation on page 7.) It is therefore important to follow only Llewellyn's *Moon Sign Book* or our *Astrological Calendar* for timing events defined in this book.

The Moon is the most important planet in any election. Time and experience have proven that anything started when the Moon is weak by sign and aspect is unlikely to prosper.

What Makes the Moon Weak or Strong?

When astrologers talk about the Moon's strength, they are not referring to physical strength, nor to emotional strength or weakness. The Moon's strength is an assessment of its energy in a particular sign—its attitude—when compared to how the Moon is expressed in Cancer, the sign it rules and where it enjoys its purest form of expression. The Moon is said to be strong in Cancer because her symbolism is closely associated with Cancer's traits of mothering, nurturing, feeling, and intuiting. On the other hand, the Moon's expression in Capricorn is thought to be weak because the qualities of goal setting, detachment, and achieving, which are common to Capricorn, are not in sync with the Moon's natural mode of expression.

When the Moon is not in its home sign of Cancer or the sign of its exaltation, Taurus, its strength is judged according to its position in the chart. If it is in the first, fourth, seventh, or tenth house, it will have more impact on the outcome of the election than it would have if located in the third, sixth, ninth, or twelfth house.

The Moon is considered weak when she is void-of-course (near the end of a sign and not aspecting other planets). Experience has proven that activities begun during a void-of-course Moon often have a different ending than what was expected.

In electional astrology, the worst zodiacal position of the Moon is the 30 degrees referred to as the "Via Combusta" (15 degrees Libra to 15 degrees Scorpio). This is especially unfavorable for buying, selling, traveling, and marrying.

The Moon's affect is weakened if it is in difficult aspect to Saturn, Mars, Uranus, Neptune, or Pluto.

Moon Phases

The Moon's phase is important to the success of your election, too. Some elections will have better success if the Moon is in its waxing (increasing) phase, while other elections will benefit from having the Moon in its waning (decreasing) phase.

The first twelve hours after the exact moment of the New Moon are considered unfavorable for many things. The next seventy-two hours (until the time of the first quarter) are considered favorable. The twelve hours beginning with the exact time of the first quarter are unfortunate. This pattern continues throughout the Moon's cycle.

The Moon Tables (pages 68–90) or Llewellyn's *Astrological Calendar* can show you what sign the Moon is in and when it changes quarter phase; and the tables on pages 95–100 show when it goes void-of-course.

First Quarter

The first quarter begins at the New Moon, when the Sun and Moon are conjoined (the Sun and Moon are in the same degree of the same zodiac sign). The New Moon phase is a time for new beginnings that favor growth and a time to draw things to you. During this phase, the lunar and solar forces work together, pulling things in the same direction. Toward the end of the first quarter is the best time to finalize plans. In nature, it is the time when things germinate and begin to emerge.

Second Quarter

The second quarter begins when the Sun and Moon are ninety degrees apart (about seven days into the lunation cycle), and it ends with the Full Moon. This half Moon rises about noontime and sets near midnight, and it can be seen in the western sky during the first half of the night. It represents growth, development, and the expression of things that already exist.

If your plans are taking shape, concentrate on completing or adding to projects at this time. It should be noted that every thing has its own timeline. Events occurring now may be the result of something initiated in a different lunation cycle, year, or even a different "season" of life.

Third Quarter

The third quarter begins at the Full Moon (about fourteen days into the lunation cycle), when the Sun and Moon are opposite, which allows the Sun's full light to shine on the Moon. Early in this phase, the Moon can be seen rising in the east at sunset, and then rising a little later each evening. The Full Moon stands for illumination, completion, unrest, and using what we worked to create. Toward the end of the third quarter is a time of maturity, fruition, and fulfillment.

Fourth Quarter

The fourth quarter begins about day twenty-one of the lunation cycle, or halfway between the Full Moon and next New Moon. The Sun and Moon are again ninety degrees apart, or in square aspect. A waning Moon rises at midnight and it can be seen in the east during the last half of the night, reaching the overhead position at about the time the Sun is rising. The fourth quarter is a time of disintegration, drawing back for reorganization, reflecting on what has passed, and ridding yourself of what has become unnecessary in order to make room for what is new to come in.

Moon Aspects

The aspects the Moon will make during the times you are considering are also important. A trine or sextile, and sometimes a conjunction, are considered favorable aspects. A trine or sextile between the Sun and Moon is an excellent foundation for success. Whether or not a conjunction is considered favorable depends upon the planet the Moon is making a conjunction to. If it's joining the Sun, Venus, Mercury, Jupiter, or even Saturn, the aspect is favorable. If the Moon joins Pluto or Mars, however, that would not be considered favorable. There may be exceptions, but it would depend on what you are electing to do. For example, a trine to Pluto might hasten the end of a relationship you want to be free of.

It is important to avoid times when the Moon makes an aspect to or is conjoining any retrograde planet, unless, of course, you want the thing started to end in failure.

After the Moon has completed an aspect to a planet, that planetary energy has passed. For example, if the Moon squares Saturn at 10:00 am, you can disregard Saturn's influence on your activity if it will occur after that time. You should always look ahead at aspects the Moon will make on the day in question, though, because if the Moon opposes Mars at 11:30 pm on that day, you can expect events that stretch into the evening to be affected by the Moon-Mars aspect. A testy conversation might lead to an argument, or more.

Moon Signs

Much agricultural work is ruled by earth signs—Virgo, Capricorn, and Taurus; and the air signs—Gemini, Aquarius, and Libra—rule flying and intellectual pursuits.

Each planet has one or two signs in which its characteristics are enhanced or "dignified," and the planet is said to "rule" that sign. The Sun rules Leo and the Moon rules Cancer, for example. The ruling planet for each sign is listed below. These should not be considered complete lists. We recommend that you purchase a book of planetary rulerships for more complete information.

Aries Moon

The energy of an Aries Moon is masculine, dry, barren, and fiery. Aries provides great start-up energy, but things started at this time may be the result of impulsive action that lacks research or necessary support. Aries lacks staying power.

Use this assertive, outgoing Moon sign to initiate change, but have a plan in place for someone to pick up the reins when you're impatient to move on to the next thing. Work that requires skillful, but not necessarily patient, use of tools—hammering, cutting down trees, etc.—is appropriate in Aries. Expect things to occur rapidly but to also quickly pass. If you are prone to injury or accidents, exercise caution and good judgment in Aries-related activities.

RULER: Mars

IMPULSE: Action

RULES: Head and face

PLANTS: Aloe, buttercup, and star thistle

LOCATIONS: Large cities, corner houses, east, east corner rooms, east walls, and entryways

MOST COMPATIBLE WITH: Gemini, Leo, Sagittarius, and Aquarius

Taurus Moon

A Taurus Moon's energy is feminine, semi-fruitful, and earthy. The Moon is exalted—very strong—in Taurus. Taurus is known as the farmer's sign because of its associations with farmland and precipitation that is the typical day-long "soaker" variety. Taurus energy is good to incorporate into your plans when patience, practicality, and perseverance are needed. Be aware, though, that you may also experience stubbornness in this sign.

Things started in Taurus tend to be long lasting and to increase in value. This can be very supportive energy in a marriage election. On the downside, the fixed energy of this sign resists change or the letting go of even the most difficult situations. A divorce following a marriage that occurred during a Taurus Moon may be difficult and costly to end. Things begun now tend to become habitual and hard to alter. If you want to make changes in something you start, it would be better to wait for Gemini. This is a good time to get a loan, but expect the people in charge of money to be cautious and slow to make decisions.

RULER: Venus

IMPULSE: Stability

RULES: Neck, throat, and voice

PLANTS: Columbine, daisy, cow-slip, goldenrod, and violet

LOCATIONS: Quiet places, center rooms, middle of the block, fields, landscaped areas near a building, safes, storerooms, and southeast

MOST COMPATIBLE WITH: Cancer, Virgo, Capricorn, and Pisces

Gemini Moon

A Gemini Moon's energy is masculine, dry, barren, and airy. People are more changeable than usual and may prefer to follow intellectual pursuits and play mental games rather than apply themselves to practical concerns.

This sign is not favored for agricultural matters, but it is an excellent time to prepare for activities, to run errands, and write letters. Plan to use a Gemini Moon to exchange ideas, meet people, go on vacations that include walking or biking, or be in situations that require versatility and quick thinking on your feet.

RULER: Mercury

IMPULSE: Versatility

SIGN RULES: Shoulders, hands, arms, lungs, and nervous system

PLANTS: Ferns, lily of the valley, vervain, yarrow, and woodbine

LOCATIONS: High places, grain elevators, roads of all kinds, subways, schools, and upper rooms

MOST COMPATIBLE WITH: Aries, Leo, Aquarius, and Libra

Cancer Moon

A Cancer Moon's energy is feminine, fruitful, moist, and very strong. Use this sign when you want to grow things—flowers, fruits, vegetables, commodities, stocks, or collections—for example. This sensitive sign stimulates rapport between people. Considered the most fertile of the signs, it is often associated with mothering. You can use this moontime to build personal friendships that support mutual growth.

Cancer is associated with emotions and feelings. Prominent Cancer energy promotes growth, but it can also turn people pouty and prone to withdrawing into their shells.

RULER: The Moon

IMPULSE: Tenacity

RULES: Chest area, breasts, and stomach

PLANTS: Iris, lotus, white rose, white lily, night-blooming and water plants

LOCATIONS: Near water, gardens, shady places, ditches, kitchens, eating areas, grocery stores, warehouses, cellars, north, and north walls

MOST COMPATIBLE WITH: Virgo, Scorpio, Pisces, or Taurus,

Leo Moon

A Leo Moon's energy is masculine, hot, dry, fiery, and barren. Use it whenever you need to put on a show, make a presentation, or entertain colleagues or guests. This is a proud yet playful energy that exudes self-confidence and is often associated with romance.

This is an excellent time for fund-raisers and ceremonies, or to be straight forward, frank, and honest about something. It is advisable not to put yourself in a position of needing public approval or where you might have to cope with underhandedness, as trouble in these areas can bring out the worst Leo traits. There is a tendency in this sign to become arrogant or self-centered.

RULER: The Sun

IMPULSE: I am

RULES: Heart, upper back

PLANTS: Daffodil, dill, poppy, eye-bright, fennel, red rose, mistletoe, marigolds, sunflower, and saffron

LOCATIONS: Outdoors, mountains, ballrooms, castles, dance halls, forests, stadiums, and sunrooms

MOST COMPATIBLE WITH: Aries, Gemini, Libra, and Sagittarius

Virgo Moon

A Virgo Moon is feminine, dry, barren, earthy energy. It is favorable for anything that needs painstaking attention—especially those things where exactness rather than innovation is preferred.

Use this sign for activities when you must analyze information, or when you must determine the value of something. Virgo is the sign of bargain hunting. It's friendly toward agricultural matters with an emphasis on animals and harvesting vegetables. It is an excellent time to care for animals, especially training them and veterinary work.

This sign is most beneficial when decisions have already been made and now need to be carried out. The inclination here is to see details rather than the bigger picture.

There is a tendency in this sign to overdo. Precautions should be taken to avoid becoming too dull from all work and no play. Build a little relaxation and pleasure into your routine from the beginning.

RULER: Mercury

IMPULSE: Discriminating

RULES: Abdomen and intestines

PLANTS: Azalea, lavender, skullcap, woodbine, and grains

LOCATIONS: Rural areas, closets, dairies, gardens, lands that are level and productive, meadows, pantries, sick rooms, rooms that are kept locked, and southwest

MOST COMPATIBLE WITH: Cancer, Scorpio, Capricorn, and Taurus

Libra Moon

A Libra Moon's energy is masculine, semi-fruitful, and airy. This energy will benefit any attempt to bring beauty to a place or thing. Libra is considered good energy for starting things of an intellectual nature. Libra is the sign of partnership and unions, which make it an excellent time to form partnerships of any kind, to make agreements, and to negotiate. Even though this sign is good for initiating things, it is crucial to work with a partner who will provide incentive and encouragement, however. A Libra Moon accentuates teamwork (particularly teams of two) and artistic work (especially work that involves color). Make use of this sign when you are decorating your home or shopping for better quality clothing.

RULER: Venus

IMPULSE: Balance

RULES: Lower back, kidneys, and buttocks

PLANTS: Lemon-thyme, strawberries, flowers

LOCATIONS: Beauty salons, bedrooms, boutiques, corner building facing west, west corner room, west wall of room, garrets, and upper airy rooms

MOST COMPATIBLE WITH: Aquarius, Sagittarius, Gemini, and Leo

Scorpio Moon

The energy of a Scorpio Moon is feminine, fruitful, cold, and moist. It is useful when intensity (that sometimes borders on obsession) is needed. Scorpio is considered a very psychic sign. Use this Moon sign when you must back up something you strongly believe in, such as union or employer relations. There is strong group loyalty here, but a Scorpio Moon is also a good time to end connections thoroughly. This is also a good time to conduct research.

The desire nature is so strong here that there is a tendency to manipulate situations to get what one wants, or to not see one's responsibility in an act.

RULER: Pluto, Mars (traditional)

IMPULSE: Transformation

RULES: Reproductive organs, genitals, groin, and pelvis

PLANTS: Honeysuckle, heather, thistle, wormwood, and poisonous plants

LOCATIONS: Near stagnant water, cemeteries, morgues and mortuaries, drugstores, bathrooms, rubbish dumps, north-east, and northeast walls

MOST COMPATIBLE WITH: Cancer, Virgo, Capricorn, and Pisces

Sagittarius Moon

The Moon's energy is dry, barren, and fiery in Sagittarius, encouraging flights of imagination and confidence in the flow of life. Sagittarius is the most philosophical sign. Candor and honesty are enhanced when the Moon is here. This is an excellent time to "get things off your chest," to deal with institutions of higher learning, publishing companies, and the law. It's also a good time for sport and adventure.

Sagittarians are the crusaders of this world. This is a good time to tackle things that need improvement, but don't try to be the diplomat while influenced by this energy. Opinions can run strong and the tendency to proselytize is increased.

RULER: Jupiter

IMPULSE: Expansion

RULES: Thighs and hips

PLANTS: Mallow, feverfew, holly, and carnation

LOCATIONS: High and airy places, army barracks, banks, churches, foreign countries, universities, racetracks, upper rooms, and ships

MOST COMPATIBLE WITH: Libra, Aries, Leo, and Aquarius

Capricorn Moon

In Capricorn the Moon's energy is feminine, semi-fruitful, and earthy. Because Cancer and Capricorn are polar opposites, the Moon's energy is thought to be weakened here. This energy encourages the need for structure, discipline, and organization. This is a good time to set goals and plan for the future, tend to family business, and to take care of details requiring patience or a businesslike manner. Institutional activities are favored. This sign should be avoided if you're seeking favors as those in authority can be insensitive under this influence.

RULER: Saturn

IMPULSE: Ambitious

RULES: Bones, skin, and knees

PLANTS: Moss, amaranth, plantain, black poppies, and hemlock

LOCATIONS: Abandoned places, old churches, tombs, ore mines, places hard to reach, pyramids, south, south rooms, south wall of room, vaults, and vaulted passages

MOST COMPATIBLE WITH: Taurus, Virgo, and Pisces

Aquarius Moon

An Aquarius Moon's energy is masculine, barren, dry, and airy. Activities that are unique, individualistic, concerned with humanitarian issues, society as a whole, and making improvements are favored under this Moon. It is this quality of making improvements that has caused this sign to be associated with inventors and new inventions.

An Aquarius Moon promotes the gathering of social groups for friendly exchanges. People tend to react and speak from an intellectual rather than emotional viewpoint when the Moon is in this sign.

RULER: Uranus, Saturn

IMPULSE: Reformer

RULES: Calves and ankles

PLANTS: Frankincense

LOCATIONS: High places where there is activity, movie theaters, airplanes, airplane hangers, and lecture halls

MOST COMPATIBLE WITH: Aries, Libra, Sagittarius, and Gemini

Pisces Moon

A Pisces Moon is feminine, fruitful, cool, and moist. This is an excellent time to retreat, meditate, sleep, pray, or make that dreamed-of escape into a fantasy vacation. However, things are not always what they seem to be with the Moon in Pisces. Personal boundaries tend to be fuzzy, and you may not be seeing things clearly. People tend to be idealistic under this sign, which can prevent them from seeing reality.

There is a live and let live philosophy attached to this sign, which in the idealistic world may work well enough, but chaos is frequently the result. That's why this sign is also associated with alcohol and drug abuse, drug trafficking, and counterfeiting. On the lighter side, many musicians and artists are ruled by Pisces. It's only when they move too far away from reality that the dark side of substance abuse, suicide, or crime takes away life.

RULER: Jupiter and Neptune

IMPULSE: Empathetic

RULES: Feet

PLANTS: Water lily, water ferns, and mosses that grow in water

LOCATIONS: Ponds, oceans, convents, gasoline stations, hospitals, institutions, rooms with low ceilings, southeast, southeast wall, and submarines

MOST COMPATIBLE WITH: Taurus, Capricorn, Cancer, and Scorpio

More About Zodiac Signs
Element (Triplicity)

Each of the zodiac signs is classified as belonging to the element of fire, earth, air, or water. These are the four basic elements. The fire signs—Aries, Sagittarius, and Leo—are action oriented, outgoing, energetic, and spontaneous. The earth signs—Taurus, Capricorn, and Virgo—are stable, conservative, practical, and oriented to the physical and material realm. The air signs—Gemini, Aquarius, and Libra—are sociable, critical, and tend to represent intellectual responses rather than feelings. The water signs—Cancer, Scorpio, and Pisces are—are emotional, receptive, intuitive, and can be very sensitive.

Quality (Quadruplicity)

Each zodiac sign is further classified as being cardinal, mutable, or fixed. There are four signs in each quadruplicity, one sign from each element.

Cardinal signs—Aries, Cancer, Libra, and Capricorn—represent beginnings and initiate new action. They initiate each new season in the cycle of the year.

Fixed signs—Taurus, Leo, Scorpio, and Aquarius—want to maintain the status quo through stubbornness and persistence. represent that "between" time. For example, Leo is the month when summer really feels like summer.

Mutable signs—Pisces, Gemini, Virgo, and Sagittarius—adapt to change and tolerate situations. They represent the last month of each season, when things are changing in preparation for the coming season.

Nature and Fertility

In addition to a sign's element and quality, each sign is further classified as either fruitful, semi-fruitful, or barren. This classification is the most important for readers who use the gardening information in the *Moon Sign Book* because the timing of most events depends on the fertility of the sign occupied by the Moon. The water signs of Cancer, Scorpio, and Pisces are the most fruitful. The semi-fruitful signs are the earth signs Taurus and Capricorn, and the air sign Libra. The barren signs correspond to the fire signs Aries, Leo, and Sagittarius; the air signs Gemini and Aquarius; and the earth sign Virgo.

Planetary Rulerships

Each sign and planet rules many things, including specific parts of the body. A bird's nest and the eggs are Moon-ruled, while a small bird is Mercury-ruled, and the maple tree the nest is built in is Jupiter-ruled. A pine tree, on the other hand, is Saturn-ruled. The lists that begin on the following page are not meant to be complete, but they will give you some idea about what activities are ruled over by each planet. We recommend that you refer to a book of planetary and sign rulerships if you are going to use electional astrology. There are several books on planet rulerships available, including Rex E. Bills' *The Rulership Book* and Dr. Lee Lehman's *The Book of Rulerships*. Maria K. Simms' book *A Time for Magick* is another excellent resource if you want help with timing elections.

The Moon

Moon-ruled things are constantly changing, like the tides, emotions, feelings, and fluctuating character. She also rules the public, in general. Other Moon-ruled things include:

Babies
Bakers and bakeries
Bars, bartenders
Baths
Breasts
Cafes
Childbirth
Cleaning
Collectors and collections
Dairies
Domestic life
Ferries
Fish
Fortunetellers
Furniture
Germination
Homes
Houseboats
Kitchens
Land
Landscape gardeners
Lamps
Mariners
Midwives
Monday
Nurses
Oceans
Pantries
Procreation
Public opinion
Reproduction
Water pipes
Water-related occupations
Women, in general

Mercury

Travel is Mercury-ruled, as are most forms of communication. Hard aspects to Mercury or Mercury retrograde may result in lost letters, snarled traffic, delayed mail delivery, and faulty office equipment. Other Mercury-ruled things include:

Advertising
Agents
Amnesia
Animals, small and domestic
Animals, training
Audits
Bookcases
Books and bookstores
Briefcases
Communications
Commuting
Conferences
Contracts
Coughs
Editors

Early education
Employees
Eyeglasses
Fennel
Hay fever
Humor and humorists
Insomnia
Interviews
Invoices
Manuscripts
Neighbors
Research
Telephones
Socializing
Traffic
Vehicles
Veterinarians
Wednesday
Writing
Written agreements

Venus

Venus rules parties and social events, and plans made when Venus is receiving good aspects from other planets are more apt to be successful. When she is receiving less favorable aspects, events are likely to be boring or poorly attended. Other things ruled by Venus include:

Apparel, women's
Art
Art dealers and museums
Artists
Ballrooms
Banks, banking, bankers
Bank notes
Brokers
Brides, bridegrooms
Brotherhoods
Carpets
Cashiers
Chimes
Costumes
Customers
Dressmakers
Friday
Furnishings
Hairdressers
Handicrafts
Gardens, gardeners
Hotels
Interest, interest rates
Jewelry
Maids, servants
Opera, opera singers
Paperhangers
Popularity
Profits
Romance
Shops, shopping
Social gatherings
Vacations
Wallets
Wine

Sun

You will make a more favorable impression when meetings or interviews are scheduled at times the Sun makes a favorable aspect to your natal Ascendant. If the Sun is afflicted by hard aspects to Saturn or Mars, however, business dealings should be avoided. Things ruled by the Sun include:

Authorities
Ballrooms
Bragging
Casinos
Chief executives
Commanders
Confidence
Coronations
Empires
Favors
Foremen
Games, professional
Gambling, gamblers
Grants
Government
Government service
Honors
Leadership
Managers
Moneylenders
Parks, park keepers
Playgrounds
Politicians
Principals
Recreation
Resorts
Self-expression
Showboats
Solariums
Speculation, speculators
Stock brokering
Stock market
Sunday
Theaters

Mars

Avoid or postpone potential confrontations when Mars is squaring a sensitive point in your birthchart as power struggles will likely be the outcome. However, when Mars is transiting your Ascendant, it will often bring a strong sense of self-confidence to you. Mars rules over:

Accidents
Ambition
Ammunition
Arenas
Armed forces
Athletes
Barbers
Battles

Blacksmiths
Blemishes
Carpenters
Chimneys
Crime, criminals
Dentists, dentistry
Enemies
Fire
Firefighters, fire departments
Furnaces
Guards
Leadership
Piercing
Prizefighters
Sports, competitive
Surgery, surgeons
Tattoos
Tools, sharp
Wreckers
Wrenches
Wrestlers

Jupiter

When you make important life changes, Jupiter is the most important planet to consider. Favorable Jupiter aspects are beneficial if you are starting an education program or publishing. Jupiter can bring about excesses such as agreeing to too much, or overspending. Other things Jupiter rules include:

Accumulation
Advertising, long-range
Animals, large
Appraisals, appraisers
Assessors
Attorneys
Banquets
Benefactors
Bondsmen
Capitalism, capitalists
Celebrations
Clergy
Commerce, general
Costumes
Courts of law
Exports
Financial gain
Indorsements
Inheritances
Journeys, long
Law, legal affairs
Plaintiffs
Profits
Publishing
Reimbursement
Shops and shopkeepers
Sports enthusiasts
Taxation
Vows

Saturn

You are apt to succeed at projects that require a long-term

commitment if Saturn is making good aspects to your birth chart when the work begins. If Saturn is squaring your Midheaven or Sun, though, failure is more likely to be the outcome. Saturn-ruled things are:

Abandoned places
Aging people
Archeology
Architects
Bankruptcy
Basements
Barriers
Blood clots
Bones
Builders, buildings in general
Buyers
Cement
Clothing, work
Constrictions
Contraction
Day laborers
Decomposition
Earthy occupations
Embargoes
Employment
Engineers
Farms, farmhands
Foreclosures
Grudges
Government buildings
Harshness

Hoarding
Knees
Landowners
Ore
Reunions
Refrigeration
Rejection
Reservoirs
Saturday
Self-control
Solitude
Subways
Tenements
Watches, watchmakers

Uranus

This energy tends to create unstable conditions. Your ability to adjust to change will determine if the energy is felt positively or negatively. Uranus' ability to time events is impressive. Squares from this planet to your natal planets can bring disruption in your life. Other things Uranus rules include:

Aeronautics
Agitators
Aloofness
Airplanes, airports
Astrologers
Boycotts
Cartoons, cartoonists

Colleagues
Computers
Convulsion
Discrepancies
Electricians
Electricity
Elevators
Explorers
Flying
Free trade
Garages, repair
Gasoline stations
Hearing aids
Helicopters
Highways
Immigration
Inventions
Inversions
Magic and magicians
Mechanisms
Miracles
Music (electronic)
Passports
Radio
Repair people
Research, researchers
Revolution
Science, scientists
Telephones
Television
Transformation
Violations

Neptune

Neptune transits are subtle. Changes that occur under Neptune's influence are so gradual they often go undetected until some time has passed. Neptune rules:

Actors, actresses
Addicts
Admirals
Alcohol, alcoholism
Aquariums
Artists
Baptism
Barges
Bartenders
Baths, bathing
Bayous, bays, beaches
Boats
Butterflies
Camouflage
Charity
Chemicals
Cigarettes
Confessions
Con artists
Drains
Dreams
Espionage
Fog
Liars
Magicians

Missionaries
Obsession
Prisoners
Secrets
Ships
Wasting diseases

Pluto

Pluto transits are profound and have lasting effects. You may experience big changes in life direction when this transit is interacting with your natal birth chart. Pluto rules:

Abduction
Ambulances
Autopsies
Betrayal
Coffins
Coroners
Death
Decay
Destruction
Detectives
Disasters

Espionage
Funerals
Gangs, gang leaders
Garbage
Legacies
Lewdness
Massacres
Pestilence
Petroleum
Plutonium
Poisons
Pornography
Puzzles
Rape
Satire
Septic systems
Snakes
Vandals
Viruses
Wars

Zodiac Signs and Their Corresponding Body Parts

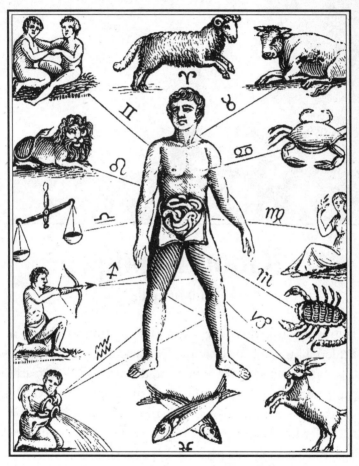

♈	= Aries	♎	= Libra
♉	= Taurus	♏	= Scorpio
♊	= Gemini	♐	= Sagittarius
♋	= Cancer	♑	= Capricorn
♌	= Leo	♒	= Aquarius
♍	= Virgo	♓	= Pisces

Good Timing

by Sharon Leah

E lectional astrology is the art of electing times to begin any
undertaking. Say, for example, you want to start a business.
That business will experience ups and downs, as well as reach its
potential, according to the promise held in the universe at the time
the business was started—its birth time. The horoscope (birth
chart) set for the date, time, and place that a business starts would
indicate the outcome—its potential to succeed.

So, you might ask yourself the question: If the horoscope for a
business start can show success or failure, why not begin at a
time that is more favorable to the venture? Well, you can.

While no time is perfect, there are better times and better days
to undertake specific activities. There are thousands of examples

that prove electional astrology is not only practical, but that it can make a difference in our lives. If you could schedule meetings so that attendees would be awake, attentive, and cooperative, wouldn't you do it? And wouldn't most of us prefer to enjoy the clothing we buy for a longer time than only the day we bought them? There are rules for electing times to begin various activities—even shopping. You'll find detailed instructions about how to make elections beginning on page 40.

Personalizing Elections

The election rules in this almanac are based upon the planetary positions at the time for which the election is made. They do not depend on any type of birth chart. However, a birth chart based upon the time, date, and birthplace of an event has advantages.

Why is a birth chart important if you can make elections without one? Because no election is effective for every person. For example, you may leave home to begin a trip at the same time as a friend, but each of you will have a different experience according to whether or not your birth chart favors the trip.

Not all elections require a birth chart, but the timing of very important events—business starts, marriages, etc.—would benefit from the additional accuracy a birth chart provides. To order a birth chart for yourself or a planned event, visit our Web site at www.llewellyn.com.

Some Things to Consider

You've probably experienced good timing in your life. Maybe you were at the right place at the right time to meet a friend whom you hadn't seen in years. Frequently, when something like that happens, it is the result of following an intuitive impulse—that "gut instinct." Consider for a moment that you were actually responding to planetary energies.Electional astrology is a tool that can help you to align with energies, present and future, that are available to us through planetary placements.

Significificators

Decide upon the important significators (planet, sign, and house ruling the matter) for which the election is being made. The Moon is the most important significator in any election, so the Moon should always be fortified (strong by sign, and making favorable aspects to other planets). The Moon's aspects to other planets are more important than the sign the Moon is in.

Other important considerations are the significators of the Ascendant and Midheaven—the house ruling the election matter, and the ruler of the sign on that house cusp. Finally, any planet or sign that has a general rulership over the matter in question should be taken into consideration. A list of significators (rulerships) begins on page 24.

Nature and Fertility

Determine the general nature of the sign that is appropriate for your election. For example, much agricultural work is ruled by the earth signs of Virgo, Capricorn, and Taurus; while the air signs—Gemini, Aquarius, and Libra—rule intellectual pursuits.

One Final Comment

Use common sense. If you must do something, like plant your garden or take an airplane trip on a day that doesn't have the best aspects, proceed anyway, but try to minimize problems. For example, leave early for the airport to avoid being left behind due to delays in the security lanes. When you have no other choice, do the best that you can under the circumstances at the time.

Planetary Hours

Choosing the "best" time to have an event begin—buying a home, a meeting, marriage, taking a trip—is one of the great benefits you can gain from using electional astrology. You've read that planets have rulership over specific days and things. Planets have rulership over specific times during each day, too.

The astrological day begins at the exact moment of local sunrise in your area, and the night begins at local sunset. The first planetary hour of the day depends on what day of the week it is. Sunday and the first planetary hour of Sunday are ruled by the Sun, the second hour is ruled by the Moon, the third hour by Mars, and so on, until the eighth hour after sunrise, which is again ruled by the Sun.

Monday and the first hour after sunrise on Monday are ruled by the Moon. The second hour is ruled by Mars, the third by Mercury, and so on. Tuesday and the first hour after sunrise on Tuesday are ruled by Mars. Wednesday and the first hour after sunrise on Wednesday are ruled by Mercury. Thursday and the first hour after sunrise on Thursday are ruled by Jupiter. Friday and the first hour after sunrise on Friday are ruled by Venus. Saturday and the first hour after sunrise on Saturday are ruled by Saturn.

The length of a planetary hour varies, depending on the time of the year, because days are longer in summer than they are in winter (in the Northern Hemisphere). So to find the length of a planetary hour, you must first know the length of time between sunrise and sunset in hours and minutes. You divide that time by twelve, which gives you the length of a planetary hour on a specific date. It is easier to work with the time if you convert hours to sixty-minute segments. Divide the total time by twelve. Do the same to find the length of a nighttime planetary hour.

The Advantage of Using Planetary Hours

It is easier and less time consuming to figure out an hour table than it is to learn how to set up an election chart. There are books available, including Maria K. Simms *A Time for Magick* (Llewellyn, 2001), that have the hour tables already figured out for you. You will also find more complete information on planetary hours in the book.

Your may also find information about planetary hours on various Web sites. An Internet search at the time of this writing turned up several resources. It would be best if you conducted your own search, though, because Internet addresses change frequently and without warning.

If you elect to begin an activity that involves writing, for example, you could start the letter or project on a Wednesday (Mercury rules writing and communications), or during a Mercury hour. But if you wanted to begin a courtship or some other activity that involves a woman, choosing to begin on a Friday (Venus rules courtship, women, and matters relating to women) or during a Venus hour would be to your advantage.

Houses in the Horoscope

You'll find this information more useful if you have a horoscope (birth chart) for yourself or the event in question. If you do not have access to a horoscope, please do not attempt to apply these additional qualifications to your elections.

Each house in the horoscope represents an area of life, and the planets found in a house will have direct bearing on the outcome of your elections. For example, if Saturn is in the first house, you might expect something to hinder the election. Things may go slower than expected, there might be restrictions or obstacles you didn't expect, and so on. The planets and their aspects to other planets in other houses also influence the election.

The House Ruling the Election Is Important

The ruling house is the house that relates strongly to your event. If your personal interests are important, you would look to the first house for information. If your concern is about career or reputation, the tenth house would be the ruling house. Following is general list of the houses and what they rule.

- The first house relates to you and your personal interests in an election; the business or organization in question; the home team in sports; the head

- The second house relates to budgets, finances, earnings, and spending power; personal possessions or resources; person(s) who handles financial matters; the ears and throat

- The third house relates to travel by taxi, bus, bike, car, walking, and running; siblings and neighbors; communications; shoulders, arms, lungs, and nervous system

- The fourth house relates to buildings, property, and real estate investments; family, the father; endings; breasts, stomach, and digestive organs

- The fifth house relates to children; recreation and entertaining activities; developing resources and products for speculation; gambling; creative work; the heart and upper part of the back

- The sixth house relates to daily routine, habits, and schedules; employees and labor unions; small animals; personal well-being and illness; the solar plexus and bowels

- The seventh house relates to partnerships, mergers, agreements, your opponent, and competitive relationships; the public; kidneys, ovaries, and lower back

- The eighth house relates to loans, debts, joint finances, profits and losses from death or inheritance, sharing, borrowed money, and investments; divorce; sexuality; the muscular system, bladder, and sex organs

- The ninth house relates to publishing, advertising, and legal matters; foreign travel; higher education; liver and thighs

- The tenth house relates to career, management, status, reputation, one's public image; the government; mothers; the knees

- The eleventh house relates to groups of friends, organizations, and group activities; condition of employer; wishes and expectations; the ankles

- The twelfth house relates to secret activities, plots, and intelligence gathering; confinement, hospitals, institutions; large animals; occult matters; the feet

Choose the Best Time for Your Activities

When rules for elections refer to "favorable" and "unfavorable" aspects to your Sun or other planets, please refer to the Favorable and Unfavorable Days Tables and Lunar Aspectarian for more information. You'll find instructions and the tables beginning on page 61.

The material in this section came from several sources including: *The New A to Z Horoscope Maker and Delineator* by Llewellyn George (Llewellyn, 1999), *Moon Sign Book* (Llewellyn, 1945), and *Electional Astrology* (Slingshot Publishing, 2000) by Vivian Robson. Robson's book was originally published in 1937.

Advertise (Internet)
The Moon should be conjunct, sextile, or trine Mercury or Uranus; and in the sign of Gemini, Capricorn, or Aquarius.

Advertise (Print)
Write ads on a day favorable to your Sun. The Moon should be conjunct, sextile, or trine Mercury or Venus. Avoid hard aspects to Mars and Saturn. Ad campaigns produce the best results when the Moon is well aspected in Gemini (to enhance communication) or Capricorn (to build business).

Automobiles
When buying an automobile, select a time when the Moon is conjunct, sextile, or trine to Mercury, Saturn, or Uranus; and in the sign Gemini or Capricorn.

Animals
Take home new pets when the day is favorable to your Sun, or when the Moon is trine, sextile, or conjunct Mercury, Venus, or

Jupiter, or in the sign of Virgo or Pisces. However, avoid days when the Moon is either square or opposing the Sun, Mars, Saturn, Uranus, Neptune, or Pluto. When selecting a pet, have the Moon well aspected by the planet that rules the animal. Cats are ruled by the Sun, dogs by Mercury, birds by Venus, horses by Jupiter, and fish by Neptune. Buy large animals when the Moon is in Sagittarius or Pisces, and making favorable aspects to Jupiter or Mercury. Buy animals smaller than sheep when the Moon is in Virgo with favorable aspects to Mercury or Venus.

Animals (Breed)

Animals are easiest to handle when the Moon is in Taurus, Cancer, Libra, or Pisces, but try to avoid the Full Moon. To encourage healthy births, animals should be mated so births occur when the Moon is increasing in Taurus, Cancer, Pisces, or Libra. Those born during a semi-fruitful sign (Taurus and Capricorn) will produce leaner meat. Libra yields beautiful animals for showing and racing.

Animals (Declaw)

Declaw cats in the dark of the Moon. Avoid the week before and after the Full Moon and the sign of Pisces.

Animals (Neuter or spay)

Have livestock and pets neutered or spayed when the Moon is in Sagittarius, Capricorn, or Pisces; after it has passed through Scorpio, the sign that rules reproductive organs. Avoid the week before and after the Full Moon.

Animals (Sell or buy)

In either buying or selling, it is important to keep the Moon and Mercury free from any aspect to Mars. Aspects to Mars will create discord and increase the likelihood of wrangling over price and quality. The Moon should be passing from the first quarter to full and sextile or trine Venus or Jupiter. When buying racehorses, let the Moon be in an air sign. The Moon should be in air signs when you buy birds. If the birds are to be pets, let the Moon be in good aspect to Venus.

Animals (Train)

Train pets when the Moon is in Virgo or when the Moon trines Mercury.

Animals (Train dogs to hunt)

Let the Moon be in Aries in conjunction with Mars, which makes them courageous and quick to learn. But let Jupiter also be in aspect to preserve them from danger in hunting.

Baking Cakes

Your cakes will be have a lighter texture if you see that the Moon is in Gemini, Libra, or Aquarius, and in good aspect to Venus or Mercury. If you are decorating a cake or confections are being made, have the Moon placed in Libra.

Beauty Treatments (Massage, etc.)

See that the Moon is in Taurus, Cancer, Leo, Libra, or Aquarius, and in favorable aspect to Venus. In the case of plastic surgery, aspects to Mars should be avoided, and the Moon should not be in the sign ruling the part to be operated on.

Borrow (Money or goods)

See that the Moon is not placed between 15 degrees Libra and 15 degrees Scorpio. Let the Moon be waning and in Leo, Scorpio (16 to 30 degrees), Sagittarius, or Pisces. Venus should be in good aspect to the Moon, and the Moon should not be square, opposing, or conjunct either Saturn or Mars.

Brewing

Start brewing during the third or fourth quarter, when the Moon is in Cancer, Scorpio, or Pisces.

Build (Start foundation)

Turning the first sod for the foundation marks the beginning of the building. For best results, excavate the site when the Moon is in the first quarter of a fixed sign and making favorable aspects to Saturn.

Business (Start new)

When starting a business, have the Moon be in Taurus, Virgo, or Capricorn, and increasing. The Moon should be sextile or trine Jupiter or Saturn, but avoid oppositions or squares. The planet ruling the business should be well aspected, too.

Buy Goods

Buy during the third quarter, when the Moon is in Taurus for quality, or in a mutable sign (Gemini, Sagittarius, Virgo, or Pisces) for savings. Good aspects to Venus or the Sun are desirable. If you are buying for yourself, it is good if the day is favorable for your Sun sign. You may also apply rules for buying specific items.

Canning

Can fruits and vegetables when the Moon is in either the third or fourth quarter, and in the water sign Cancer or Pisces. Preserves and jellies use the same quarters and the signs Cancer, Pisces, or Taurus.

Clothing

Buy clothing on a day that is favorable for your Sun sign, and when Venus or Mercury is well aspected. Avoid aspects to Mars and Saturn. Buy your clothing when the Moon is in Taurus if you want to remain satisfied. Do not buy clothing or jewelry when the Moon is in Scorpio or Aries. See that the Moon is sextile or trine the Sun during the first or second quarters.

Collections

Try to make collections on days when your Sun is well aspected. Avoid days when the Moon is opposing or square Mars or Saturn. If possible, the Moon should be in a cardinal sign (Aries, Cancer, Libra, or Capricorn). It is more difficult to collect when the Moon is in Taurus or Scorpio.

Concrete

Pour concrete when the Moon is in the third quarter of the fixed sign Taurus, Leo, or Aquarius.

Construction (Begin new)

The Moon should be sextile or trine Jupiter. According to Hermes, no building should be begun when the Moon is in Scorpio or Pisces. The best time to begin building is when the Moon is in Aquarius.

Consultants (Work with)

The Moon should be conjunct, sextile, or trine Mercury or Jupiter.

Contracts (Bid on)

The Moon should be in Gemini or Capricorn, and either the Moon or Mercury should be conjunct, sextile, or trine Jupiter.

Copyrights/Patents

The Moon should be conjunct, trine, or sextile Mercury or Jupiter.

Coronations and Installations

Let the Moon be in Leo and in favorable aspect to Venus, Jupiter, or Mercury. The Moon should be applying to these planets.

Cultivate

Cultivate when the Moon is in a barren sign and waning, ideally the fourth quarter in Aries, Gemini, Leo, Virgo, or Aquarius. The third quarter in the sign of Sagittarius will also work.

Cut Timber

Timber cut during the waning Moon does not become worm-eaten, it will season well, and not warp, decay, or snap during burning. Cut when the Moon is in Taurus, Gemini, Virgo, or Capricorn—especially in August. Avoid the water signs. Look for favorable aspects to Mars.

Decorating or Home Repairs

Have the Moon waxing, and in the sign of Libra, Gemini, or Aquarius. Avoid squares or oppositions to either Mars or Saturn. Venus in good aspect to Mars or Saturn is beneficial.

Demolition

Let the waning Moon be in Leo, Sagittarius, or Aries.

Dental and Dentists

Visit the dentist when the Moon is in Virgo, or pick a day marked favorable for your Sun sign. Mars should be marked sextile, conjunct, or trine; and avoid squares or oppositions to Saturn, Uranus, or Jupiter.

Teeth are best removed when the Moon is in Gemini, Virgo, Sagittarius, or Pisces, and during the first or second quarter. Avoid the Full Moon! The day should be favorable for your lunar cycle, and Mars and Saturn should be marked conjunct, trine, or sextile. Fillings should be done in the third or fourth quarters in the sign of Taurus, Leo, Scorpio, or Pisces. The same applies for dentures.

Dressmaking

William Lilly wrote in 1676: "Make no new clothes, or first put them on when the Moon is in Scorpio or afflicted by Mars, for they will be apt to be torn and quickly worn out." Design, repair, and sew clothes in the first and second quarters of Taurus, Leo, or Libra on a day marked favorable for your Sun sign. Venus, Jupiter, and Mercury should be favorably aspected, but avoid hard aspects to Mars or Saturn.

Egg-setting

Eggs should be set so chicks will hatch during fruitful signs. To set eggs, subtract the number of days given for incubation or gestation from the fruitful dates. Chickens incubate in twenty-one days, turkeys and geese in twenty-eight days.

A freshly laid egg loses quality rapidly if it is not handled properly. Use plenty of clean litter in the nests to reduce the number of dirty or cracked eggs. Gather eggs daily in mild weather and at least two times daily in hot or cold weather. The eggs should be placed in a cooler immediately after gathering and stored at 50 to 55° F. Do not store eggs with foods or products that give off pungent odors since eggs may absorb the odors.

Eggs saved for hatching purposes should not be washed. Only clean and slightly soiled eggs should be saved for hatching. Dirty eggs should not be incubated. Eggs should be stored in a cool place with the large ends up. It is not advisable to store the eggs longer than one week before setting them in an incubator.

Electronic (Repair)

The Moon should be sextile or trine Mars or Uranus, and in a fixed sign (Taurus, Leo, Scorpio, Aquarius).

Electronics (Buying)

Choose a day when the Moon is in an air sign (Gemini, Libra, Aquarius) and well aspected by Mercury and/or Uranus when buying electronics.

Electricity and Gas (Install)

The Moon should be in a fire sign, and there should be no squares, oppositions, or conjunctions with Uranus (ruler of electricity), Neptune (ruler of gas), Saturn, or Mars. Hard aspects to Mars can cause fires.

Entertain Friends

Let the Moon be in Leo or Libra and making good aspects to Venus. Avoid squares or oppositions to either Mars or Saturn by the Moon or Venus.

Eyes and Eyeglasses

Have your eyes tested and glasses fitted on a day marked favorable for your Sun sign, and on a day that falls during your favorable lunar cycle. Mars should not be in aspect with the Moon. The same applies for any treatment of the eyes, which should also be started during the Moon's first or second quarter.

Fence Posts

Set posts when the Moon is in the third or fourth quarter of the fixed sign Taurus or Leo.

Fertilize and Compost

Fertilize when the Moon is in a fruitful sign (Cancer, Scorpio, Pisces). Organic fertilizers are best when the Moon is waning. Use chemical fertilizers when the Moon is waxing. Start compost when the Moon is in the fourth quarter in a water sign.

Find Hidden Treasure

Let the Moon be in good aspect to Jupiter or Venus. If you erect a horoscope for this election, place the Moon in the fourth house.

Find Lost Articles

Search for lost articles during the first quarter and when your Sun sign is marked favorable. Also check to see that the planet ruling the lost item is trine, sextile, or conjunct the Moon. The Moon rules household utensils; Mercury rules letters and books; and Venus rules clothing, jewelry, and money.

Fishing

During the summer months, the best time of the day to fish is from sunrise to three hours after, and from two hours before sunset until one hour after. Fish do not bite in cooler months until the air is warm, from noon to 3 pm. Warm, cloudy days are good. The most favorable winds are from the south and southwest. Easterly winds are unfavorable. The best days of the month for fishing are when the Moon changes quarters, especially if the change occurs on a day when the Moon is in a water sign (Cancer, Scorpio, Pisces). The best period in any month is the day after the Full Moon.

Friendship

The need for friendship is greater when the Moon is in Aquarius, or when Uranus aspects the Moon. Friendship prospers when Venus or Uranus is trine, sextile, or conjunct the Moon. The Moon in Gemini facilitates the chance meeting of acquaintances and friends.

Grafting or Budding

Grafting is the process of introducing new varieties of fruit on less desirable trees. For this process you should use the increasing phase of the Moon in fruitful signs such as Cancer, Scorpio, or Pisces. Capricorn may be used, too. Cut your grafts while trees are dormant, from December to March. Keep them in a cool, dark, not too dry or too damp place. Do the grafting before the sap starts to flow and while the Moon is waxing, and preferably while it is in Cancer, Scorpio, or Pisces. The type of plant should determine both cutting and planting times.

Habit (Breaking)

To end an undesirable habit, and this applies to ending everything from a bad relationship to smoking, start on a day when the Moon is in the fourth quarter and in the barren sign of Gemini, Leo, or Aquarius. Aries, Virgo, and Capricorn may be suitable as well, depending on the habit you want to be rid of. Make sure that your lunar cycle is favorable. Avoid lunar aspects to Mars or Jupiter. However, favorable aspects to Pluto are helpful.

Haircuts

Cut hair when the Moon is in Gemini, Sagittarius, Pisces, Taurus, or Capricorn, but not in Virgo. Look for favorable aspects to Venus. For faster growth, cut hair when the Moon is increasing in Cancer or Pisces. To make hair grow thicker, cut when the Moon is full in the signs of Taurus, Cancer, or Leo. If you want your hair to grow more slowly, have the Moon be decreasing in Aries, Gemini, or Virgo, and have the Moon square or opposing Saturn.

Permanents, straightening, and hair coloring will take well if the Moon is in Taurus or Leo and trine or sextile Venus. Avoid hair treatments if Mars is marked as square or in opposition, especially if heat is to be used. For permanents, a trine to Jupiter is helpful. The Moon also should be in the first quarter. Check the lunar cycle for a favorable day in relation to your Sun sign.

Harvest Crops

Harvest root crops when the Moon is in a dry sign (Aries, Leo, Sagittarius, Gemini, Aquarius) and waning. Harvest grain for storage just after the Full Moon, avoiding Cancer, Scorpio, or Pisces. Harvest in the third and fourth quarters in dry signs. Dry crops in the third quarter in fire signs.

Health

A diagnosis is more likely to be successful when the Moon is in Aries, Cancer, Libra, or Capricorn; and less so when in Gemini, Sagittarius, Pisces, or Virgo. Begin a recuperation program when the Moon is in a cardinal or fixed sign and the day is favorable to your Sun sign. Enter hospitals at these times, too. For surgery, see "Surgical Procedures." Buy medicines when the Moon is in Virgo or Scorpio.

Home Furnishings (Buy new)

Saturn days (Saturday) are good for buying, and Jupiter days (Thursday) are good for selling. Items bought on days when Saturn is well aspected tend to wear longer and purchases tend to be more conservative.

Home (Buy new)

If you desire a permanent home, buy when the New Moon is in a fixed sign—Taurus or Leo—for example. Each sign will affect your decision in a different way. A house bought when the Moon is in Taurus is likely to be more practical and have a country look—right down to the split-rail fence. A house purchased when the Moon is in Leo will more likely be a real showplace.

If you're buying for speculation and a quick turnover, be certain that the Moon is in a cardinal sign (Aries, Cancer, Libra, Capricorn). Avoid buying when the Moon is in a fixed sign (Leo, Scorpio, Aquarius, Taurus).

Home (Make repairs)

In all repairs, avoid squares, oppositions, or conjunctions to the planet ruling the place or thing to be repaired. For example, bathrooms are ruled by Scorpio and Cancer. You would not want to start a project in those rooms when the Moon or Pluto is receiving hard aspects. The front entrance, hall, dining room, and porch are ruled by the Sun. So you would want to avoid times when Saturn or Mars are square, opposing, or conjunct the Sun. Also, let the Moon be waxing.

Home (Sell)
Make a strong effort to list your property for sale when the Sun is marked favorable in your sign and in good aspect to Jupiter. Avoid adverse aspects to as many planets as possible.

Job (Start new)
Jupiter and Venus should be sextile, trine, or conjunct the Moon. A day when your Sun is receiving favorable aspects is preferred.

Legal Matters
Good Moon-Jupiter aspects improve the outcome in legal decisions. To gain damages through a lawsuit, begin the process during the increasing Moon. To avoid paying damages, a court date during the decreasing Moon is desirable. Good Moon-Sun aspects strengthen your chance of success. A well-aspected Moon in Cancer or Leo, making good aspects to the Sun, brings the best results in custody cases. In divorce cases, a favorable Moon-Venus aspect is best.

Loan (Ask for)
A first and second quarter phase favors the lender, the third and fourth quarters favor the borrower. Good aspects of Jupiter and Venus to the Moon are favorable to both, as is having the Moon in Leo or Taurus.

Machinery, Appliances, or Tools (Buy)
Tools, machinery, and other implements should be bought on days when your lunar cycle is favorable and when Mars and Uranus are trine, sextile, or conjunct the Moon. Any quarter of

the Moon is suitable. When buying gas or electrical appliances, the Moon should be in Aquarius.

Make a Will

Let the Moon be in a fixed sign (Taurus, Leo, Scorpio, or Aquarius) to ensure permanence. If the Moon is in a cardinal sign (Aries, Cancer, Libra, or Capricorn), the will could be altered. Let the Moon be waxing—increasing in light—and in good aspect to Saturn, Venus, or Mercury. In the case the will is made in an emergency during illness, and the Moon is slow in motion, void-of-course, combust, or under the Sun's beams, the testator will die and the will remain unaltered. There is some danger that it will be lost or stolen, however.

Marriage

The best time for marriage to take place is when the Moon is increasing, but not yet full. Good signs for the Moon to be in are Taurus, Cancer, Leo, or Libra.

The Moon in Taurus produces the most steadfast marriages, but if the partners later want to separate, they may have a difficult time. Make sure that the Moon is well aspected, especially to Venus or Jupiter. Avoid aspects to Mars, Uranus, or Pluto, and the signs Aries, Gemini, Virgo, Scorpio, or Aquarius.

The values of the signs are as follows:

- Aries is not favored for marriage
- Taurus from 0 to 19 degrees is good, the remaining degrees are less favorable
- Cancer is unfavorable unless you are marrying a widow
- Leo is favored, but it may cause one party to deceive the other as to his or her money or possessions
- Virgo is not favored except when marrying a widow
- Libra is good for engagements but not for marriage
- Scorpio from 0 to 15 degrees is good, but the last fifteen

degrees are entirely unfortunate. The woman may be fickle, envious, and quarrelsome
- Sagittarius is neutral
- Capricorn, from 0 to 10 degrees, is difficult for marriage; however, the remaining degrees are favorable, especially when marrying a widow
- Aquarius is not favored
- Pisces is favored, although marriage under this sign can incline a woman to chatter a lot

These effects are strongest when the Moon is in the sign. If the Moon and Venus are in a cardinal sign, happiness between the couple may not continue long.

On no account should the Moon apply to Saturn or Mars, even by good aspect.

Medical Treatment for the Head

If possible, have Mars and Saturn free of hard aspects. Let the Moon be in Aries or Taurus, decreasing in light, in conjunction or aspect with Venus or Jupiter, and free of hard aspects. The Sun should not be in any aspect to the Moon.

Medical Treatment for the Eyes

Let the Moon be increasing in light and motion and making favorable aspects to Venus or Jupiter, and be unaspected by Mars. Keep the Moon out of Taurus, Capricorn, or Virgo. If an aspect between the Moon and Mars is unavoidable, let it be separating.

Medical Treatment for the Nose

Let the Moon be in Cancer, Leo, or Virgo, and not aspecting Mars or Saturn, and not in conjunction with a weak or retrograde planet.

Mining

Saturn rules mining. Begin work when Saturn is marked conjunct, trine, or sextile. Mine for gold when the Sun is marked conjunct, trine, or sextile. Mercury rules quicksilver, Venus rules copper, Jupiter rules tin, Saturn rules lead and coal, Uranus rules radioactive elements, Neptune rules oil, the Moon rules water. Mine for these items when the ruling planet is marked conjunct, trine, or sextile.

Mow Lawn

Mow in the first and second quarters (waxing phase) to increase growth and lushness, and in the third and fourth quarters (waning phase) to decrease growth.

Move to New Home

If you have a choice, and sometimes we don't, make sure that Mars is not aspecting the Moon. Move on a day favorable to your Sun sign, or when the Moon is conjunct, sextile, or trine the Sun.

Negotiate

When you are choosing a time to negotiate, consider what the meeting is about and what you want to have happen. If it is agreement or compromise between two parties that you desire, have the Moon be in the sign of Libra. When you are making contracts, it is best to have the Moon in  the same element. For example, if your concern is communication, then elect a time when the Moon is in an air sign. If, on the other hand, your concern is about possessions, an earth sign would be more appropriate. Fixed signs are unfavorable, with the exception of Leo; so are cardinal signs, except for Capricorn. If you are negotiating the end of something, use the rules that apply to ending habits.

Occupational Training

When you begin training, see that your lunar cycle is favorable that day, and that the planet ruling your occupation is marked conjunct or trine.

Paint

Paint buildings during the waning Libra or Aquarius Moon. If the weather is hot, paint when the Moon is in Taurus. If the weather is cold, paint when the Moon is in Leo. Schedule the painting to start in the fourth quarter as the wood is drier and paint will penetrate wood better. Avoid painting around the New Moon, though, as the wood is likely to be damp, making the paint subject to scalding when hot weather hits it. If the temperature is below 70° F, it is not advisable to paint while the Moon is in Cancer, Scorpio, or Pisces as the paint is apt to creep, check, or run.

Party (Host or attend)

A party timed so the Moon is in Gemini, Leo, Libra, or Sagittarius, with good aspects to Venus and Jupiter, will be fun and well attended. There should be no aspects between the Moon and Mars or Saturn.

Pawn

Do not pawn any article when Jupiter is receiving a square or opposition from Saturn or Mars, or when Jupiter is within seventeen degrees of the Sun, for you will have little chance to redeem the items.

Pick Mushrooms

Mushrooms, one of the most promising traditional medicines in the world, should be gathered at the Full Moon.

Plant

Root crops, like carrots and potatoes, are best if planted in the sign Taurus or Capricorn. Beans, peas, tomatoes, peppers, and other fruit-bearing plants are best if planted in a sign that supports seed growth. Leaf plants, like lettuce, broccoli, or cauliflower, are best planted when the Moon is in a water sign.

It is recommended that you transplant during a decreasing Moon, when forces are streaming into the lower part of the plant. This helps root growth. For complete instructions on planting by the Moon, see Gardening by the Moon on page 262, A Guide to Planting (pages 271–76), Gardening Dates (pages 306–13), and Companion Planting Guide (pages 317–19).

Promotion (Ask for)

Choose a day favorable to your Sun sign. Mercury should be marked conjunct, trine, or sextile. Avoid days when Mars or Saturn is aspected.

Prune

Prune during the third and fourth quarter of a Scorpio Moon to retard growth and to promote better fruit. Prune when the Moon is in cardinal Capricorn to promote healing.

Reconcile with People

If the reconciliation be with a woman, let Venus be strong and well aspected. If elders or superiors are involved, see that Saturn is receiving good aspects; if the reconciliation is between young people or between an older and younger person, see that Mercury is well aspected.

Roof a Building

Begin roofing a building during the third or fourth quarter, when the Moon is in Aries or Aquarius. Shingles laid during the New Moon have a tendency to curl at the edges.

Romance

There is less control of when a romance starts, but romances begun under an increasing Moon are more likely to be permanent or satisfying, while those begun during the decreasing Moon will tend to transform the participants. The tone of the relationship can be guessed from the sign the Moon is in. Romances begun with the Moon in Aries may be impulsive. Those begun in Capricorn will take greater effort to bring to a desirable conclusion, but they may be very rewarding. Good aspects between the Moon and Venus will have a positive influence on the relationship. Avoid unfavorable aspects to Mars, Uranus, and Pluto. A decreasing Moon, particularly the fourth quarter, facilitates ending a relationship, and causes the least pain.

Sauerkraut

The best-tasting sauerkraut is made just after the Full Moon in the fruitful signs of Cancer, Scorpio, or Pisces.

Select a Child's Sex

Count from the last day of menstruation to the first day of the next cycle and divide the interval between the two dates in half. Pregnancy in the first half produces females, but copulation should take place with the Moon in a feminine sign. Pregnancy in the latter half, up to three days before the beginning of menstruation, produces males, but copulation should take place with the Moon in a masculine sign. The three-day period before the next period again produces females.

Sell or Canvas

Begin these activities during a day favorable to your Sun sign. Otherwise, sell on days when Jupiter, Mercury, or Mars is trine, sextile, or conjunct the Moon. Avoid days when Saturn is square or opposing the Moon, for that always hinders business and causes discord. If the Moon is passing from the first quarter to full, it is best to have the Moon swift in motion and in good aspect with Venus and/or Jupiter.

Sign Papers

Sign contracts or agreements when the Moon is increasing in a fruitful sign and on a day when the Moon is making favorable aspects to Mercury. Avoid days when Mars, Saturn, or Neptune are square or opposite the Moon.

Spray and Weed

Spray pests and weeds during the fourth quarter when the Moon is in the barren sign Leo or Aquarius, and making favorable aspects to Pluto. Weed during a waning Moon in a barren sign. For the best days to kill weeds and pests, see pages 314–15.

Staff (Fire)

Have the Moon in the third or fourth quarter, but not full. The Moon should not be square any planets.

Staff (Hire)

The Moon should be in the first or second quarter, and preferably in the sign of Gemini or Virgo. The Moon should be conjunct, trine, or sextile Mercury or Jupiter.

Stocks (Buy)

The Moon should be in Taurus or Capricorn, and there should be a sextile or trine to Jupiter or Saturn.

Surgical Procedures

Blood flow, like ocean tides, appears to be related to Moon phases. To reduce hemorrhage after a surgery, schedule it within one week before or after a New Moon. Schedule surgery to occur during the increase of the Moon if possible, as wounds heal better and vitality is greater than during the decrease of the Moon. Avoid surgery within one week before or after the Full Moon.

Select a date when the Moon is past the sign governing the part of the body involved in the operation. For example, abdominal operations should be done when the Moon is in Sagittarius, Capricorn, or Aquarius. To find the signs and the body parts they rule, turn to the chart on page 31. The further removed the Moon sign is from the sign ruling the afflicted part of the body, the better.

For successful operations, avoid times when the Moon is applying to any aspect of Mars. (This tends to promote inflammation and complications.) See the Lunar Aspectarian on pages 69–91 to find days with negative Mars aspects and positive Venus and Jupiter aspects. Never operate with the Moon in the same sign as a person's Sun sign or Ascendant. Let the Moon be in a fixed sign and avoid square or opposing aspects. The Moon should not be void-of-course.

Cosmetic surgery should be done in the increase of the Moon, when the Moon is not square or in opposition to Mars. Avoid days when the Moon is square or opposing Saturn or the Sun.

Travel (Air)

Start long trips when the Moon is making favorable aspects to the Sun. For enjoyment, aspects to Jupiter are preferable; for visiting, look for favorable aspects to Mercury. To prevent accidents, avoid squares or oppositions to Mars, Saturn, Uranus, or Pluto. Choose a day when the Moon is in Sagittarius or Gemini and well aspected to Mercury, Jupiter, or Uranus. Avoid adverse aspects of Mars, Saturn, or Uranus.

Travel (Automobile)

Start your journey on a day when the Moon is not in a fixed sign, and when it is marked favorable to your ruler, or to Mercury or Uranus. For automobile travels, choose a day when the Moon is in Gemini and making good aspects to Mercury.

If a speedy return from a journey is desired, have Jupiter square the Sun and Venus in sextile to Jupiter, or place the Moon in Leo increasing in light and motion.

Visit

On setting out to visit a person, let the Moon be in aspect with any retrograde planet, for this ensures that the person you're visiting will be at home. If you desire to stay a long time in a place, let the Moon be in good aspect to Saturn. If you desire to leave the place quickly, let the Moon be in a cardinal sign.

Wean Children

To wean a child successfully, do so when the Moon is in Sagittarius, Capricorn, Aquarius, or Pisces—signs that do not rule vital human organs. By observing this astrological rule, much trouble for parents and child may be avoided.

Weight (Reduce)

If you want to lose weight, the best time to get started is when the Moon is in the third or fourth quarter, and in the barren sign of Virgo. Review the section on How to Use the Moon Tables and Lunar Aspectarian beginning on page 61 to help you select a date that is favorable to begin your weight-loss program.

Wine and Drink Other Than Beer

It is best to start brewing when the Moon is in Pisces or Taurus. Sextiles or trines to Venus are favorable, but avoid aspects to Mars or Saturn.

Write

Write for pleasure or publication when the Moon is in Gemini. Mercury should be making favorable aspects to Uranus and Neptune.

How to Use the Moon Tables and Lunar Aspectarian

Timing activities is one of the most important things you can do to ensure success. In many eastern countries, timing by the planets is so important that practically no event takes place without first setting up a chart for it. Weddings have occurred in the middle of the night because the influences were best then. You may not want to take it that far, but you can still make use of the influences of the Moon whenever possible. It's easy and it works!

In the *Moon Sign Book* is information to help you plan just about any activity: weddings, fishing, making purchases, cutting your hair, traveling, and more. We provide the guidelines you need to pick the best day out of the several from which you have to choose. The Moon Tables are the *Moon Sign Book's* primary method for choosing dates. Following are instructions, examples, and directions on how to read the Moon Tables. More advanced information on using the tables containing the Lunar Aspectarian and favorable and unfavorable days (found on odd-numbered pages opposite the Moon Tables), Moon void-of-course, and retro-grade information to choose the dates best for you is also included.

We highly recommend reading the sections of this book called Our Almanac is Different from Some Almanacs on page 7, How Important Is the Moon? on page 9, Moon Void-of-Course on page 94, and Retrograde Periods on page 103. It's not essential that you read these before you try the examples below, but reading them will deepen your understanding of the date-choosing process.

The Five Basic Steps

Step 1: Directions for Choosing Dates

Look up the directions for choosing dates for the activity that you wish to begin, then go to step 2.

Step 2: Check the Moon Tables

You'll find two tables for each month of the year beginning on page 68. The Moon Tables (on the left-hand pages) include the day, date, and sign the Moon is in; the element and nature of the sign; the Moon's phase; and when it changes sign or phase. If there is a time listed after a date, that time is the time when the Moon moves into that zodiac sign. Until then, the Moon is considered to be in the sign for the previous day.

The abbreviation Full signifies Full Moon and New signifies New Moon. The times listed with dates indicate when the Moon changes sign. The times listed after the phase indicate when the Moon changes phase.

Turn to the month you would like to begin your activity. You will be using the Moon's sign and phase information most often when you begin choosing your own dates. Use the Time Zone Conversions map and table on pages 92–93 to convert time to your own time zone.

When you find dates that meet the criteria for the correct Moon phase and sign for your activity, you may have completed the process. For certain simple activities, such as getting a haircut, the phase and sign information is all that is needed. If the directions for your activity include information on certain lunar aspects, however, you should consult the Lunar Aspectarian. An example of this would be if the directions told you not to perform a certain activity when the Moon is square (Q) Jupiter.

Step 3: Check the Lunar Aspectarian

On the pages opposite the Moon Tables you will find tables containing the Lunar Aspectarian and Favorable and Unfavorable Days. The Lunar Aspectarian gives the aspects (or angles) of the Moon to other planets. Some aspects are favorable, while others are not. To use the Lunar Aspectarian, find the planet that the directions list as favorable for your activity, and run down the column to the date desired. For example, you should avoid aspects to Mars if you are planning surgery. So you would look for Mars across the top and then run down that column looking for days where there are no aspects to Mars (as signified by empty boxes). If you want to find a favorable aspect (sextile (X) or trine (T)) to Mercury, run your finger down the column under Mercury until you find an X or T. Adverse aspects to planets are squares (Q) or oppositions (O). A conjunction (C) is sometimes beneficial, sometimes not, depending on the activity or planets involved.

Step 4: Favorable and Unfavorable Days

The tables listing favorable and unfavorable days are helpful when you want to choose your personal best dates because your Sun sign is taken into consideration. The twelve Sun signs are listed on the right side of the tables. Once you have determined which days meet your criteria for phase, sign, and aspects, you can determine whether or not those days are positive for you by checking the favorable and unfavorable days for your Sun sign.

To find out if a day is positive for you, find your Sun sign and then look down the column. If it is marked F, it is very favorable.

The Moon is in the same sign as your Sun on a favorable day. If it is marked f, it is slightly favorable; U is very unfavorable; and u means slightly unfavorable. A day marked very unfavorable (U) indicates that the Moon is in the sign opposing your Sun.

Once you have selected good dates for the activity you are about to begin, you can go straight to the examples section beginning on the next page. To learn how to fine-tune your selections even further, read on.

Step 5: Void-of-Course Moon and Retrogrades

This last step is perhaps the most advanced portion of the procedure. It is generally considered poor timing to make decisions, sign important papers, or start special activities during a Moon void-of-course period or during a Mercury retrograde. Once you have chosen the best date for your activity based on steps one through four, you can check the Void-of-Course tables, beginning on page 95, to find out if any of the dates you have chosen have void periods.

The Moon is said to be void-of-course after it has made its last aspect to a planet within a particular sign, but before it has moved into the next sign. Put simply, the Moon is "resting" during the void-of-course period, so activities initiated at this time generally don't come to fruition. You will notice that there are many void periods during the year, and it is nearly impossible to avoid all of them. Some people choose to ignore these altogether and do not take them into consideration when planning activities.

Next, you can check the Retrograde Periods tables on page 103 to see what planets are retrograde during your chosen date(s).

A planet is said to be retrograde when it appears to move backward in the sky as viewed from the Earth. Generally, the farther a planet is away from the Sun, the longer it can stay retrograde. Some planets will retrograde for several months at a time. Avoiding retrogrades is not as important in lunar planning as avoiding the Moon void-of-course, with the exception of the planet Mercury.

Mercury rules thought and communication, so it is advisable not to sign important papers, initiate important business or legal work, or make crucial decisions during these times. As with the Moon void-of-course, it is difficult to avoid all planetary retrogrades when beginning events, and you may choose to ignore this step of the process. Following are some examples using some or all of the steps outlined above.

Using What You've Learned

Let's say it's a new year and you want to have your hair cut. It's thin and you would like it to look fuller, so you find the directions for hair care and you see that for thicker hair you should cut hair while the Moon is Full and in the sign of Taurus, Cancer, or Leo. You should avoid the Moon in Aries, Gemini, or Virgo. Look at the January Moon Table on page 68. You see that the Full Moon is on January 14 at 4:48 am. The Moon moves into the sign of Leo that same day, and remains in Leo until January 17 at 4:49 am; so January 14–16 meets both the phase and sign criteria.

Let's move on to a more difficult example using the sign and phase of the Moon. You want to buy a permanent home. After checking the instructions for purchasing a house: "Home (Buy new)" on page 50. You see that you should buy a home when the Moon is in Taurus, Cancer, or Leo. You need to get a loan, so you should also look under "Loan (Ask for)" on page 51.Here it says that the third and fourth quarters favor the borrower (you). You are going to buy the house in May so go to page 76. The Moon is in the third quarter May 14–19, the fourth quarter May 20–26. The Moon is in Taurus from 12:00 pm on May 24 until 3:19 pm on May 26. The best days for obtaining a loan would be May 24–25, while the Moon is in Taurus.

Just match up the best sign and phase (quarter) to come up with the best date. With all activities, be sure to check the favorable and unfavorable days for your Sun sign in the table adjoining the Lunar Aspectarian. If there is a choice between several dates, pick the one most favorable for you. Because buying a home is an important business decision, you may also wish to see if the Moon is void or if Mercury is retrograde during these dates.

Now let's look at an example that uses signs, phases, and aspects. Our example is starting new home construction. We will use month of June. Look under "Build (Start foundation)" on page 43 and you'll see that the Moon should be in the first quarter of Taurus or Leo. You should select a time when the Moon is not making unfavorable aspects to Saturn. (Conjunctions are usually considered good if they are not to Mars, Saturn, or Neptune.) Look in the June Moon Table. You will see that the Moon is in the first quarter June 1–2 and June 26–30. The Moon is in Leo until 4:17 pm on June 2, and from 1:09 pm on June 27 until 12:15 pm on June 29. Now, look to the Lunar Aspectarian for June. We see that there are no squares or oppositions to Saturn on any of these dates, but there is a conjunction with Mars on June 28. If you wanted to start building your house in June, the best dates would be June 1, 2, 26, 27, 29, or 30.

A Note About Time and Time Zones

All tables in the *Moon Sign Book* use Eastern Time. You must calculate the difference between your time zone and the Eastern Time Zone. Please refer to the Time Zone Conversions chart on page 93 for help with time conversions.

How Does the Time Matter?

Due to the three-hour time difference between the east and west coasts of the United States, those of you living on the East Coast may be, for example, under the influence of a Virgo Moon, while those of you living on the West Coast will still have a Leo Moon influence.

We follow a commonly held belief among astrologers: whatever sign the Moon is in at the start of a day—12:00 am Eastern Time—is considered the dominant influence of the day. That sign is indicated in the Moon Tables. If the date you select for an activity shows the Moon changing signs, you can decide how important the sign change may be for your specific election and adjust your election date and time accordingly.

Use Common Sense

Some activities depend on outside factors. Obviously, you can't go out and plant when there is a foot of snow on the ground. You should adjust to the conditions at hand. If the weather was bad during the first quarter, when it was best to plant crops, do it during the second quarter while the Moon is in a fruitful sign. If the Moon is not in a fruitful sign during the first or second quarter, choose a day when it is in a semi-fruitful sign. The best advice is to choose either the sign or phase that is most favorable, when the two don't coincide.

To Summarize

First, look up the activity under the proper heading, then look for the information given in the tables (the Moon Tables, Lunar Aspectarian, or Favorable and Unfavorable Days). Choose the best date considering the number of positive factors in effect. If most of the dates are favorable, there is no problem choosing the one that will fit your schedule. However, if there aren't any really good dates, pick the ones with the least number of negative influences. Please keep in mind that the information found here applies in the broadest sense to the events you want to plan or are considering. To be the most effective, when you use electional astrology, you should also consider your own birthchart in relation to a chart drawn for the time or times you have under consideration. The best advice we can offer you is: read the entire introduction to each section.

January Moon Table

Date	Sign	Element	Nature	Phase
1 Sun. 7:14 am	Aquarius	Air	Barren	1st
2 Mon.	Aquarius	Air	Barren	1st
3 Tue. 7:43 am	Pisces	Water	Fruitful	1st
4 Wed.	Pisces	Water	Fruitful	1st
5 Thu. 9:44 am	Aries	Fire	Barren	1st
6 Fri.	Aries	Fire	Barren	2nd 1:56 pm
7 Sat. 2:09 pm	Taurus	Earth	Semi-fruitful	2nd
8 Sun.	Taurus	Earth	Semi-fruitful	2nd
9 Mon. 8:58 pm	Gemini	Air	Barren	2nd
10 Tue.	Gemini	Air	Barren	2nd
11 Wed.	Gemini	Air	Barren	2nd
12 Thu. 5:50 am	Cancer	Water	Fruitful	2nd
13 Fri.	Cancer	Water	Fruitful	2nd
14 Sat. 4:31 pm	Leo	Fire	Barren	Full 4:48 am
15 Sun.	Leo	Fire	Barren	3rd
16 Mon.	Leo	Fire	Barren	3rd
17 Tue. 4:49 am	Virgo	Earth	Barren	3rd
18 Wed.	Virgo	Earth	Barren	3rd
19 Thu. 5:49 pm	Libra	Air	Semi-fruitful	3rd
20 Fri.	Libra	Air	Semi-fruitful	3rd
21 Sat.	Libra	Air	Semi-fruitful	3rd
22 Sun. 5:28 am	Scorpio	Water	Fruitful	4th 10:14 am
23 Mon.	Scorpio	Water	Fruitful	4th
24 Tue. 1:38 pm	Sagittarius	Fire	Barren	4th
25 Wed.	Sagittarius	Fire	Barren	4th
26 Thu. 5:31 pm	Capricorn	Earth	Semi-fruitful	4th
27 Fri.	Capricorn	Earth	Semi-fruitful	4th
28 Sat. 6:09 pm	Aquarius	Air	Barren	4th
29 Sun.	Aquarius	Air	Barren	New 9:15 am
30 Mon. 5:32 pm	Pisces	Water	Fruitful	1st
31 Tue.	Pisces	Water	Fruitful	1st

Aspectarian/Favorable & Unfavorable Days

	Sun	Mercury	Venus	Mars	Jupiter	Saturn	Uranus	Neptune	Pluto	Aries	Taurus	Gemini	Cancer	Leo	Virgo	Libra	Scorpio	Sagittarius	Capricorn	Aquarius	Pisces
1			C			0				u	f		U		f	u	f		F		f
2				Q	Q			C	X	f	u	f		U		f	u	f		F	
3		X				C				f	u	f		U		f	u	f		F	
4	X			X	T						f	u	f		U		f	u	f		F
5		Q	X						Q		f	u	f		U		f	u	f		F
6	Q				T			X		F		f	u	f		U		f	u	f	
7		Q						T		F		f	u	f		U		f	u	f	
8		T		C	0	Q	X		Q		F		f	u	f		U		f	u	f
9	T		T								F		f	u	f		U		f	u	f
10					X	Q				f		F		f	u	f		U		f	u
11						T	0			f		F		f	u	f		U		f	u
12						T				f		F		f	u	f		U		f	u
13		0		X	T					u	f		F		f	u	f		U		f
14	0		0							u	f		F		f	u	f		U		f
15			Q	Q	C					f	u	f		F		f	u	f		U	
16							0	T		f	u	f		F		f	u	f		U	
17							0			f	u	f		F		f	u	f		U	
18		T	T	X							f	u	f		F		f	u	f		U
19	T	T							Q		f	u	f		F		f	u	f		U
20				X						U		f	u	f		F		f	u	f	
21		Q					T	X		U		f	u	f		F		f	u	f	
22	Q	Q				Q	T			U		f	u	f		F		f	u	f	
23			X	0	C			Q			U		f	u	f		F		f	u	f
24	X	X									U		f	u	f		F		f	u	f
25						T	Q	X		f		U		f	u	f		F		f	u
26									C	f		U		f	u	f		F		f	u
27			C	X		X				u	f		U		f	u	f		F		f
28			T							u	f		U		f	u	f		F		f
29	C	C			Q	0		C		f	u	f		U		f	u	f		F	
30			Q						X	f	u	f		U		f	u	f		F	
31			X		T		C				f	u	f		U		f	u	f		F

February Moon Table

Date	Sign	Element	Nature	Phase
1 Wed. 5:46 pm	Aries	Fire	Barren	1st
2 Thu.	Aries	Fire	Barren	1st
3 Fri. 8:31 pm	Taurus	Earth	Semi-fruitful	1st
4 Sat.	Taurus	Earth	Semi-fruitful	1st
5 Sun.	Taurus	Earth	Semi-fruitful	2nd 1:29 am
6 Mon. 2:32 am	Gemini	Air	Barren	2nd
7 Tue.	Gemini	Air	Barren	2nd
8 Wed. 11:33 am	Cancer	Water	Fruitful	2nd
9 Thu.	Cancer	Water	Fruitful	2nd
10 Fri. 10:44 pm	Leo	Fire	Barren	2nd
11 Sat.	Leo	Fire	Barren	2nd
12 Sun.	Leo	Fire	Barren	Full 11:44 pm
13 Mon. 11:13 am	Virgo	Earth	Barren	3rd
14 Tue.	Virgo	Earth	Barren	3rd
15 Wed.	Virgo	Earth	Barren	3rd
16 Thu. 12:09 am	Libra	Air	Semi-fruitful	3rd
17 Fri.	Libra	Air	Semi-fruitful	3rd
18 Sat. 12:11 pm	Scorpio	Water	Fruitful	3rd
19 Sun.	Scorpio	Water	Fruitful	3rd
20 Mon. 9:38 pm	Sagittarius	Fire	Barren	3rd
21 Tue.	Sagittarius	Fire	Barren	4th 2:17 am
22 Wed.	Sagittarius	Fire	Barren	4th
23 Thu. 3:16 am	Capricorn	Earth	Semi-fruitful	4th
24 Fri.	Capricorn	Earth	Semi-fruitful	4th
25 Sat. 5:14 am	Aquarius	Air	Barren	4th
26 Sun.	Aquarius	Air	Barren	4th
27 Mon. 4:56 am	Pisces	Water	Fruitful	New 7:31 pm
28 Tue.	Pisces	Water	Fruitful	1st

Aspectarian/Favorable & Unfavorable Days

	Sun	Mercury	Venus	Mars	Jupiter	Saturn	Uranus	Neptune	Pluto	Aries	Taurus	Gemini	Cancer	Leo	Virgo	Libra	Scorpio	Sagittarius	Capricorn	Aquarius	Pisces
1				X					Q		f	u	f		U		f	u	f		F
2	S		Q			T		X		F		f	u	f		U		f	u	f	
3		X							T	F		f	u	f		U		f	u	f	
4					Q	X					F		f	u	f		U		f	u	f
5	Q	Q	T	C	0			Q			F		f	u	f		U		f	u	f
6						X	Q				F		f	u	f		U		f	u	f
7	T							T		f		F		f	u	f		U		f	u
8		T							0	f		F		f	u	f		U		f	u
9			0		T		T			u	f		F	f	u	f		U			f
10				X						u	f		F	f	u	f		U			f
11					C					f	u	f		F	f	u	f		U		
12	0				Q			0		f	u	f		F	f	u	f		U		
13			Q						T	f	u	f		F	f	u	f		U		
14		0						0			f	u	f		F	f	u	f			U
15			T	T	X				Q		f	u	f		F	f	u	f			U
16				X							f	u	f		F	f	u	f			U
17			Q					T		U		f	u	f		F	f	u	f		
18	T								X	U		f	u	f		F	f	u	f		
19					Q	T	Q				U		f	u	f		F		f	u	f
20		T	X		C						U		f	u	f		F		f	u	f
21	S		0			T	Q			f		U		f	u	f		F		f	u
22		Q						X	C	f		U		f	u	f		F		f	u
23							X			f		U		f	u	f		F		f	u
24		X	C	X						u	f		U		f	u	f		F		f
25			T		0					u	f		U		f	u	f		F		f
26				Q				C	X	f	u	f			U	f	u	f		F	
27	C		Q				C			f	u	f			U	f	u	f		F	
28		C	X		T				Q		f	u	f		U	f	u	f			F

March Moon Table

Date	Sign	Element	Nature	Phase
1 Wed. 4:18 am	Aries	Fire	Barren	1st
2 Thu.	Aries	Fire	Barren	1st
3 Fri. 5:22 am	Taurus	Earth	Semi-fruitful	1st
4 Sat.	Taurus	Earth	Semi-fruitful	1st
5 Sun. 9:37 am	Gemini	Air	Barren	1st
6 Mon.	Gemini	Air	Barren	2nd 3:16 pm
7 Tue. 5:38 pm	Cancer	Water	Fruitful	2nd
8 Wed.	Cancer	Water	Fruitful	2nd
9 Thu.	Cancer	Water	Fruitful	2nd
10 Fri. 4:42 am	Leo	Fire	Barren	2nd
11 Sat.	Leo	Fire	Barren	2nd
12 Sun. 5:23 pm	Virgo	Earth	Barren	2nd
13 Mon.	Virgo	Earth	Barren	2nd
14 Tue.	Virgo	Earth	Barren	Full 6:35 pm
15 Wed. 6:12 am	Libra	Air	Semi-fruitful	3rd
16 Thu.	Libra	Air	Semi-fruitful	3rd
17 Fri. 5:59 pm	Scorpio	Water	Fruitful	3rd
18 Sat.	Scorpio	Water	Fruitful	3rd
19 Sun.	Scorpio	Water	Fruitful	3rd
20 Mon. 3:43 am	Sagittarius	Fire	Barren	3rd
21 Tue.	Sagittarius	Fire	Barren	3rd
22 Wed. 10:36 am	Capricorn	Earth	Semi-fruitful	4th 2:10 pm
23 Thu.	Capricorn	Earth	Semi-fruitful	4th
24 Fri. 2:21 pm	Aquarius	Air	Barren	4th
25 Sat.	Aquarius	Air	Barren	4th
26 Sun. 3:33 pm	Pisces	Water	Fruitful	4th
27 Mon.	Pisces	Water	Fruitful	4th
28 Tue. 3:31 pm	Aries	Fire	Barren	4th
29 Wed.	Aries	Fire	Barren	New 5:15 am
30 Thu. 4:00 pm	Taurus	Earth	Semi-fruitful	1st
31 Fri.	Taurus	Earth	Semi-fruitful	1st

Aspectarian/Favorable & Unfavorable Days

	Sun	Mercury	Venus	Mars	Jupiter	Saturn	Uranus	Neptune	Pluto	Aries	Taurus	Gemini	Cancer	Leo	Virgo	Libra	Scorpio	Sagittarius	Capricorn	Aquarius	Pisces
1				X		T					f	u	f		U		f	u	f		F
2								X	T	F		f	u	f		U		f	u	f	
3			Q			Q	X			F		f	u	f		U		f	u	f	
4	X				0			Q			F		f	u	f		U		f	u	f
5		X	T			X					F		f	u	f		U		f	u	f
6	Q			C		Q	T			f		F		f	u	f		U		f	u
7		Q							0	f		F		f	u	f		U		f	u
8						T				u	f		F		f	u	f		U		f
9	T	T				T				u	f		F		f	u	f		U		f
10			0				C			u	f		F		f	u	f		U		f
11				X	Q				0	f	u	f		F		f	u	f		U	
12									T	f	u	f		F		f	u	f		U	
13			Q					0			f	u	f		F		f	u	f		U
14	0	0			X			Q			f	u	f		F		f	u	f		U
15					X						f	u	f		F		f	u	f		U
16			T	T				T		U		f	u	f		F		f	u	f	
17								X		U		f	u	f		F		f	u	f	
18		T	Q			Q	T				U		f	u	f		F		f	u	f
19				C				Q			U		f	u	f		F		f	u	f
20	T					T					U		f	u	f		F		f	u	f
21		Q	X	0				Q	X	f		U		f	u	f		F		f	u
22	Q								C	f		U		f	u	f		F		f	u
23		X			X	X				u	f		U		f	u	f		F		f
24	X				0					u	f		U		f	u	f		F		f
25			C	T	Q			C		f	u	f		U		f	u	f		F	
26									X	f	u	f		U		f	u	f		F	
27		C			T		C				f	u	f		U		f	u	f		F
28			Q			T		Q			f	u	f		U		f	u	f		F
29	C						X			F		f	u	f		U		f	u	f	
30			X	X	Q				T	F		f	u	f		U		f	u	f	
31		X			0		X				F		f	u	f		U		f	u	f

April Moon Table

Date	Sign	Element	Nature	Phase
1 Sat. 6:49 pm	Gemini	Air	Barren	1st
2 Sun.	Gemini	Air	Barren	1st
3 Mon.	Gemini	Air	Barren	1st
4 Tue. 2:15 am	Cancer	Water	Fruitful	1st
5 Wed.	Cancer	Water	Fruitful	2nd 8:01 am
6 Thu. 12:25 pm	Leo	Fire	Barren	2nd
7 Fri.	Leo	Fire	Barren	2nd
8 Sat.	Leo	Fire	Barren	2nd
9 Sun. 12:58 am	Virgo	Earth	Barren	2nd
10 Mon.	Virgo	Earth	Barren	2nd
11 Tue. 1:46 pm	Libra	Air	Semi-fruitful	2nd
12 Wed.	Libra	Air	Semi-fruitful	2nd
13 Thu.	Libra	Air	Semi-fruitful	Full 12:40 pm
14 Fri. 1:08 am	Scorpio	Water	Fruitful	3rd
15 Sat.	Scorpio	Water	Fruitful	3rd
16 Sun. 10:19 am	Sagittarius	Fire	Barren	3rd
17 Mon.	Sagittarius	Fire	Barren	3rd
18 Tue. 5:13 pm	Capricorn	Earth	Semi-fruitful	3rd
19 Wed.	Capricorn	Earth	Semi-fruitful	3rd
20 Thu. 9:56 pm	Aquarius	Air	Barren	4th 11:28 pm
21 Fri.	Aquarius	Air	Barren	4th
22 Sat.	Aquarius	Air	Barren	4th
23 Sun. 12:43 am	Pisces	Water	Fruitful	4th
24 Mon.	Pisces	Water	Fruitful	4th
25 Tue. 2:12 am	Aries	Fire	Barren	4th
26 Wed.	Aries	Fire	Barren	4th
27 Thu. 3:27 am	Taurus	Earth	Semi-fruitful	New 3:44 pm
28 Fri.	Taurus	Earth	Semi-fruitful	1st
29 Sat. 5:58 am	Gemini	Air	Barren	1st
30 Sun.	Gemini	Air	Barren	1st

Aspectarian/Favorable & Unfavorable Days

	Sun	Mercury	Venus	Mars	Jupiter	Saturn	Uranus	Neptune	Pluto	Aries	Taurus	Gemini	Cancer	Leo	Virgo	Libra	Scorpio	Sagittarius	Capricorn	Aquarius	Pisces
1			Q					Q			F		f	u	f		U			f	u	f
2	X					X	Q			f		F		f	u	f		U			f	u
3		Q	T	C				T	0	f		F		f	u	f		U			f	u
4										f		F		f	u	f		U			f	u
5	Q	T			T		T			u	f		F		f	u	f		U			f
6						C				u	f		F		f	u	f		U			f
7					Q					f	u	f		F		f	u	f		U		
8	T			X				0	T	f	u	f		F		f	u	f		U		
9			0							f	u	f		F		f	u	f		U		
10		0		X		0					f	u	f		F		f	u	f			U
11			Q		X			Q			f	u	f		F		f	u	f			U
12										U		f	u	f		F		f	u	f		
13	0						T	X		U		f	u	f		F		f	u	f		
14			T	T				Q		U		f	u	f		F		f	u	f		
15					C		T	Q			U		f	u	f		F		f	u	f
16		T					T				U		f	u	f		F		f	u	f
17			Q					Q	X	f		U		f	u	f		F			f	u
18	T	Q		0					C	f		U		f	u	f		F			f	u
19			X	X	X					u	f		U		f	u	f		F			f
20	Q									u	f		U		f	u	f		F			f
21		X			Q	0				f	u	f		U		f	u	f		F		
22						C	X			f	u	f		U		f	u	f		F		
23	X			T		C					f	u	f		U		f	u	f			F
24		C		T				Q			f	u	f		U		f	u	f			F
25			Q		T						f	u	f		U		f	u	f			F
26		C					X	T		F		f	u	f		U		f	u	f		
27	C			X		Q				F		f	u	f		U		f	u	f		
28			X	0		X	Q				F		f	u	f		U			f	u	f
29						X					F		f	u	f		U			f	u	f
30		X				Q	T			f		F		f	u	f		U			f	u

May Moon Table

Date	Sign	Element	Nature	Phase
1 Mon. 11:17 am	Cancer	Water	Fruitful	1st
2 Tue.	Cancer	Water	Fruitful	1st
3 Wed. 8:18 pm	Leo	Fire	Barren	1st
4 Thu.	Leo	Fire	Barren	1st
5 Fri.	Leo	Fire	Barren	2nd 1:13 am
6 Sat. 8:20 am	Virgo	Earth	Barren	2nd
7 Sun.	Virgo	Earth	Barren	2nd
8 Mon. 9:10 pm	Libra	Air	Semi-fruitful	2nd
9 Tue.	Libra	Air	Semi-fruitful	2nd
10 Wed.	Libra	Air	Semi-fruitful	2nd
11 Thu. 8:24 am	Scorpio	Water	Fruitful	2nd
12 Fri.	Scorpio	Water	Fruitful	2nd
13 Sat. 4:56 pm	Sagittarius	Fire	Barren	Full 2:51 am
14 Sun.	Sagittarius	Fire	Barren	3rd
15 Mon. 10:59 pm	Capricorn	Earth	Semi-fruitful	3rd
16 Tue.	Capricorn	Earth	Semi-fruitful	3rd
17 Wed.	Capricorn	Earth	Semi-fruitful	3rd
18 Thu. 3:19 am	Aquarius	Air	Barren	3rd
19 Fri.	Aquarius	Air	Barren	3rd
20 Sat. 6:39 am	Pisces	Water	Fruitful	4th 5:20 am
21 Sun.	Pisces	Water	Fruitful	4th
22 Mon. 9:24 am	Aries	Fire	Barren	4th
23 Tue.	Aries	Fire	Barren	4th
24 Wed. 12:00 pm	Taurus	Earth	Semi-fruitful	4th
25 Thu.	Taurus	Earth	Semi-fruitful	4th
26 Fri. 3:19 pm	Gemini	Air	Barren	4th
27 Sat.	Gemini	Air	Barren	New 1:25 am
28 Sun. 8:33 pm	Cancer	Water	Fruitful	1st
29 Mon.	Cancer	Water	Fruitful	1st
30 Tue.	Cancer	Water	Fruitful	1st
31 Wed. 4:51 am	Leo	Fire	Barren	1st

Aspectarian/Favorable & Unfavorable Days

	Sun	Mercury	Venus	Mars	Jupiter	Saturn	Uranus	Neptune	Pluto	Aries	Taurus	Gemini	Cancer	Leo	Virgo	Libra	Scoprio	Sagittarius	Capricorn	Aquarius	Pisces
1			Q						0	f		F		f	u	f		U		f	u
2	X				C	T		T		u	f		F		f	u	f		U		f
3		Q	T							u	f		F		f	u	f		U		f
4					Q	C				f	u	f		F		f	u	f		U	
5	Q							0		f	u	f		F		f	u	f		U	
6		T							T	f	u	f		F		f	u	f		U	
7	T				X	X		0			f	u	f		F		f	u	f		U
8									Q		f	u	f		F		f	u	f		U
9			0				X			U		f	u	f		F		f	u	f	
10				Q				T		U		f	u	f		F		f	u	f	
11					Q				X	U		f	u	f		F		f	u	f	
12		0		T	C		T	Q			U		f	u	f		F		f	u	f
13	0										U		f	u	f		F		f	u	f
14			T			T	Q			f		U		f	u	f		F		f	u
15							X	C		f		U		f	u	f		F		f	u
16				X		X				u	f		U		f	u	f		F		f
17	T	T	Q	0						u	f		U		f	u	f		F		f
18						0				u	f		U		f	u	f		F		f
19			X		Q			C		f	u	f		U		f	u	f		F	
20	Q	Q							X	f	u	f		U		f	u	f		F	
21				T	T		C				f	u	f		U		f	u	f		F
22	X	X				T			Q		f	u	f		U		f	u	f		F
23							X			F		f	u	f		U		f	u	f	
24		C	Q		Q			T		F		f	u	f		U		f	u	f	
25				0		X	Q				F		f	u	f		U		f	u	f
26			X								F		f	u	f		U		f	u	f
27	C	C			X	Q				f		F		f	u	f		U		f	u
28		X				T	0			f		F		f	u	f		U		f	u
29			T		T					u	f		F		f	u	f		U		f
30										u	f		F		f	u	f		U		f
31		Q	C	C						u	f		F		f	u	f		U		f

June Moon Table

Date	Sign	Element	Nature	Phase
1 Thu.	Leo	Fire	Barren	1st
2 Fri. 4:17 pm	Virgo	Earth	Barren	1st
3 Sat.	Virgo	Earth	Barren	2nd 7:06 pm
4 Sun.	Virgo	Earth	Barren	2nd
5 Mon. 5:08 am	Libra	Air	Semi-fruitful	2nd
6 Tue.	Libra	Air	Semi-fruitful	2nd
7 Wed. 4:41 pm	Scorpio	Water	Fruitful	2nd
8 Thu.	Scorpio	Water	Fruitful	2nd
9 Fri.	Scorpio	Water	Fruitful	2nd
10 Sat. 1:05 am	Sagittarius	Fire	Barren	2nd
11 Sun.	Sagittarius	Fire	Barren	Full 2:03 pm
12 Mon. 6:19 am	Capricorn	Earth	Semi-fruitful	3rd
13 Tue.	Capricorn	Earth	Semi-fruitful	3rd
14 Wed. 9:32 am	Aquarius	Air	Barren	3rd
15 Thu.	Aquarius	Air	Barren	3rd
16 Fri. 12:05 pm	Pisces	Water	Fruitful	3rd
17 Sat.	Pisces	Water	Fruitful	3rd
18 Sun. 2:54 pm	Aries	Fire	Barren	4th 10:08 am
19 Mon.	Aries	Fire	Barren	4th
20 Tue. 6:23 pm	Taurus	Earth	Semi-fruitful	4th
21 Wed.	Taurus	Earth	Semi-fruitful	4th
22 Thu. 10:49 pm	Gemini	Air	Barren	4th
23 Fri.	Gemini	Air	Barren	4th
24 Sat.	Gemini	Air	Barren	4th
25 Sun. 4:48 am	Cancer	Water	Fruitful	New 12:05 pm
26 Mon.	Cancer	Water	Fruitful	1st
27 Tue. 1:09 pm	Leo	Fire	Barren	1st
28 Wed.	Leo	Fire	Barren	1st
29 Thu. 12:15 pm	Virgo	Earth	Barren	1st
30 Fri.	Virgo	Earth	Barren	1st

Aspectarian/Favorable & Unfavorable Days

	Sun	Mercury	Venus	Mars	Jupiter	Saturn	Uranus	Neptune	Pluto	Aries	Taurus	Gemini	Cancer	Leo	Virgo	Libra	Scorpio	Sagittarius	Capricorn	Aquarius	Pisces
1	X				Q			0		f	u	f		F		f	u	f		U	
2		X							T	f	u	f		F		f	u	f		U	
3	Q		T		X		0				f	u	f		F		f	u	f		U
4									Q		f	u	f		F		f	u	f		U
5		Q		X		X					f	u	f		F		f	u	f		U
6	T							T		U		f	u	f		F		f	u	f	
7					Q				X	U		f	u	f		F		f	u	f	
8		T	0			C	Q	T			U		f	u	f		F		f	u	f
9						Q					U		f	u	f		F		f	u	f
10			T			T					U		f	u	f		F		f	u	f
11	0						Q	X	C	f		U		f	u	f		F		f	u
12					X					f		U		f	u	f		F		f	u
13		0	T				X			u	f		U		f	u	f		F		f
14				0		0				u	f		U		f	u	f		F		f
15			Q		Q			C		f	u	f		U		f	u	f		F	
16	T								X	f	u	f		U		f	u	f		F	
17					T		C				f	u	f		U		f	u	f		F
18	Q	T	X						Q		f	u	f		U		f	u	f		F
19				T	T					F		f	u	f		U		f	u	f	
20		Q						X	T	F		f	u	f		U		f	u	f	
21			Q	0	Q	X					F		f	u	f		U		f	u	f
22		X	C					Q			F		f	u	f		U		f	u	f
23				X		X				f		F		f	u	f		U		f	u
24						Q	T	0		f		F		f	u	f		U		f	u
25	C					T				f		F		f	u	f		U		f	u
26						T				u	f		F		f	u	f		U		f
27		C	X							u	f		F		f	u	f		U		f
28			C	Q		C				f	u	f		F		f	u	f		U	
29								0	T	f	u	f		F		f	u	f		U	
30	X		Q		X						f	u	f		F		f	u	f		U

July Moon Table

Date	Sign	Element	Nature	Phase
1 Sat.	Virgo	Earth	Barren	1st
2 Sun. 1:06 pm	Libra	Air	Semi-fruitful	1st
3 Mon.	Libra	Air	Semi-fruitful	2nd 12:37 am
4 Tue.	Libra	Air	Semi-fruitful	2nd
5 Wed. 1:13 am	Scorpio	Water	Fruitful	2nd
6 Thu.	Scorpio	Water	Fruitful	2nd
7 Fri. 10:13 am	Sagittarius	Fire	Barren	2nd
8 Sat.	Sagittarius	Fire	Barren	2nd
9 Sun. 3:25 pm	Capricorn	Earth	Semi-fruitful	2nd
10 Mon.	Capricorn	Earth	Semi-fruitful	Full 11:02 pm
11 Tue. 5:46 pm	Aquarius	Air	Barren	3rd
12 Wed.	Aquarius	Air	Barren	3rd
13 Thu. 6:59 pm	Pisces	Water	Fruitful	3rd
14 Fri.	Pisces	Water	Fruitful	3rd
15 Sat. 8:39 pm	Aries	Fire	Barren	3rd
16 Sun.	Aries	Fire	Barren	3rd
17 Mon. 11:44 pm	Taurus	Earth	Semi-fruitful	4th 3:12 pm
18 Tue.	Taurus	Earth	Semi-fruitful	4th
19 Wed.	Taurus	Earth	Semi-fruitful	4th
20 Thu. 4:38 am	Gemini	Air	Barren	4th
21 Fri.	Gemini	Air	Barren	4th
22 Sat. 11:28 am	Cancer	Water	Fruitful	4th
23 Sun.	Cancer	Water	Fruitful	4th
24 Mon. 8:24 pm	Leo	Fire	Barren	4th
25 Tue.	Leo	Fire	Barren	New 12:31 pm
26 Wed.	Leo	Fire	Barren	1st
27 Thu. 7:36 am	Virgo	Earth	Barren	1st
28 Fri.	Virgo	Earth	Barren	1st
29 Sat. 8:27 pm	Virgo	Earth	Barren	1st
30 Sun.	Libra	Air	Semi-fruitful	1st
31 Mon.	Libra	Air	Semi-fruitful	1st

Aspectarian/Favorable & Unfavorable Days

	Sun	Mercury	Venus	Mars	Jupiter	Saturn	Uranus	Neptune	Pluto	Aries	Taurus	Gemini	Cancer	Leo	Virgo	Libra	Scorpio	Sagittarius	Capricorn	Aquarius	Pisces
1							0				f	u	f		F		f	u	f		U
2		X							Q		f	u	f		F		f	u	f		U
3	Q		T			X				U		f	u	f		F		f	u	f	
4				X				T	X	U		f	u	f		F		f	u	f	
5		Q			C	Q				U		f	u	f		F		f	u	f	
6	T			Q				T	Q		U		f	u	f		F		f	u	f
7		T									U		f	u	f		F		f	u	f
8			0			T	Q	X		f		U		f	u	f		F		f	u
9			T						C	f		U		f	u	f		F		f	u
10	0				X		X			u	f		U		f	u	f		F		f
11		0								u	f		U		f	u	f		F		f
12					Q	0				f	u	f		U		f	u	f		F	
13			T	0				C	X	f	u	f		U		f	u	f		F	
14				T			C				f	u	f		U		f	u	f		F
15	T	T	Q						Q		f	u	f		U		f	u	f		F
16						T				F		f	u	f		U		f	u	f	
17	Q	Q	X	T				X	T	F		f	u	f		U		f	u	f	
18					0	Q					F		f	u	f		U		f	u	f
19		X					X	Q			F		f	u	f		U		f	u	f
20			Q								F		f	u	f		U		f	u	f
21						X	Q	T		f		F		f	u	f		U		f	u
22		C	X						0	f		F		f	u	f		U		f	ú
23				T		T				u	f		F		f	u	f		U		f
24		C								u	f		F		f	u	f		U		f
25	C				Q	C				f	u	f		F		f	u	f		U	
26								0	T	f	u	f		F		f	u	f		U	
27			C							f	u	f		F		f	u	f		U	
28		X		X			0				f	u	f		F		f	u	f		U
29		X							Q		f	u	f		F		f	u	f		U
30	X									U		f	u	f		F		f	u	f	
31		Q	Q			X		T	X	U		f	u	f		F		f	u	f	

August Moon Table

Date	Sign	Element	Nature	Phase
1 Tue. 9:08 am	Scorpio	Water	Fruitful	1st
2 Wed.	Scorpio	Water	Fruitful	2nd 4:46 am
3 Thu. 7:13 pm	Sagittarius	Fire	Barren	2nd
4 Fri.	Sagittarius	Fire	Barren	2nd
5 Sat.	Sagittarius	Fire	Barren	2nd
6 Sun. 1:19 am	Capricorn	Earth	Semi-fruitful	2nd
7 Mon.	Capricorn	Earth	Semi-fruitful	2nd
8 Tue. 3:47 am	Aquarius	Air	Barren	2nd
9 Wed.	Aquarius	Air	Barren	Full 6:54 am
10 Thu. 4:10 am	Pisces	Water	Fruitful	3rd
11 Fri.	Pisces	Water	Fruitful	3rd
12 Sat. 4:22 am	Aries	Fire	Barren	3rd
13 Sun.	Aries	Fire	Barren	3rd
14 Mon. 6:00 am	Taurus	Earth	Semi-fruitful	3rd
15 Tue.	Taurus	Earth	Semi-fruitful	4th 9:51 pm
16 Wed. 10:07 am	Gemini	Air	Barren	4th
17 Thu.	Gemini	Air	Barren	4th
18 Fri. 5:03 pm	Cancer	Water	Fruitful	4th
19 Sat.	Cancer	Water	Fruitful	4th
20 Sun.	Cancer	Water	Fruitful	4th
21 Mon. 2:33 am	Leo	Fire	Barren	4th
22 Tue.	Leo	Fire	Barren	4th
23 Wed. 2:08 pm	Virgo	Earth	Barren	New 3:10 pm
24 Thu.	Virgo	Earth	Barren	1st
25 Fri.	Virgo	Earth	Barren	1st
26 Sat. 3:01 am	Libra	Air	Semi-fruitful	1st
27 Sun.	Libra	Air	Semi-fruitful	1st
28 Mon. 3:56 pm	Scorpio	Water	Fruitful	1st
29 Tue.	Scorpio	Water	Fruitful	1st
30 Wed.	Scorpio	Water	Fruitful	1st
31 Thu. 3:00 am	Sagittarius	Fire	Barren	2nd 6:56 pm

Aspectarian/Favorable & Unfavorable Days

	Sun	Mercury	Venus	Mars	Jupiter	Saturn	Uranus	Neptune	Pluto	Aries	Taurus	Gemini	Cancer	Leo	Virgo	Libra	Scorpio	Sagittarius	Capricorn	Aquarius	Pisces
1				X						U		f	u	f		F		f	u	f	
2	Q		T		C	Q	T	Q			U		f	u	f		F		f	u	f
3		T									U		f	u	f		F		f	u	f
4	T			Q		T	Q			f		U		f	u	f		F		f	u
5								X	C	f		U		f	u	f		F		f	u
6				T	X					f		U		f	u	f		F		f	u
7		0	0					X		u	f		U		f	u	f		F		f
8					Q					u	f		U		f	u	f		F		f
9	0				0			C	X	f	u	f		U		f	u	f		F	
10			0	T						f	u	f		U		f	u	f		F	
11						C			Q		f	u	f		U		f	u	f		F
12		T	T								f	u	f		U		f	u	f		F
13					T			X	T	F		f	u	f		U		f	u	f	
14		Q	Q							F		f	u	f		U		f	u	f	
15	Q			T	0	Q	X	Q			F		f	u	f		U		f	u	f
16		X									F		f	u	f		U		f	u	f
17		X		Q	X	Q	T			f		F		f	u	f		U		f	u
18	X							0		f		F		f	u	f		U		f	u
19				T		T				u	f		F		f	u	f		U		f
20				X						u	f		F		f	u	f		U		f
21										u	f		F		f	u	f		U		f
22		C	C		Q	C		0		f	u	f		F		f	u	f		U	
23	C							T		f	u	f		F		f	u	f		U	
24				X			0				f	u	f		F		f	u	f		U
25			C						Q		f	u	f		F		f	u	f		U
26											f	u	f		F		f	u	f		U
27			X		X			T		U		f	u	f		F		f	u	f	
28		X						X		U		f	u	f		F		f	u	f	
29	X				C		T				U		f	u	f		F		f	u	f
30			Q	X	Q		Q				U		f	u	f		F		f	u	f
31	Q	Q									U		f	u	f		F		f	u	f

September Moon Table

Date	Sign	Element	Nature	Phase
1 Fri.	Sagittarius	Fire	Barren	2nd
2 Sat. 10:34 am	Capricorn	Earth	Semi-fruitful	2nd
3 Sun.	Capricorn	Earth	Semi-fruitful	2nd
4 Mon. 2:15 pm	Aquarius	Air	Barren	2nd
5 Tue.	Aquarius	Air	Barren	2nd
6 Wed. 2:56 pm	Pisces	Water	Fruitful	2nd
7 Thu.	Pisces	Water	Fruitful	Full 2:42 pm
8 Fri. 2:23 pm	Aries	Fire	Barren	3rd
9 Sat.	Aries	Fire	Barren	3rd
10 Sun. 2:30 pm	Taurus	Earth	Semi-fruitful	3rd
11 Mon.	Taurus	Earth	Semi-fruitful	3rd
12 Tue. 4:59 pm	Gemini	Air	Barren	3rd
13 Wed.	Gemini	Air	Barren	3rd
14 Thu. 10:53 pm	Cancer	Water	Fruitful	4th 7:15 am
15 Fri.	Cancer	Water	Fruitful	4th
16 Sat.	Cancer	Water	Fruitful	4th
17 Sun. 8:15 am	Leo	Fire	Barren	4th
18 Mon.	Leo	Fire	Barren	4th
19 Tue. 8:07 pm	Virgo	Earth	Barren	4th
20 Wed.	Virgo	Earth	Barren	4th
21 Thu.	Virgo	Earth	Barren	4th
22 Fri. 9:06 am	Libra	Air	Semi-fruitful	New 7:45 am
23 Sat.	Libra	Air	Semi-fruitful	1st
24 Sun. 9:54 pm	Scorpio	Water	Fruitful	1st
25 Mon.	Scorpio	Water	Fruitful	1st
26 Tue.	Scorpio	Water	Fruitful	1st
27 Wed. 9:16 am	Sagittarius	Fire	Barren	1st
28 Thu.	Sagittarius	Fire	Barren	1st
29 Fri. 6:01 pm	Capricorn	Earth	Semi-fruitful	1st
30 Sat.	Capricorn	Earth	Semi-fruitful	2nd 7:04 am

Aspectarian/Favorable & Unfavorable Days

	Sun	Mercury	Venus	Mars	Jupiter	Saturn	Uranus	Neptune	Pluto	Aries	Taurus	Gemini	Cancer	Leo	Virgo	Libra	Scoprio	Sagittarius	Capricorn	Aquarius	Pisces
1						T	Q	X	C	f		U		f	u	f		F		f	u
2			T	Q						f		U		f	u	f		F		f	u
3	T	T			X		X			u	f		U	f	u	f			F		f
4				T						u	f		U	f	u	f			F		f
5					Q	0		C		f	u	f		U		f	u	f		F	
6		0							X	f	u	f		U		f	u	f		F	
7	0				T			C		f	u	f		U		f	u	f			F
8		0		0					Q	f	u	f		U		f	u	f			F
9						T	X			F		f	u	f		U		f	u	f	
10								T		F		f	u	f		U		f	u	f	
11	T		T		0	Q	X	Q			F		f	u	f		U		f	u	f
12		T		T							F		f	u	f		U		f	u	f
13			Q			Q				f		F		f	u	f		U		f	u
14	Q				X			T	0	f		F		f	u	f		U		f	u
15		Q	X	Q				T		u	f		F	f	u	f			U		f
16	X			T						u	f		F	f	u	f			U		f
17			X							u	f		F	f	u	f			U		f
18		X			Q	C		0		f	u	f		F		f	u	f		U	
19						0			T	f	u	f		F		f	u	f		U	
20						0				f	u	f		F		f	u	f			U
21			C	X					Q	f	u	f		F		f	u	f			U
22	C									f	u	f		F		f	u	f			U
23		C		C			T			U		f	u	f		F		f	u	f	
24					X				X	U		f	u	f		F		f	u	f	
25							T				U		f	u	f		F		f	u	f
26					C	Q		Q			U		f	u	f		F		f	u	f
27	C		X								U		f	u	f		F		f	u	f
28				X			Q	X		f		U		f	u	f		F		f	u
29		X	Q			T			C	f		U		f	u	f		F		f	u
30	Q			Q			X			u	f		U	f	u	f			F		f

October Moon Table

Date	Sign	Element	Nature	Phase
1 Sun. 11:24 pm	Aquarius	Air	Barren	2nd
2 Mon.	Aquarius	Air	Barren	2nd
3 Tue.	Aquarius	Air	Barren	2nd
4 Wed. 1:33 am	Pisces	Water	Fruitful	2nd
5 Thu.	Pisces	Water	Fruitful	2nd
6 Fri. 1:32 am	Aries	Fire	Barren	Full 11:13 pm
7 Sat.	Aries	Fire	Barren	3rd
8 Sun. 1:04 am	Taurus	Earth	Semi-fruitful	3rd
9 Mon.	Taurus	Earth	Semi-fruitful	3rd
10 Tue. 2:06 am	Gemini	Air	Barren	3rd
11 Wed.	Gemini	Air	Barren	3rd
12 Thu. 6:21 am	Cancer	Water	Fruitful	3rd
13 Fri.	Cancer	Water	Fruitful	4th 8:25 pm
14 Sat. 2:38 pm	Leo	Fire	Barren	4th
15 Sun.	Leo	Fire	Barren	4th
16 Mon.	Leo	Fire	Barren	4th
17 Tue. 2:15 am	Virgo	Earth	Barren	4th
18 Wed.	Virgo	Earth	Barren	4th
19 Thu. 3:19 pm	Libra	Air	Semi-fruitful	4th
20 Fri.	Libra	Air	Semi-fruitful	4th
21 Sat.	Libra	Air	Semi-fruitful	4th
22 Sun. 3:54 am	Scorpio	Water	Fruitful	New 1:14 am
23 Mon.	Scorpio	Water	Fruitful	1st
24 Tue. 2:53 pm	Sagittarius	Fire	Barren	1st
25 Wed.	Sagittarius	Fire	Barren	1st
26 Thu. 11:47 pm	Capricorn	Earth	Semi-fruitful	1st
27 Fri.	Capricorn	Earth	Semi-fruitful	1st
28 Sat.	Capricorn	Earth	Semi-fruitful	1st
29 Sun. 5:17 am	Aquarius	Air	Barren	2nd 4:25 pm
30 Mon.	Aquarius	Air	Barren	2nd
31 Tue. 9:10 am	Pisces	Water	Fruitful	2nd

Aspectarian/Favorable & Unfavorable Days

	Sun	Mercury	Venus	Mars	Jupiter	Saturn	Uranus	Neptune	Pluto	Aries	Taurus	Gemini	Cancer	Leo	Virgo	Libra	Scoprio	Sagittarius	Capricorn	Aquarius	Pisces
1		Q			X					u	f		U		f	u	f		F		f
2	T		T							f	u	f		U		f	u	f		F	
3				T	Q	0		C	X	f	u	f		U		f	u	f		F	
4		T					C			f	u	f		U		f	u	f		F	
5					T				Q	f	u	f		U		f	u	f			F
6	0		0							f	u	f		U		f	u	f			F
7			0			T		X	T	F		f	u	f		U	f	u	f		
8		0					X			F		f	u	f		U	f	u	f		
9				0	Q		Q				F		f	u	f		U		f	u	f
10							Q				F		f	u	f		U		f	u	f
11	T		T	T		X		T	0	f		F		f	u	f		U		f	u
12										f		F		f	u	f		U		f	u
13	Q	T	Q		T		T			u	f		F	f	u	f			U		f
14				Q						u	f		F	f	u	f			U		f
15										f	u	f		F		f	u	f		U	
16	X	Q	X	X	Q	C		0	T	f	u	f		F		f	u	f		U	
17										f	u	f		F		f	u	f		U	
18		X			X	0					f	u	f		F	f	u	f			U
19									Q		f	u	f		F	f	u	f			U
20										U	f	u	f			F	f	u	f		
21			C		X		T		X	U	f	u	f			F	f	u	f		
22	C		C							U	f	u	f			F	f	u	f		
23						T	Q				U		f	u	f		F		f	u	f
24		C			C	Q					U		f	u	f		F		f	u	f
25						Q	X			f			U	f	u	f		F		f	u
26						T			C	f			U	f	u	f		F		f	u
27	X		X	X		X				u	f		U		f	u	f		F		f
28		X		X						u	f		U		f	u	f		F		f
29	Q		Q	Q						u	f		U		f	u	f		F		f
30							0	C		f	u	f		U		f	u	f		F	
31		Q			T	Q			X	f	u	f		U		f	u	f		F	

November Moon Table

Date	Sign	Element	Nature	Phase
1 Wed.	Pisces	Water	Fruitful	2nd
2 Thu. 10:46 am	Aries	Fire	Barren	2nd
3 Fri.	Aries	Fire	Barren	2nd
4 Sat. 11:05 am	Taurus	Earth	Semi-fruitful	2nd
5 Sun.	Taurus	Earth	Semi-fruitful	Full 7:58 am
6 Mon. 11:46 am	Gemini	Air	Barren	2nd
7 Tue.	Gemini	Air	Barren	2nd
8 Wed. 2:46 pm	Cancer	Water	Fruitful	2nd
9 Thu.	Cancer	Water	Fruitful	2nd
10 Fri. 9:34 pm	Leo	Fire	Barren	2nd
11 Sat.	Leo	Fire	Barren	2nd
12 Sun.	Leo	Fire	Barren	4th 12:45 pm
13 Mon. 8:18 am	Virgo	Earth	Barren	4th
14 Tue.	Virgo	Earth	Barren	4th
15 Wed. 9:14 pm	Libra	Air	Semi-fruitful	4th
16 Thu.	Libra	Air	Semi-fruitful	4th
17 Fri.	Libra	Air	Semi-fruitful	4th
18 Sat. 9:46 am	Scorpio	Water	Fruitful	4th
19 Sun.	Scorpio	Water	Fruitful	4th
20 Mon. 8:15 pm	Sagittarius	Fire	Barren	New 5:18 pm
21 Tue.	Sagittarius	Fire	Barren	1st
22 Wed.	Sagittarius	Fire	Barren	1st
23 Thu. 4:25 am	Capricorn	Earth	Semi-fruitful	1st
24 Fri.	Capricorn	Earth	Semi-fruitful	1st
25 Sat. 10:41 am	Aquarius	Air	Barren	1st
26 Sun.	Aquarius	Air	Barren	1st
27 Mon. 3:20 pm	Pisces	Water	Fruitful	1st
28 Tue.	Pisces	Water	Fruitful	2nd 1:29 am
29 Wed. 6:30 pm	Aries	Fire	Barren	2nd
30 Thu.	Aries	Fire	Barren	2nd

Aspectarian/Favorable & Unfavorable Days

	Sun	Mercury	Venus	Mars	Jupiter	Saturn	Uranus	Neptune	Pluto	Aries	Taurus	Gemini	Cancer	Leo	Virgo	Libra	Scorpio	Sagittarius	Capricorn	Aquarius	Pisces
1			T				C				f	u	f		U		f	u	f		F
2		T				T			Q		f	u	f		U		f	u	f		F
3								X		F		f	u	f		U		f	u	f	
4						T			T	F		f	u	f		U		f	u	f	
5	0	0	0	0				X	Q		F		f	u	f		U		f	u	f
6					0	Q					F		f	u	f		U		f	u	f
7								Q	T	f		F		f	u	f		U		f	u
8							X		0	f		F		f	u	f		U		f	u
9	T	T		T				T		u	f		F		f	u	f		U		f
10		T		T						u	f		F		f	u	f		U		f
11		Q		Q						f	u	f		F		f	u	f		U	
12		Q				C		0	T	f	u	f		F		f	u	f		U	
13				Q						f	u	f		F		f	u	f		U	
14		X		X		0					f	u	f		F		f	u	f		U
15	X	X		X					Q		f	u	f		F		f	u	f		U
16										U		f	u	f		F		f	u	f	
17							X	T		U		f	u	f		F		f	u	f	
18								X		U		f	u	f		F		f	u	f	
19		C		C				T	Q		U		f	u	f		F		f	u	f
20	C				C	Q					U		f	u	f		F		f	u	f
21			C				Q			f		U		f	u	f		F		f	u
22						T		X	C	f		U		f	u	f		F		f	u
23										f		U		f	u	f		F		f	u
24		X	X			X				u	f		U		f	u	f		F		f
25						X				u	f		U		f	u	f		F		f
26		Q	X					C		f	u	f		U		f	u	f		F	
27			Q	Q	0				X	f	u	f		U		f	u	f		F	
28	Q	T	Q			C					f	u	f		U		f	u	f		F
29				T	T				Q		f	u	f		U		f	u	f		F
30	T		T					X		F		f	u	f		U		f	u	f	

December Moon Table

Date	Sign	Element	Nature	Phase
1 Fri. 8:26 pm	Taurus	Earth	Semi-fruitful	2nd
2 Sat.	Taurus	Earth	Semi-fruitful	2nd
3 Sun. 10:05 pm	Gemini	Air	Barren	2nd
4 Mon.	Gemini	Air	Barren	Full 7:25 pm
5 Tue.	Gemini	Air	Barren	3rd
6 Wed. 1:00 am	Cancer	Water	Fruitful	3rd
7 Thu.	Cancer	Water	Fruitful	3rd
8 Fri. 6:52 am	Leo	Fire	Barren	3rd
9 Sat.	Leo	Fire	Barren	3rd
10 Sun. 4:31 pm	Virgo	Earth	Barren	3rd
11 Mon.	Virgo	Earth	Barren	3rd
12 Tue.	Virgo	Earth	Barren	4th 9:32 am
13 Wed. 5:00 am	Libra	Air	Semi-fruitful	4th
14 Thu.	Libra	Air	Semi-fruitful	4th
15 Fri. 5:42 pm	Scorpio	Water	Fruitful	4th
16 Sat.	Scorpio	Water	Fruitful	4th
17 Sun.	Scorpio	Water	Fruitful	4th
18 Mon. 4:10 am	Sagittarius	Fire	Barren	4th
19 Tue.	Sagittarius	Fire	Barren	4th
20 Wed. 11:39 am	Capricorn	Earth	Semi-fruitful	New 9:01 am
21 Thu.	Capricorn	Earth	Semi-fruitful	1st
22 Fri. 4:49 pm	Aquarius	Air	Barren	1st
23 Sat.	Aquarius	Air	Barren	1st
24 Sun. 8:43 pm	Pisces	Water	Fruitful	1st
25 Mon.	Pisces	Water	Fruitful	1st
26 Tue.	Pisces	Water	Fruitful	1st
27 Wed. 12:04 am	Aries	Fire	Barren	2nd 9:48 am
28 Thu.	Aries	Fire	Barren	2nd
29 Fri. 3:08 am	Taurus	Earth	Semi-fruitful	2nd
30 Sat.	Taurus	Earth	Semi-fruitful	2nd
31 Sun.	Taurus	Earth	Semi-fruitful	2nd

Aspectarian/Favorable & Unfavorable Days

	Sun	Mercury	Venus	Mars	Jupiter	Saturn	Uranus	Neptune	Pluto	Aries	Taurus	Gemini	Cancer	Leo	Virgo	Libra	Scorpio	Sagittarius	Capricorn	Aquarius	Pisces
1						T			T	F		f	u	f		U		f	u	f	
2							X			F		f	u	f		U		f	u	f	
3			O		O	Q		Q		F		f	u	f		U		f	u	f	
4	O				O	Q				f		F		f	u	f		U		f	u
5		O				X		T	O	f		F		f	u	f		U		f	u
6						T				f		F		f	u	f		U		f	u
7										u	f		F		f	u	f		U		f
8		T		T	T					u	f		F		f	u	f		U		f
9	T							O		f	u	f		F		f	u	f		U	
10			T	Q		C			T	f	u	f		F		f	u	f		U	
11		Q			Q	O					f	u	f		F		f	u	f		U
12	Q							Q			f	u	f		F		f	u	f		U
13		X	Q	X	X						f	u	f		F		f	u	f		U
14								T		U		f	u	f		F		f	u	f	
15	X					X			X	U		f	u	f		F		f	u	f	
16			X					T			U		f	u	f		F		f	u	f
17						Q		Q			U		f	u	f		F		f	u	f
18				C	C						U		f	u	f		F		f	u	f
19		C				Q	X			f		U		f	u	f		F		f	u
20	C					T			C	f		U		f	u	f		F		f	u
21			C				X			u	f		U		f	u	f		F		f
22										u	f		U		f	u	f		F		f
23			X	X				C		f	u	f		U		f	u	f		F	
24		X			O				X	f	u	f		U		f	u	f		F	
25	X			Q	Q	C					f	u	f		U		f	u	f		F
26		Q	X						Q		f	u	f		U		f	u	f		F
27	Q				T						f	u	f		U		f	u	f		F
28			Q	T		T		X	T	F		f	u	f		U		f	u	f	
29	T	T					X			F		f	u	f		U		f	u	f	
30			T			Q		Q		F		f	u	f		U		f	u	f	
31							O			F		f	u	f		U		f	u	f	

Time Zone Map

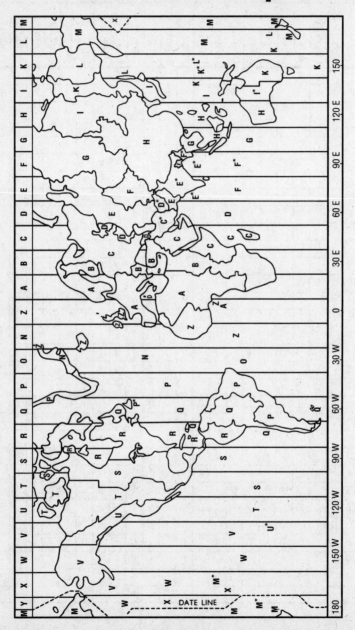

Time Zone Conversions

World Time Zones Compared to Eastern Time

(R)	EST—Used	(C*)	Add 8½ hours
(S)	CST—Subtract 1 hour	(D)	Add 9 hours
(T)	MST—Subtract 2 hours	(D*)	Add 9½ hours
(U)	PST—Subtract 3 hours	(E)	Add 10 hours
(V)	Subtract 4 hours	(E*)	Add 10½ hours
(U*)	Subtract 4½ hours	(F)	Add 11 hours
(W)	Subtract 5 hours	(F*)	Add 11½ hours
(X)	Subtract 6 hours	(G)	Add 12 hours
(Y)	Subtract 7 hours	(H)	Add 13 hours
(Q)	Add 1 hour	(I)	Add 14 hours
(P)	Add 2 hours	(I*)	Add 14½ hours
(P*)	Add 2½ hours	(K)	Add 15 hours
(O)	Add 3 hours	(K*)	Add 15½ hours
(N)	Add 4 hours	(L)	Add 16 hours
(Z)	Add 5 hours	(L*)	Add 16½ hours
(A)	Add 6 hours	(M)	Add 17 hours
(B)	Add 7 hours	(M*)	Add 17½ hours
(C)	Add 8 hours		

Important!

All times given in the *Moon Sign Book* are set in Eastern Time. The conversions shown here are for standard times only. Use the time zone conversions map and table to calculate the difference in your time zone. You must make the adjustment for your time zone and adjust for Daylight Saving Time where applicable.

Moon Void-of-Course

by Kim Rogers-Gallagher

The Moon circles the Earth in about twenty-eight days, moving through each zodiac sign in two-and-a-half days. As she passes through the thirty degrees of each sign, she "visits" with the planets in numerical order, forming aspects with them. Because she moves one degree in just two to two-and-a-half hours, her influence on each planet lasts only a few hours. She eventually reaches the planet that's in the highest degree of any sign, and forms what will be her final aspect before leaving the sign. From this point until she enters the next sign, she is referred to as void-of-course.

Think of it this way: the Moon is the emotional "tone" of the day, carrying feelings with her particular to the sign she's "wearing" at the moment. After she has contacted each of the planets, she symbolically "rests" before changing her costume, so her instinct is temporarily on hold. It's during this time that many people feel "fuzzy" or "vague." Plans or decisions made now often do not pan out. Without the instinctual "knowing" the Moon provides as she touches each planet, we tend to be unrealistic or exercise poor judgment. The traditional definition of the void Moon is that "nothing will come of this." Actions initiated under a void Moon are often wasted, irrelevant, or incorrect—usually because information is hidden, missing, or has been overlooked.

Although it's not a good time to initiate plans, routine tasks seem to go along just fine. This period is ideal for reflection. On the lighter side, remember there are good uses for the void Moon. It is the period when the universe seems to be most open to loopholes. It's a great time to make plans you don't want to fulfill or schedule things you don't want to do. See the table on pages 95–100 for a schedule of the Moon's void-of-course times in 2006.

Moon Void-of-Course Tables

Last Aspect   **Moon enters New Sign**

		January			
3	6:44 am	3	Pisces	7:43 am	
5	7:10 am	5	Aries	9:44 am	
7	9:34 am	7	Taurus	2:09 pm	
9	1:56 pm	9	Gemini	8:58 pm	
11	8:46 pm	12	Cancer	5:50 am	
14	7:20 am	14	Leo	4:31 pm	
16	10:28 pm	17	Virgo	4:49 am	
19	5:12 pm	19	Libra	5:49 pm	
22	3:53 am	22	Scorpio	5:28 am	
23	4:53 pm	24	Sagittarius	1:38 pm	
26	10:24 am	26	Capricorn	5:31 pm	
28	2:57 am	28	Aquarius	6:09 pm	
30	11:00 am	30	Pisces	5:32 pm	
		February			
1	11:06 am	1	Aries	5:46 pm	
3	1:33 pm	3	Taurus	8:31 pm	
5	7:14 pm	6	Gemini	2:32 am	
8	10:04 am	8	Cancer	11:33 am	
10	3:53 pm	10	Leo	10:44 pm	
13	6:48 am	13	Virgo	11:13 am	
15	10:21 pm	16	Libra	12:09 am	
18	11:59 am	18	Scorpio	12:11 pm	
20	5:02 am	20	Sagittarius	9:38 pm	
22	9:06 pm	23	Capricorn	3:16 am	
24	7:58 pm	25	Aquarius	5:14 am	
26	11:25 pm	27	Pisces	4:56 am	
28	11:14 pm	1	Aries	4:18 am	
		March			
3	2:42 am	3	Taurus	5:22 am	

Last Aspect   Moon enters New Sign

5	3:30 am	5	Gemini	9:37 am
7	11:09 am	7	Cancer	5:38 pm
9	10:00 pm	10	Leo	4:42 am
12	10:38 am	12	Virgo	5:23 pm
14	11:33 pm	15	Libra	6:12 am
17	12:00 pm	17	Scorpio	5:59 pm
20	2:54 am	20	Sagittarius	3:43 am
22	4:47 am	22	Capricorn	10:36 am
23	6:30 pm	24	Aquarius	2:21 pm
26	10:18 am	26	Pisces	3:33 pm
28	10:20 am	28	Aries	3:31 pm
30	10:41 am	30	Taurus	4:00 pm
		April		
1	1:10 pm	1	Gemini	6:49 pm
3	10:24 pm	4	Cancer	2:15 am
6	5:56 am	6	Leo	12:25 am
8	7:02 pm	8	Virgo	12:58 pm
11	10:59 am	11	Libra	1:46 pm
13	6:53 pm	14	Scorpio	1:08 am
16	3:08 am	16	Sagittarius	10:19 am
18	2:41 pm	18	Capricorn	5:13 pm
19	9:15 pm	20	Aquarius	9:56 pm
22	7:03 pm	22	Pisces	12:43 pm
24	8:35 pm	25	Aries	2:12 am
26	9:44 pm	27	Taurus	3:27 am
28	11:58 pm	29	Gemini	5:58 am
		May		
1	7:13 am	1	Cancer	11:17 am
3	2:35 pm	3	Leo	8:18 pm
6	1:01 am	6	Virgo	8:20 am

Last Aspect　　　Moon enters New Sign

8	1:49 pm	8	Libra	9:10 pm
11	1:15 am	11	Scorpio	8:24 am
13	2:51 am	13	Sagittarius	4:56 pm
15	4:15 pm	15	Capricorn	10:59 pm
17	10:10 pm	18	Aquarius	3:19 am
20	5:20 am	20	Pisces	6:39 am
22	2:45 am	22	Aries	9:24 am
24	5:16 am	24	Taurus	12:00 am
26	8:20 am	26	Gemini	3:19 pm
28	7:23 pm	28	Cancer	8:33 pm
30	12:42 pm	31	Leo	4:51 am
		June		
2	1:34 pm	2	Virgo	4:17 pm
4	8:30 pm	5	Libra	5:08 am
7	8:15 am	7	Scorpio	4:41 pm
9	6:10 am	10	Sagittarius	1:05 am
11	10:34 pm	12	Capricorn	6:19 am
13	9:29 pm	14	Aquarius	9:32 am
16	4:24 am	16	Pisces	12:05 am
18	10:08 am	18	Aries	2:54 pm
20	5:20 pm	20	Taurus	6:23 pm
22	8:44 pm	22	Gemini	10:49 pm
24	8:02 pm	25	Cancer	4:48 am
27	12:02 am	27	Leo	1:09 pm
29	2:24 pm	29	Virgo	12:15 pm
		July		
2	2:58 am	2	Libra	1:06 pm
4	3:17 pm	5	Scorpio	1:13 am
6	3:54 pm	7	Sagittarius	10:13 am
9	6:31 am	9	Capricorn	3:25 pm

Last Aspect   Moon enters New Sign

11	4:58 pm	11	Aquarius	5:46 pm
13	4:25 pm	13	Pisces	6:59 pm
15	3:56 pm	15	Aries	8:39 pm
17	9:33 pm	17	Taurus	11:44 pm
20	1:48 am	20	Gemini	4:38 am
22	11:17 am	22	Cancer	11:28 am
24	9:50 am	24	Leo	8:24 pm
26	8:32 pm	27	Virgo	7:36 am
29	9:05 am	29	Libra	8:27 pm
31	9:54 pm	1	Scorpio	9:08 am
		August		
3	5:08 am	3	Sagittarius	7:13 pm
5	3:22 pm	6	Capricorn	1:19 am
7	9:44 pm	8	Aquarius	3:47 am
10	2:17 am	10	Pisces	4:10 am
12	3:17 am	12	Aries	4:22 am
13	8:14 pm	14	Taurus	6:00 am
15	11:47 pm	16	Gemini	10:07 am
18	8:30 am	18	Cancer	5:03 pm
20	3:08 pm	21	Leo	2:33 am
23	2:19 am	23	Virgo	2:08 pm
25	3:00 pm	26	Libra	3:01 am
28	4:01 am	28	Scorpio	3:56 pm
30	4:41 pm	31	Sagittarius	3:00 am
		September		
2	3:49 am	2	Capricorn	10:34 am
4	10:52 am	4	Aquarius	2:15 pm
6	1:27 pm	6	Pisces	2:56 pm
8	5:02 am	8	Aries	2:23 pm
10	7:42 am	10	Taurus	2:30 pm

Last Aspect   Moon enters New Sign

12	4:58 pm	12	Gemini	4:59 pm
14	12:00 pm	14	Cancer	10:53 pm
16	8:46 pm	17	Leo	8:15 am
19	8:16 am	19	Virgo	8:07 pm
22	7:45 am	22	Libra	9:06 am
24	10:11 am	24	Scorpio	9:54 pm
27	1:32 am	27	Sagittarius	9:16 am
29	4:45 pm	29	Capricorn	6:01 pm
		October		
1	11:16 pm	1	Aquarius	11:24 pm
3	4:14 pm	4	Pisces	1:33 am
5	4:33 pm	6	Aries	1:32 am
7	4:05 pm	8	Taurus	1:04 am
9	4:45 pm	10	Gemini	2:06 am
11	8:22 pm	12	Cancer	6:21 am
14	4:00 am	14	Leo	2:38 pm
16	5:00 pm	17	Virgo	2:15 am
19	4:18 am	19	Libra	3:19 pm
22	1:57 am	22	Scorpio	3:54 am
24	2:56 am	24	Sagittarius	2:53 pm
26	2:02 pm	26	Capricorn	11:47 pm
28	9:30 pm	29	Aquarius	5:17 am
31	12:31 am	31	Pisces	9:10 am
		November		
2	2:54 am	2	Aries	10:46 am
4	4:02 am	4	Taurus	11:05 am
6	5:17 am	6	Gemini	11:46 am
8	8:42 am	8	Cancer	2:46 pm
10	3:58 pm	10	Leo	9:34 pm
13	3:29 am	13	Virgo	8:18 am

Last Aspect   Moon enters New Sign

	Last Aspect		Moon enters New Sign	
15	5:41 pm	15	Libra	9:14 pm
18	12:41 am	18	Scorpio	9:46 am
20	6:54 pm	20	Sagittarius	8:15 pm
22	8:19 pm	23	Capricorn	4:25 am
25	1:41 am	25	Aquarius	10:41 am
27	8:00 am	27	Pisces	3:20 pm
29	11:29 am	29	Aries	6:30 pm
		December		
1	3:22 pm	1	Taurus	8:26 pm
3	7:31 pm	3	Gemini	10:05 pm
5	7:23 pm	6	Cancer	1:00 am
7	11:50 pm	8	Leo	6:52 am
10	3:35 pm	10	Virgo	4:31 pm
12	9:32 pm	13	Libra	5:00 am
15	10:33 am	15	Scorpio	5:42 pm
17	6:31 pm	18	Sagittarius	4:10 am
20	9:01 am	20	Capricorn	11:39 am
22	7:45 am	22	Aquarius	4:49 pm
24	3:09 pm	24	Pisces	8:43 pm
26	10:05 pm	27	Aries	12:04 am
28	9:54 pm	29	Taurus	3:08 am
31	1:08 am	31	Gemini	6:16 am

Eclipse Dates in 2006

Dates are given in parentheses for eclipses that fall across two days due to time zone differences. Times are in Eastern Time and are rounded off to the nearest minute. The exact time of an eclipse generally differs from the exact time of a New or Full Moon. For solar eclipses, "greatest eclipse" represents the time (converted from Local Mean Time) of the Moon's maximum obscuration of the Sun as viewed from the Earth. For lunar eclipses, "middle of eclipse" represents the time at which the Moon rests at the centermost point of its journey through the shadow cast by the Earth passing between it and the Sun. Data is from *Astronomical Phenomena for the Year 2006*, prepared by the United States Naval Observatory and Her Majesty's Nautical Almanac Office (United Kingdom).

March 14

Penumbral lunar eclipse at 6:49 pm EST: 24° ♍ 15'

Eclipse enters penumbra	4:21 pm	159°
Middle of eclipse	6:49 pm	
Eclipse leaves penumbra	9:14 pm	259°

March 29

Total solar eclipse at 5:33 am EST: 8° ♈ 35'

Eclipse begins	2:36 am	22° E	15° S
Greatest eclipse	5:33 am	23° W	30° N
Eclipse ends	7:45 am	83° W	44° N

September 7

Partial lunar eclipse at 2:52 pm EDT: 15° ♓ 01'

Eclipse enters penumbra	2:05 pm	358°
Middle of eclipse	2:52 pm	
Eclipse leaves penumbra	3:37 pm	306°

September 22

Annular solar eclipse at 7:41 am EDT: 29° ♍ 20'

Eclipse begins	4:40 am	42° E	14° N
Greatest eclipse	7:41 am	04° E	28° S
Eclipse ends	10:40 am	67° W	17° S

Retrograde Periods

Planet	Begin	EST	PST	End	EST	PST
Saturn	11/22/05	4:01 am	**1:01 am**	04/05/06	8:54 am	**5:54 am**
Venus	12/24/05	4:36 am	**1:36 am**	02/03/06	4:18 am	**1:18 am**
Mercury	03/02/06	3:29 pm	**12:29 pm**	03/25/06	8:42 am	**5:42 am**
Jupiter	03/04/06	1:02 pm	**10:02 am**	07/06/06	3:19 am	**12:19 am**
Pluto	03/29/06	7:40 am	**4:40 am**	09/04/06	7:21 pm	**4:21 pm**
Neptune	05/22/06	9:05 am	**6:05 am**	10/28/06	2:56 am	**12:56 am**
Uranus	06/19/06	3:40 am	**12:40 am**	11/19/06		**10:09 pm**
				11/20/06	1:09 am	
Mercury	07/04/06	3:33 pm	**12:33 pm**	07/28/06	8:39 pm	**5:39 pm**
Mercury	10/28/06	3:16 pm	**12:16 pm**	11/17/06	7:25 pm	**4:25 pm**
Saturn	12/05/06	11:06 pm	**8:06 pm**	04/19/07	5:24 pm	**2:24 pm**

Eastern Time in plain type, **Pacific Time in bold type**

	05 Dec	06 Jan	Feb	Mar	Apr	May	Jun	Jul	Aug	Sep	Oct	Nov	06 Dec	07 Jan
☿				▓				▓				▓		
♀		▓												
♂														
♃				▓	▓	▓	▓							
♄	▓	▓	▓	▓	▓								▓	▓
♅							▓	▓	▓	▓	▓	▓		
♆						▓	▓	▓	▓	▓	▓			
♇				▓	▓	▓	▓	▓	▓	▓				

2006 Planetary Phenomena

The planets below are referenced to the constellations (astronomical or sidereal zodiac) and not to the tropical zodiac signs. This may result in planets being located in different signs than are shown throughout the remainder of the book. Information on Uranus and Neptune assumes the use of a telescope. Resource: *Astronomical Phenomena for the Year 2006*, prepared by the U.S. Naval Observatory and the Royal Greenwich Observatory.

Planets in Morning and Evening Twilight

	Morning	Evening
Venus	01/19–10/19	01/01–01/08
	12/08–12/31	
Mars	12/10–12/31	01/01–09/07
Jupiter	01/01–05/04	05/04–11/09
	12/05–12/31	
Saturn	01/01–12/27	01/27–07/20
	08/26–12/31	

Mercury can be seen low in the east before sunrise, or low in the west after sunset. It is visible in the mornings between the following approximate dates: January 1–12, March 19–May 11, July 26–August 24, and November 15–December 21. The planet is brighter at the end of each period. It is visible in the evenings between the following approximate dates: February 8–March 6, May 26–July 11, and September 12–November 3. The planet is brighter at the beginning of each period. Mercury transits the Sun on November 8–9. The event is visible from South America; North America, except the extreme north of Canada, Antarctica; New Zealand; Australia; and eastern Asia.

Venus is visible in the evening sky until the beginning of the second week in January. It reappears in the third week of January as a morning star and can be seen in the morning sky until mid-September. From early December until the end of the year it is visible in the evening sky. Venus is in conjunction with Saturn on August 26.

Mars is in Aries at the beginning of the year, and can be seen for more than half the night until around mid-February, after which it can only be seen in the evening sky. It passes too close to the Sun for observation September through mid-December, after which it reappears as a morning star. Mars is in conjunction with Saturn on June 17, with Mercury on September 15 and December 9, and with Jupiter on December 12.

Jupiter rises shortly after midnight in Libra at the beginning of the year and it can be seen for more than half the night in early February. Its westward elongation increases until May 4, when it is visible throughout the night. From late July until early November, it can only be seen in the evening sky. It reappears at the beginning of December in the morning sky. Jupiter is in conjunction with Mercury on October 25, October 28, and December 10; and with Mars on December 12.

Saturn can be seen in Cancer from the beginning of the year for most of the night. From the end of April to late July, it is visible only in the evening sky. It reappears in the morning sky in late August and moves into Leo in September. By mid-November it can be seen for more than half the night. Saturn is in conjunction with Mars on June 17, with Mercury on August 20, and with Venus on August 26.

Uranus is visible from the beginning of the year until early February in the evening sky in Aquarius and remains in this constellation throughout the year. From early February it becomes too close to the Sun for observation and reappears in late March in the morning sky. It is at opposition on September 5. From early December, it can only be seen in the evening sky.

Neptune is visible for the first half of January in the evening sky. Then it is too close to the Sun for observation until late February, when it reappears in the morning sky.

Find Your Moon Sign

Every year we give tables for the position of the Moon during that year, but it is more complicated to provide tables for the Moon's position in any given year because of its continuous movement. However, the problem was solved by Grant Lewi in *Astrology for the Millions*, which is available from Llewellyn Worldwide.

Grant Lewi's System
Step 1:
Find your birth year in the tables on pages 110–119.

Step 2:
Run down the left-hand column and see if your birth date is there. If your birth date is in the left-hand column, run over this line until you come to the column under your birth year. Here you will find a number. This is your base number. Write it down, and go directly to the direction under the heading "What to Do with Your Base Number" on page 107.

Step 3:
If your birth date is not in the left-hand column, get a pencil and paper. Your birth date falls between two numbers in the left-hand column. Look at the date closest after your birth date; run across this line to your birth year. Write down the number you find there, and label it "top number." Directly beneath it on your piece of paper write the number printed just above it in the table. Label this "bottom number." Subtract the bottom number from the top number. If the top number is smaller, add 360 and subtract. The result is your difference.

Step 4:
Go back to the left-hand column and find the date before your birth date. Determine the number of days between this date and your birth date. Write this down and label it "intervening days."

Step 5:
Note which group your difference falls in.

Difference	Daily Motion
80–87	12 degrees
88–94	13 degrees
95–101	14 degrees
102–106	15 degrees

Note: If you were born in a leap year and use the difference between February 26 and March 5, then the daily motion is slightly different. If you fall into this category use the figures below.

Difference	Daily Motion
94–99	12 degrees
100–108	13 degrees
109–115	14 degrees
116–122	15 degrees

Step 6:
Write down the "daily motion" corresponding to your place in the proper table of difference above. Multiply daily motion by the number labeled "intervening days" (found at step 5).

Step 7:
Add the result of step 6 to your bottom number. This is your base number. If it is more than 360, subtract 360 from it and call the result your base number.

What to Do with Your Base Number

Locate your base number in the Table of Base Numbers. At the top of the column you will find the sign your Moon was in. In the far left-hand column you will find the degree the Moon occupied at 7:00 am of your birth date if you were born under Eastern Standard Time (EST). Refer to the Time Zone Conversions chart and table on page 92–93 to adjust information for your time zone.

If you don't know the hour of your birth, accept this as your Moon's sign and degree. If you do know the hour of your birth, get the exact degree as follows:

If you were born after 7:00 am EST, determine the number of hours after the time that you were born. Divide this by two, rounding up if necessary. Add this to your base number, and the result in the table will be the exact degree and sign of the Moon on the year, month, date, and hour of your birth.

If you were born before 7:00 am EST, determine the number of hours before the time that you were born. Divide this by two. Subtract this from your base number, and the result in the table will be the exact degree and sign of the Moon on the year, month, date, and hour of your birth.

Table of Base Numbers

	♈ (13)	♉ (14)	♊ (15)	♋ (16)	♌ (17)	♍ (18)	♎ (19)	♏ (20)	♐ (21)	♑ (22)	♒ (23)	♓ (24)
0°	0	30	60	90	120	150	180	210	240	270	300	330
1°	1	31	61	91	121	151	181	211	241	271	301	331
2°	2	32	62	92	122	152	182	212	242	272	302	332
3°	3	33	63	93	123	153	183	213	243	273	303	333
4°	4	34	64	94	124	154	184	214	244	274	304	334
5°	5	35	65	95	125	155	185	215	245	275	305	335
6°	6	36	66	96	126	156	186	216	246	276	306	336
7°	7	37	67	97	127	157	187	217	247	277	307	337
8°	8	38	68	98	128	158	188	218	248	278	308	338
9°	9	39	69	99	129	159	189	219	249	279	309	339
10°	10	40	70	100	130	160	190	220	250	280	310	340
11°	11	41	71	101	131	161	191	221	251	281	311	341
12°	12	42	72	102	132	162	192	222	252	282	312	342
13°	13	43	73	103	133	163	193	223	253	283	313	343
14°	14	44	74	104	134	164	194	224	254	284	314	344
15°	15	45	75	105	135	165	195	225	255	285	315	345
16°	16	46	76	106	136	166	196	226	256	286	316	346
17°	17	47	77	107	137	167	197	227	257	287	317	347
18°	18	48	78	108	138	168	198	228	258	288	318	248
19°	19	49	79	109	139	169	199	229	259	289	319	349
20°	20	50	80	110	140	170	200	230	260	290	320	350
21°	21	51	81	111	141	171	201	231	261	291	321	351
22°	22	52	82	112	142	172	202	232	262	292	322	352
23°	23	53	83	113	143	173	203	233	263	293	323	353
24°	24	54	84	114	144	174	204	234	264	294	324	354
25°	25	55	85	115	145	175	205	235	265	295	325	355
26°	26	56	86	116	146	176	206	236	266	296	326	356
27°	27	57	87	117	147	177	207	237	267	297	327	357
28°	28	58	88	118	148	178	208	238	268	298	328	358
29°	29	59	89	119	149	179	209	239	269	299	329	359

Month	Date	1911	1912	1913	1914	1915	1916	1917	1918	1919	1920
Jan.	1	289	57	211	337	100	228	23	147	270	39
Jan.	8	20	162	299	61	192	332	110	231	5	143
Jan.	15	122	251	23	158	293	61	193	329	103	231
Jan.	22	214	335	120	256	23	145	290	68	193	316
Jan.	29	298	66	221	345	108	237	32	155	278	49
Feb.	5	31	170	308	69	203	340	118	239	16	150
Feb.	12	130	260	32	167	302	70	203	338	113	239
Feb.	19	222	344	128	266	31	154	298	78	201	325
Feb.	26	306	75	231	353	116	248	41	164	286	60
Mar.	5	42	192	317	77	214	2	127	248	26	172
Mar.	12	140	280	41	176	311	89	212	346	123	259
Mar.	19	230	5	136	276	39	176	308	87	209	346
Mar.	26	314	100	239	2	124	273	49	173	294	85
Apr.	2	52	200	326	86	223	10	135	257	35	181
Apr.	9	150	288	51	184	321	97	222	355	133	267
Apr.	16	238	14	146	286	48	184	318	96	218	355
Apr.	23	322	111	247	11	132	284	57	181	303	96
Apr.	30	61	208	334	96	232	19	143	267	43	190
May	7	160	296	60	192	331	105	231	4	142	275
May	14	246	22	156	294	56	192	329	104	227	3
May	21	331	122	255	20	141	294	66	190	312	105
May	28	69	218	342	106	240	29	151	277	51	200
Jun.	4	170	304	69	202	341	114	240	14	151	284
Jun.	11	255	30	167	302	65	200	340	112	235	11
Jun.	18	340	132	264	28	151	304	74	198	322	114
Jun.	25	78	228	350	115	249	39	159	286	60	209
Jul.	2	179	312	78	212	349	122	248	25	159	293
Jul.	9	264	39	178	310	74	209	350	120	244	20
Jul.	16	349	141	273	36	161	312	84	206	332	123
Jul.	23	87	237	358	125	258	48	168	295	70	218
Jul.	30	187	321	86	223	357	131	256	36	167	302
Aug.	6	272	48	188	319	82	219	360	129	252	31
Aug.	13	359	150	282	44	171	320	93	214	342	131
Aug.	20	96	246	6	133	268	57	177	303	81	226
Aug.	27	195	330	94	234	5	140	265	46	175	310
Sep.	3	281	57	198	328	90	229	9	138	260	41
Sep.	10	9	158	292	52	180	329	102	222	351	140
Sep.	17	107	255	15	141	279	65	186	312	91	234
Sep.	24	203	339	103	244	13	149	274	56	184	319
Oct.	1	288	68	206	337	98	240	17	148	268	52
Oct.	8	18	167	301	61	189	338	111	231	360	150
Oct.	15	118	263	24	149	290	73.	195	320	102	242
Oct.	22	212	347	113	254	22	157	284	65	193	326
Oct.	29	296	78	214	346	106	250	25	157	276	61
Nov.	5	26	177	309	70	197	348	119	240	7	161
Nov.	12	129	271	33	158	300	81	203	329	112	250
Nov.	19	221	355	123	262	31	164	295	73	202	334
Nov.	26	305	88	223	355	115	259	34	165	285	70
Dec.	3	34	187	317	79	205	359	127	249	16	171
Dec.	10	138	279	41	168	310	89	211	340	120	259
Dec.	17	230	3	134	270	40	172	305	81	211	343
Dec.	24	313	97	232	3	124	267	44	173	294	78
Dec.	31	42	198	325	87	214	9	135	257	25	181

Month	Date	1921	1922	1923	1924	1925	1926	1927	1928	1929	1930
Jan.	1	194	317	80	211	5	127	250	23	176	297
Jan.	8	280	41	177	313	90	211	349	123	260	22
Jan.	15	4	141	275	41	175	312	86	211	346	123
Jan.	22	101	239	3	127	272	51	172	297	83	222
Jan.	29	203	325	88	222	13	135	258	34	184	306
Feb.	5	289	49	188	321	99	220	359	131	269	31
Feb.	12	14	149	284	49	185	320	95	219	356	131
Feb.	19	110	249	11	135	281	60	181	305	93	230
Feb.	26	211	334	96	233	21	144	266	45	191	314
Mar.	5	297	58	197	343	107	230	8	153	276	41
Mar.	12	23	157	294	69	194	328	105	238	6	140
Mar.	19	119	258	19	157	292	68	190	327	104	238
Mar.	26	219	343	104	258	29	153	275	70	200	323
Apr.	2	305	68	205	352	115	240	16	163	284	51
Apr.	9	33	166	304	77	204	337	114	247	14	149
Apr.	16	130	266	28	164	303	76	198	335	115	246
Apr.	23	227	351	114	268	38	161	285	79	208	331
Apr.	30	313	78	214	1	123	250	25	172	292	61
May	7	42	176	313	85	212	348	123	256	23	160
May	14	141	274	37	173	314	84	207	344	125	254
May	21	236	359	123	277	47	169	295	88	217	339
May	28	321	88	222	11	131	259	34	181	301	70
Jun.	4	50	186	321	94	220	358	131	264	31	171
Jun.	11	152	282	45	182	324	93	215	354	135	263
Jun.	18	245	7	134	285	56	177	305	96	226	347
Jun.	25	330	97	232	20	139	268	44	190	310	78
Jul.	2	58	197	329	103	229	9	139	273	40	181
Jul.	9	162	291	54	192	333	101	223	4	144	272
Jul.	16	254	15	144	294	65	185	315	104	236	355
Jul.	23	338	106	242	28	148	276	54	198	319	87
Jul.	30	67	208	337	112	238	20	147	282	49	191
Aug.	6	171	300	62	202	341	110	231	15	152	281
Aug.	13	264	24	153	302	74	194	324	114	244	4
Aug.	20	347	114	253	36	157	285	65	206	328	95
Aug.	27	76	218	346	120	248	29	156	290	59	200
Sep.	3	179	309	70	213	350	119	239	25	161	290
Sep.	10	273	32	162	312	83	203	332	124	252	13
Sep.	17	356	122	264	44	166	293	75	214	337	105
Sep.	24	86	227	354	128	258	38	165	298	70	208
Oct.	1	187	318	78	223	358	128	248	35	169	298
Oct.	8	281	41	170	322	91	212	340	134	260	23
Oct.	15	5	132	274	52	175	303	85	222	345	115
Oct.	22	97	235	3	136	269	46	174	306	81	216
Oct.	29	196	327	87	232	7	137	257	44	179	307
Nov.	5	289	50	178	332	99	221	349	144	268	31
Nov.	12	13	142	283	61	183	313	93	231	353	126
Nov.	19	107	243	12	144	279	54	183	315	91	225
Nov.	26	206	335	96	241	17	145	266	52	189	314
Dec.	3	297	59	187	343	107	230	359	154	276	39
Dec.	10	21	152	291	70	191	324	101	240	1	137
Dec.	17	117	252	21	153	289	63	191	324	99	234
Dec.	24	216	343	105	249	28	152	275	60	199	322
Dec.	31	305	67	197	352	115	237	9	162	285	47

Month	Date	1931	1932	1933	1934	1935	1936	1937	1938	1939	1940
Jan.	1	60	196	346	107	231	8	156	277	41	181
Jan.	8	162	294	70	193	333	104	240	4	144	275
Jan.	15	257	20	158	294	68	190	329	104	239	360
Jan.	22	342	108	255	32	152	278	67	202	323	88
Jan.	29	68	207	353	116	239	19	163	286	49	191
Feb.	5	171	302	78	203	342	113	248	14	153	284
Feb.	12	267	28	168	302	78	198	339	113	248	8
Feb.	19	351	116	266	40	161	286	78	210	332	96
Feb.	26	77	217	1	124	248	29	171	294	59	200
Mar.	5	179	324	86	213	350	135	256	25	161	306
Mar.	12	276	48	176	311	86	218	347	123	256	29
Mar.	19	360	137	277	48	170	308	89	218	340	119
Mar.	26	86	241	10	132	258	52	180	302	69	223
Apr.	2	187	334	94	223	358	144	264	34	169	315
Apr.	9	285	57	185	321	95	227	355	133	264	38
Apr.	16	9	146	287	56	178	317	99	226	349	128
Apr.	23	96	250	18	140	268	61	189	310	80	231
Apr.	30	196	343	102	232	7	153	273	43	179	323
May	7	293	66	193	332	103	237	4	144	272	47
May	14	17	155	297	64	187	327	108	235	357	139
May	21	107	258	28	148	278	69	198	318	90	239
May	28	205	351	111	241	17	161	282	51	189	331
Jun.	4	301	75	201	343	111	245	13	154	280	55
Jun.	11	25	165	306	73	195	337	117	244	5	150
Jun.	18	117	267	37	157	288	78	207	327	99	248
Jun.	25	215	360	120	249	28	169	291	60	200	339
Jul.	2	309	84	211	353	119	254	23	164	289	64
Jul.	9	33	176	315	82	203	348	125	253	13	160
Jul.	16	126	276	46	165	297	87	216	336	108	258
Jul.	23	226	8	130	258	38	177	300	69	210	347
Jul.	30	317	92	221	2	128	262	33	173	298	72
Aug.	6	41	187	323	91	211	359	133	261	21	170
Aug.	13	135	285	54	175	305	97	224	346	116	268
Aug.	20	237	16	138	267	49	185	308	78	220	355
Aug.	27	326	100	232	10	136	270	44	181	307	80
Sep.	3	49	197	331	100	220	8	142	270	31	179
Sep.	10	143	295	62	184	314	107	232	355	125	278
Sep.	17	247	24	147	277	58	194	317	89	228	4
Sep.	24	335	108	243	18	145	278	55	189	316	88
Oct.	1	58	206	341	108	229	17	152	278	40	188
Oct.	8	151	306	70	193	322	117	240	4	134	288
Oct.	15	256	32	155	287	66	203	324	100	236	13
Oct.	22	344	116	253	27	154	287	64	198	324	98
Oct.	29	68	214	350	116	239	25	162	286	49	196
Nov.	5	161	316	78	201	332	126	248	12	145	297
Nov.	12	264	41	162	298	74	212	333	111	244	22
Nov.	19	353	125	262	36	162	296	73	207	332	108
Nov.	26	77	222	0	124	248	33	172	294	58	205
Dec.	3	171	325	87	209	343	135	257	19	156	305
Dec.	10	272	50	171	309	82	220	341	120	253	30
Dec.	17	1	135	271	45	170	306	81	217	340	118
Dec.	24	86	231	10	132	256	43	181	302	66	214
Dec.	31	182	333	95	217	354	142	265	27	167	313

Month	Date	1941	1942	1943	1944	1945	1946	1947	1948	1949	1950
Jan.	1	325	88	211	353	135	258	22	165	305	68
Jan.	8	50	176	315	85	219	348	126	256	29	160
Jan.	15	141	276	50	169	312	87	220	340	123	258
Jan.	22	239	12	133	258	52	182	303	69	224	352
Jan.	29	333	96	221	2	143	266	32	174	314	75
Feb.	5	57	186	323	95	227	358	134	265	37	170
Feb.	12	150	285	58	178	320	96	228	349	131	268
Feb.	19	250	20	142	267	62	190	312	78	234	359
Feb.	26	342	104	231	11	152	274	43	182	323	83
Mar.	5	65	196	331	116	236	8	142	286	46	179
Mar.	12	158	295	66	199	328	107	236	10	139	279
Mar.	19	261	28	150	290	72	198	320	102	243	8
Mar.	26	351	112	242	34	161	281	53	204	332	91
Apr.	2	74	205	340	125	244	16	152	294	55	187
Apr.	9	166	306	74	208	337	117	244	19	148	289
Apr.	16	270	36	158	300	81	206	328	112	252	17
Apr.	23	360	120	252	42	170	290	63	212	340	100
Apr.	30	83	214	350	133	254	25	162	302	64	195
May	7	174	316	82	217	346	127	252	27	158	299
May	14	279	45	166	311	90	215	336	123	260	26
May	21	9	128	261	50	179	299	72	221	349	110
May	28	92	222	1	141	263	33	173	310	73	204
Jun.	4	184	326	91	226	356	137	261	36	168	307
Jun.	11	287	54	174	322	98	224	344	134	268	34
Jun.	18	17	137	270	60	187	308	81	231	357	119
Jun.	25	102	231	11	149	272	42	183	318	82	213
Jul.	2	194	335	99	234	7	145	269	44	179	316
Jul.	9	296	63	183	332	106	233	353	144	277	43
Jul.	16	25	147	279	70	195	318	89	241	5	129
Jul.	23	110	240	21	157	280	52	192	327	91	224
Jul.	30	205	343	108	242	18	153	278	52	190	324
Aug.	6	304	71	192	341	115	241	3	153	286	51
Aug.	13	33	156	287	80	203	327	98	251	13	138
Aug.	20	119	250	30	165	289	63	201	336	99	235
Aug.	27	216	351	117	250	28	162	287	61	200	332
Sep.	3	314	80	201	350	125	249	13	161	296	59
Sep.	10	41	165	296	90	211	336	108	260	21	146
Sep.	17	127	261	39	174	297	74	209	345	107	246
Sep.	24	226	359	126	259	38	170	295	70	209	341
Oct.	1	323	88	211	358	135	257	22	170	306	67
Oct.	8	49	174	306	99	220	344	118	269	30	154
Oct.	15	135	272	47	183	305	84	217	353	116	256
Oct.	22	236	8	134	269	47	180	303	80	217	351
Oct.	29	333	95	220	7	144	265	31	179	315	75
Nov.	5	58	181	317	107	229	352	129	277	39	162
Nov.	12	143	283	55	192	314	94	225	1	125	265
Nov.	19	244	18	141	279	55	189	311	90	225	0
Nov.	26	343	104	229	16	153	274	39	189	323	84
Dec.	3	67	189	328	115	237	360	140	284	47	171
Dec.	10	153	292	64	200	324	103	234	9	136	274
Dec.	17	252	28	149	289	63	199	319	100	234	9
Dec.	24	351	112	237	27	161	282	47	199	331	93
Dec.	31	76	198	338	123	246	9	150	293	55	180

Month	Date	1951	1952	1953	1954	1955	1956	1957	1958	1959	1960
Jan.	1	194	336	115	238	6	147	285	47	178	317
Jan.	8	297	67	199	331	107	237	9	143	278	47
Jan.	15	30	150	294	70	200	320	104	242	9	131
Jan.	22	114	240	35	161	284	51	207	331	94	223
Jan.	29	204	344	124	245	17	155	294	55	189	325
Feb.	5	305	76	207	341	116	246	18	152	287	56
Feb.	12	38	159	302	80	208	330	112	252	17	140
Feb.	19	122	249	45	169	292	61	216	340	102	233
Feb.	26	215	352	133	253	27	163	303	63	199	333
Mar.	5	314	96	216	350	125	266	27	161	297	75
Mar.	12	46	180	310	91	216	351	121	262	25	161
Mar.	19	130	274	54	178	300	86	224	349	110	259
Mar.	26	225	14	142	262	37	185	312	72	208	356
Apr.	2	324	104	226	358	135	274	37	169	307	83
Apr.	9	54	189	319	100	224	360	131	271	34	170
Apr.	16	138	285	62	187	308	97	232	357	118	269
Apr.	23	235	23	150	271	46	194	320	82	217	5
Apr.	30	334	112	235	6	146	282	48	177	317	91
May	7	62	197	330	109	232	8	142	279	42	177
May	14	146	296	70	196	316	107	240	6	127	279
May	21	243	32	158	280	54	204	328	91	225	15
May	28	344	120	244	15	155	290	55	187	326	100
Jun.	4	71	205	341	117	241	16	153	288	51	186
Jun.	11	155	306	79	204	325	117	249	14	137	288
Jun.	18	252	42	166	290	63	214	336	101	234	25
Jun.	25	354	128	253	26	164	298	63	198	335	109
Jul.	2	80	214	351	125	250	24	164	296	60	195
Jul.	9	164	315	88	212	335	126	259	22	147	297
Jul.	16	260	52	174	299	72	223	344	110	243	34
Jul.	23	3	137	261	37	173	307	71	209	343	118
Jul.	30	89	222	2	134	258	33	174	304	68	205
Aug.	6	174	324	97	220	345	134	268	30	156	305
Aug.	13	270	62	182	308	82	232	353	118	254	42
Aug.	20	11	146	269	48	181	316	79	220	351	126
Aug.	27	97	232	11	143	267	43	183	314	76	215
Sep.	3	184	332	107	228	355	143	278	38	166	314
Sep.	10	280	71	191	316	92	241	2	127	265	50
Sep.	17	19	155	278	58	189	325	88	230	359	135
Sep.	24	105	242	20	152	274	54	191	323	84	225
Oct.	1	193	341	116	237	4	152	287	47	174	324
Oct.	8	291	79	200	324	103	249	11	135	276	58
Oct.	15	27	163	287	68	198	333	98	239	8	143
Oct.	22	113	252	28	162	282	64	199	332	92	235
Oct.	29	201	350	125	245	12	162	295	56	182	334
Nov.	5	302	87	209	333	114	256	19	144	286	66
Nov.	12	36	171	297	76	207	341	109	247	17	150
Nov.	19	121	262	37	171	291	73	208	341	101	244
Nov.	26	209	0	133	254	20	173	303	65	190	345
Dec.	3	312	95	217	342	124	265	27	154	295	75
Dec.	10	45	179	307	84	216	348	119	255	27	158
Dec.	17	129	271	46	180	299	82	218	350	110	252
Dec.	24	217	11	141	263	28	184	311	73	199	355
Dec.	31	321	103	225	352	132	273	35	164	303	84

Month	Date	1961	1962	1963	1964	1965	1966	1967	1968	1969	1970
Jan.	1	96	217	350	128	266	27	163	298	76	197
Jan.	8	179	315	89	217	350	126	260	27	161	297
Jan.	15	275	54	179	302	86	225	349	112	257	36
Jan.	22	18	141	264	35	189	311	74	207	359	122
Jan.	29	105	225	1	136	275	35	173	306	85	206
Feb.	5	188	323	99	225	360	134	270	35	171	305
Feb.	12	284	64	187	310	95	235	357	121	267	45
Feb.	19	26	150	272	46	197	320	81	218	7	130
Feb.	26	113	234	11	144	283	45	182	315	93	216
Mar.	5	198	331	109	245	9	142	280	54	180	313
Mar.	12	293	73	195	332	105	244	5	142	277	54
Mar.	19	34	159	280	71	205	329	90	243	15	139
Mar.	26	122	243	19	167	291	54	190	338	101	226
Apr.	2	208	340	119	253	18	151	290	63	189	323
Apr.	9	303	82	204	340	116	252	14	150	288	62
Apr.	16	42	167	288	81	213	337	99	253	23	147
Apr.	23	130	253	28	176	299	64	198	347	109	235
Apr.	30	216	349	128	261	27	161	298	71	197	333
May	7	314	90	213	348	127	260	23	158	299	70
May	14	51	176	298	91	222	345	109	262	32	155
May	21	137	263	36	186	307	74	207	357	117	245
May	28	225	359	137	270	35	172	307	80	205	344
Jun.	4	325	98	222	357	137	268	31	168	309	78
Jun.	11	60	184	308	99	231	353	119	270	42	163
Jun.	18	146	272	45	195	315	82	217	6	126	253
Jun.	25	233	10	145	279	43	183	315	89	214	355
Jul.	2	336	106	230	6	147	276	40	178	318	87
Jul.	9	70	191	318	108	241	1	129	279	51	171
Jul.	16	154	281	56	204	324	91	227	14	135	261
Jul.	23	241	21	153	288	52	193	323	98	223	5
Jul.	30	345	115	238	16	156	286	47	188	327	97
Aug.	6	79	200	327	116	250	10	138	288	60	180
Aug.	13	163	289	66	212	333	99	238	22	144	270
Aug.	20	250	32	161	296	61	203	331	106	233	14
Aug.	27	353	124	246	27	164	295	55	199	335	106
Sep.	3	88	208	336	126	259	19	147	297	68	189
Sep.	10	172	297	77	220	342	108	249	30	152	279
Sep.	17	260	41	170	304	72	212	340	114	244	23
Sep.	24	1	134	254	37	172	304	64	208	344	115
Oct.	1	97	217	344	136	267	28	155	308	76	198
Oct.	8	180	306	88	228	351	117	259	38	161	289
Oct.	15	270	50	179	312	82	220	350	122	254	31
Oct.	22	10	143	262	47	182	313	73	217	353	123
Oct.	29	105	226	352	146	275	37	163	318	84	207
Nov.	5	189	315	97	237	359	127	268	47	168	299
Nov.	12	281	58	188	320	93	228	359	130	264	39
Nov.	19	19	151	271	55	191	321	82	225	3	131
Nov.	26	113	235	1	157	282	45	172	328	92	215
Dec.	3	197	326	105	245	7	138	276	55	176	310
Dec.	10	291	66	197	328	102	237	7	139	273	48
Dec.	17	30	159	280	63	202	329	91	234	13	139
Dec.	24	121	243	11	167	291	53	183	337	101	223
Dec.	31	204	336	113	254	14	149	284	64	184	320

115

Month	Date	1971	1972	1973	1974	1975	1976	1977	1978	1979	1980
Jan.	1	335	109	246	8	147	279	56	179	318	90
Jan.	8	71	197	332	108	243	6	144	278	54	176
Jan.	15	158	283	69	207	328	93	240	18	139	263
Jan.	22	244	20	169	292	54	192	339	102	224	4
Jan.	29	344	117	255	17	156	288	64	188	327	99
Feb.	5	81	204	342	116	253	14	153	287	63	184
Feb.	12	167	291	79	216	337	101	251	26	147	271
Feb.	19	252	31	177	300	62	203	347	110	233	14
Feb.	26	353	126	263	27	164	297	72	199	334	109
Mar.	5	91	224	351	124	262	34	162	296	72	204
Mar.	12	176	312	90	224	346	122	262	34	156	203
Mar.	19	261	55	185	309	72	226	356	118	243	37
Mar.	26	1	149	270	37	172	320	80	208	343	130
Apr.	2	100	233	360	134	270	43	170	307	80	213
Apr.	9	184	320	101	232	355	131	273	42	164	302
Apr.	16	271	64	194	317	82	235	5	126	254	46
Apr.	23	9	158	278	47	181	329	88	217	352	139
Apr.	30	109	242	8	145	278	52	178	318	88	222
May	7	193	329	111	240	3	141	282	50	173	312
May	14	281	73	203	324	92	243	14	134	264	54
May	21	19	167	287	55	191	337	97	226	3	147
May	28	117	251	16	156	286	61	187	328	96	231
Jun.	4	201	339	120	249	11	151	291	59	180	323
Jun.	11	291	81	213	333	102	252	23	143	273	63
Jun.	18	29	176	296	64	201	346	106	234	13	155
Jun.	25	125	260	25	167	295	69	196	338	105	239
Jul.	2	209	349	129	258	19	162	299	68	188	334
Jul.	9	300	90	222	341	111	261	32	152	282	72
Jul.	16	40	184	305	72	212	354	115	243	24	163
Jul.	23	133	268	35	176	303	78	206	347	114	248
Jul.	30	217	0	137	267	27	172	308	77	197	344
Aug.	6	309	99	230	350	120	271	40	161	290	83
Aug.	13	51	192	314	81	223	2	124	252	34	171
Aug.	20	142	276	45	185	312	86	217	356	123	256
Aug.	27	225	10	146	276	36	182	317	86	206	353
Sep.	3	317	109	238	360	128	281	48	170	299	93
Sep.	10	61	200	322	90	232	10	132	262	43	180
Sep.	17	151	284	56	193	321	94	228	4	132	264
Sep.	24	234	20	155	284	45	191	326	94	215	2
Oct.	1	325	120	246	9	136	291	56	179	308	103
Oct.	8	70	208	330	101	241	19	140	273	51	189
Oct.	15	160	292	66	202	330	102	238	12	140	273
Oct.	22	243	28	165	292	54	199	336	102	225	10
Oct.	29	334	130	254	17	146	301	64	187	318	112
Nov.	5	79	217	338	112	249	27	148	284	59	197
Nov.	12	169	300	76	210	339	111	247	21	148	282
Nov.	19	253	36	175	300	63	207	347	110	234	18
Nov.	26	344	139	262	25	156	310	73	195	329	120
Dec.	3	87	226	346	122	257	36	157	294	67	206
Dec.	10	177	310	84	220	347	121	255	31	156	292
Dec.	17	261	45	185	308	72	216	356	118	242	28
Dec.	24	355	148	271	33	167	318	81	203	340	128
Dec.	31	95	235	355	132	265	44	166	303	76	214

Month	Date	1981	1982	1983	1984	1985	1986	1987	1988	1989	1990
Jan.	1	226	350	129	260	36	162	300	71	205	333
Jan.	8	315	89	225	346	126	260	36	156	297	72
Jan.	15	53	188	309	73	225	358	119	243	37	168
Jan.	22	149	272	35	176	319	82	206	348	129	252
Jan.	29	234	0	137	270	43	172	308	81	213	343
Feb.	5	324	98	234	354	135	270	44	164	306	82
Feb.	12	64	196	317	81	236	6	128	252	48	175
Feb.	19	157	280	45	185	328	90	217	356	138	260
Feb.	26	242	10	145	279	51	182	316	90	222	353
Mar.	5	332	108	242	15	143	280	52	185	313	93
Mar.	12	74	204	326	104	246	14	136	275	57	184
Mar.	19	166	288	55	208	337	97	227	19	147	268
Mar.	26	250	20	154	300	60	191	326	111	230	1
Apr.	2	340	119	250	24	151	291	60	194	322	103
Apr.	9	84	212	334	114	255	22	144	286	66	192
Apr.	16	175	296	66	216	346	106	237	27	156	276
Apr.	23	259	28	164	309	69	199	336	119	240	9
Apr.	30	349	130	258	33	160	302	68	203	331	113
May	7	93	221	342	124	264	31	152	297	75	201
May	14	184	304	75	225	355	114	246	36	165	285
May	21	268	36	175	317	78	207	347	127	249	18
May	28	358	140	266	41	170	311	76	211	341	122
Jun.	4	102	230	350	135	272	40	160	307	83	210
Jun.	11	193	313	84	234	3	123	255	45	173	294
Jun.	18	277	45	185	325	87	216	357	135	258	27
Jun.	25	8	149	275	49	180	320	85	219	352	130
Jul.	2	110	239	359	146	281	49	169	317	92	219
Jul.	9	201	322	93	244	11	133	263	55	181	304
Jul.	16	286	54	196	333	96	225	7	143	266	37
Jul.	23	19	158	284	57	191	328	94	227	3	138
Jul.	30	119	248	7	155	290	57	178	327	101	227
Aug.	6	210	331	101	254	19	142	272	66	189	313
Aug.	13	294	64	205	341	104	236	16	152	274	48
Aug.	20	30	166	293	66	202	337	103	236	13	147
Aug.	27	128	256	17	164	299	65	187	335	111	235
Sep.	3	218	340	110	264	27	151	281	75	197	321
Sep.	10	302	75	214	350	112	247	24	160	282	59
Sep.	17	40	174	302	74	212	345	112	245	23	156
Sep.	24	138	264	26	172	309	73	197	343	121	243
Oct.	1	226	349	119	274	36	159	292	84	206	329
Oct.	8	310	86	222	359	120	258	32	169	291	70
Oct.	15	50	183	310	84	220	354	120	255	31	165
Oct.	22	148	272	35	181	319	81	206	352	130	251
Oct.	29	234	357	130	282	44	167	303	92	214	337
Nov.	5	318	96	230	8	129	268	40	178	300	79
Nov.	12	58	193	318	93	229	4	128	265	39	175
Nov.	19	158	280	44	190	329	90	214	2	139	260
Nov.	26	243	5	141	290	53	175	314	100	223	345
Dec.	3	327	106	238	16	139	277	49	185	310	88
Dec.	10	66	203	326	103	237	14	136	274	48	185
Dec.	17	167	288	52	200	337	98	222	12	147	269
Dec.	24	252	13	152	298	62	184	324	108	232	355
Dec.	31	337	114	248	24	149	285	59	193	320	96

Month	Date	1991	1992	1993	1994	1995	1996	1997	1998	1999	2000
Jan.	1	111	242	15	145	281	53	185	317	92	223
Jan.	8	206	326	108	244	16	136	279	56	186	307
Jan.	15	289	54	210	337	99	225	21	147	270	37
Jan.	22	18	158	299	61	190	329	110	231	2	140
Jan.	29	119	252	23	155	290	62	193	326	101	232
Feb.	5	214	335	116	254	24	145	287	66	193	315
Feb.	12	298	63	220	345	108	235	31	155	278	47
Feb.	19	29	166	308	69	201	337	119	239	12	148
Feb.	26	128	260	32	164	299	70	202	335	111	240
Mar.	5	222	356	124	265	32	166	295	76	201	337
Mar.	12	306	87	229	354	116	259	39	164	285	72
Mar.	19	39	189	317	77	211	360	128	248	22	170
Mar.	26	138	280	41	172	310	90	212	343	121	260
Apr.	2	230	5	133	275	40	175	305	86	210	345
Apr.	9	314	98	237	3	123	270	47	173	294	83
Apr.	16	49	198	326	86	220	9	136	257	31	180
Apr.	23	148	288	50	180	320	98	221	351	132	268
Apr.	30	238	13	143	284	48	183	315	95	218	353
May	7	322	109	245	12	132	281	55	182	302	93
May	14	57	207	335	95	228	18	144	267	39	190
May	21	158	296	59	189	330	106	230	1	141	276
May	28	247	21	154	292	57	191	326	103	227	1
Jun.	4	330	119	253	21	141	291	64	190	311	102
Jun.	11	66	217	343	105	236	28	152	276	48	199
Jun.	18	168	304	68	199	340	114	238	11	150	285
Jun.	25	256	29	165	300	66	199	337	111	236	10
Jul.	2	339	129	262	29	150	300	73	198	321	111
Jul.	9	74	227	351	114	245	38	160	285	57	209
Jul.	16	177	313	76	210	348	123	246	22	158	293
Jul.	23	265	38	175	309	75	208	347	120	245	19
Jul.	30	349	137	272	37	160	308	83	206	331	119
Aug.	6	83	237	359	123	255	48	169	293	67	218
Aug.	13	186	322	84	221	356	132	254	33	166	302
Aug.	20	273	47	185	318	83	218	356	129	253	29
Aug.	27	358	146	282	45	169	317	93	214	340	128
Sep.	3	93	246	7	131	265	56	177	301	78	226
Sep.	10	194	331	92	231	4	141	263	43	174	311
Sep.	17	281	56	194	327	91	228	5	138	261	39
Sep.	24	8	154	292	53	178	326	102	223	349	137
Oct.	1	104	254	16	139	276	64	186	310	89	234
Oct.	8	202	339	101	241	13	149	273	53	183	319
Oct.	15	289	66	202	337	99	238	13	148	269	49
Oct.	22	16	164	301	61	187	336	111	231	357	148
Oct.	29	115	262	25	148	287	72	195	318	100	242
Nov.	5	211	347	111	250	22	157	283	61	193	326
Nov.	12	297	76	211	346	107	247	22	157	277	58
Nov.	19	24	174	309	70	194	346	119	240	5	159
Nov.	26	126	270	33	156	297	80	203	328	109	251
Dec.	3	220	355	121	258	31	165	293	69	202	334
Dec.	10	305	85	220	355	115	256	31	165	286	67
Dec.	17	32	185	317	79	203	357	127	249	13	169
Dec.	24	135	278	41	166	306	89	211	338	117	260
Dec.	31	230	3	131	266	41	173	303	78	211	343

Month	Year	2001	2002	2003	2004	2005	2006	2007	2008	2009	2010
Jan.	1	355	128	263	33	165	300	74	203	336	111
Jan.	8	89	228	355	117	260	39	165	288	71	211
Jan.	15	193	317	79	209	4	127	249	20	174	297
Jan.	22	280	41	174	310	91	211	346	121	261	21
Jan.	29	4	137	273	42	175	308	84	211	345	119
Feb.	5	97	238	3	126	268	49	173	296	80	221
Feb.	12	202	326	87	219	12	136	257	31	182	306
Feb.	19	289	49	184	319	99	220	356	130	269	31
Feb.	26	13	145	283	49	184	316	94	219	355	127
Mar.	5	106	248	11	147	278	59	181	317	90	229
Mar.	12	210	334	95	244	20	145	265	56	190	315
Mar.	19	298	58	193	342	107	229	4	153	277	40
Mar.	26	23	153	293	69	193	325	104	239	4	136
Apr.	2	116	257	20	155	289	67	190	325	101	237
Apr.	9	218	343	104	255	28	154	274	67	198	323
Apr.	16	306	68	202	351	115	239	12	162	285	50
Apr.	23	32	162	303	77	202	334	114	247	12	146
Apr.	30	127	265	29	163	300	75	199	333	112	245
May	7	226	352	113	264	37	162	284	76	207	331
May	14	314	77	210	1	123	248	21	172	293	59
May	21	40	173	312	86	210	345	122	256	20	157
May	28	138	273	38	171	311	83	207	342	123	254
Jun.	4	235	0	122	273	46	170	294	84	217	339
Jun.	11	322	87	219	11	132	257	30	181	302	68
Jun.	18	48	183	320	95	218	356	130	265	29	168
Jun.	25	149	281	46	181	321	92	216	352	132	262
Jul.	2	245	8	132	281	56	178	304	93	227	347
Jul.	9	330	95	229	20	140	266	41	190	310	76
Jul.	16	56	195	328	104	227	7	138	274	38	179
Jul.	23	158	290	54	191	330	101	224	2	140	272
Jul.	30	254	16	142	290	65	186	313	101	236	356
Aug.	6	339	103	239	28	149	274	52	198	319	84
Aug.	13	65	205	336	112	236	17	147	282	47	188
Aug.	20	167	299	62	201	338	110	232	12	149	281
Aug.	27	264	24	151	299	74	194	321	111	245	5
Sep.	3	348	112	250	36	158	282	63	206	328	93
Sep.	10	74	215	345	120	246	26	156	290	58	197
Sep.	17	176	309	70	211	347	120	240	22	157	290
Sep.	24	273	33	159	309	83	203	330	122	253	14
Oct.	1	356	120	261	44	167	291	73	214	336	103
Oct.	8	84	224	354	128	256	34	165	298	68	205
Oct.	15	184	318	78	220	355	129	248	31	167	299
Oct.	22	281	42	167	320	91	212	338	132	261	23
Oct.	29	5	129	271	52	175	301	82	222	344	113
Nov.	5	95	232	4	136	266	42	174	306	78	213
Nov.	12	193	327	87	229	5	137	257	40	177	307
Nov.	19	289	51	176	331	99	221	346	143	268	31
Nov.	26	13	139	280	61	183	312	91	231	352	123
Dec.	3	105	240	13	144	276	51	183	315	87	223
Dec.	10	203	335	96	237	15	145	267	48	188	315
Dec.	17	297	59	185	341	107	229	356	152	277	39
Dec.	24	21	150	288	70	190	322	98	240	0	134
Dec.	31	114	249	22	153	285	60	191	324	96	232

Dates to Hunt or Fish

Dates to Hunt or Fish	Qtr.	Sign
Jan. 3, 7:43 am–Jan. 5, 9:44 am	1st	Pisces
Jan. 12, 5:50 am–Jan. 14, 4:31 pm	2nd	Cancer
Jan. 22, 5:28 am–Jan. 24, 1:38 pm	3rd	Scorpio
Feb. 30, 5:32 pm–Feb. 1, 5:46 pm	1st	Pisces
Feb. 8, 11:33 am–Feb. 10, 10:44 pm	2nd	Cancer
Feb. 18, 12:11 pm–Feb. 20, 9:38 pm	3rd	Scorpio
Feb. 20, 9:38 pm–Feb. 23, 3:16 am	3rd	Sagittarius
Mar. 27, 4:56 am–Mar. 1, 4:18 am	4th	Pisces
Mar. 7, 5:38 pm–Mar. 10, 4:42 am	2nd	Cancer
Mar. 17, 5:59 pm–Mar. 20, 3:43 am	3rd	Scorpio
Mar. 20, 3:43 am–Mar. 22, 10:36 am	3rd	Sagittarius
Mar. 26, 3:33 pm–Mar. 28, 3:31 pm	4th	Pisces
Apr. 4, 2:15 am–Apr. 6, 12:25 am	1st	Cancer
Apr. 14, 1:08 am–Apr. 16, 10:19 am	3rd	Scorpio
Apr.16, 10:19 am–Apr. 18, 4:13 pm	3rd	Sagittarius
Apr. 23, 12:43 am–Apr. 25, 2:12 am	4th	Pisces
May 1, 11:17 am–May 3, 8:18 pm	1st	Cancer
May 11, 8:24 am–May 13, 4:56 pm	2nd	Scorpio
May 13, 4:56 pm–May 15, 10:59 pm	3rd	Sagittarius
May 20, 6:39 am–May 22, 9:24 am	4th	Pisces
May 28, 8:33 pm–May 31, 4:51 am	1st	Cancer
Jun. 7, 4:41 pm–Jun. 10, 1:05 am	2nd	Scorpio
Jun. 10, 1:05 am–Jun. 12, 6:19 am	2nd	Sagittarius
Jun. 16, 12:05 pm–Jun. 18, 2:54 pm	3rd	Pisces
Jun.25, 4:48 am–Jun. 27, 1:09 pm	4th	Cancer
Jul. 5, 1:13 am–Jul. 7, 10:13 am	2nd	Scorpio
Jul. 7, 10:13 am–Jul. 9, 3:25 pm	2nd	Sagittarius
Jul. 13, 6:59 pm–Jul. 15, 8:39 pm	3rd	Pisces

Dates to Hunt and Fish	Qtr.	Sign
Jul. 15, 8:39 pm–Jul. 17, 11:44 pm	3rd	Aries
Jul. 22, 11:28 am–Jul. 24, 8:24 pm	4th	Cancer
Aug. 1, 9:08 am–Aug. 3, 7:13 pm	1st	Scorpio
Aug. 3, 7:13 pm–Aug. 6, 1:19 am	2nd	Sagittarius
Aug. 10, 4:10 am–Aug. 12, 4:22 am	3rd	Pisces
Aug. 12, 4:22 am–Aug. 14, 6:00 am	3rd	Aries
Aug. 18, 5:03 pm–Aug. 21, 2:33 am	4th	Cancer
Aug. 28, 3:56 pm–Aug. 31, 3:00 am	1st	Scorpio
Sep. 6, 2:56 pm–Sep. 8, 2:23 pm	2nd	Pisces
Sep. 8, 2:23 pm–Sep. 10, 2:30 pm	3rd	Aries
Sep. 14, 10:53 pm–Sep. 17, 8:15 am	4th	Cancer
Sep. 24, 9:54 pm–Sep. 27, 9:16 am	1st	Scorpio
Oct. 4, 1:33 am–Oct. 6, 1:32 am	2nd	Pisces
Oct. 6, 1:32 am–Oct. 8, 1:04 am	2nd	Aries
Oct. 12, 6:21 am–Oct. 14, 2:38 pm	3rd	Cancer
Oct. 22, 3:54 am–Oct. 24, 2:53 pm	1st	Scorpio
Nov. 31, 9:10 am–Nov. 2, 10:46 am	2nd	Pisces
Nov. 2, 10:46 am–Nov. 4, 11:05 am	2nd	Aries
Nov 8, 2:46 pm–Nov.10, 9:34 pm	3rd	Cancer
Nov. 18, 9:46 am–Nov. 20, 8:15 pm	4th	Scorpio
Nov. 27, 3:20 pm–Nov. 29, 6:30 pm	1st	Pisces
Dec. 29, 6:30 pm–Dec. 1, 8:26 pm	2nd	Aries
Dec. 6, 1:00 am–Dec. 8, 6:52 am	3rd	Cancer
Dec. 15, 5:42 pm–Dec. 18, 4:10 am	4th	Scorpio
Dec. 24, 8:43 pm–Dec. 27, 12:04 am	1st	Pisces

Eclipses: The Turning Points

by April Elliott Kent

I became an astrological eclipse-watcher completely by accident. In the early days of my practice, I decided one week to prepare a lecture on eclipse cycles for my intermediate astrology class. I did a little research and found quite a bit that had been written about the astrology of eclipses applied to politics, natural disasters, and sundry portents of doom. I found little, though, that reflected the practical, everyday concerns of my students. So I began to develop a lesson plan based on what I knew, which, admittedly, wasn't much.

I knew, for instance, that eclipses move through the birth chart approximately every eighteen years, so that an eclipse makes the same aspect to roughly the same point in your birth chart about every eighteen years. In astrology, the quarter and halfway points in a cycle are also very potent. So if eclipses meant anything, they would presumably transmit their message across a cycle of eighteen years, with cosmic punctuation marks occurring at intervals of four and a half years. Here, at least, was a framework on which to hang my tenuous lesson plan; but unlike planets and their cycles, the astrological message of eclipses wasn't clear. What did eclipses mean?

I didn't have a clear answer for my class that week, but I was hooked. In the years that followed I peered into the charts of my clients, family, and friends to observe what happened when eclipses shook up their lives. I set about deconstructing my own life, isolating major events and listing the eclipses that occurred in the same years. And what I found was that the most pivotal events of my life tended to have something in common: eclipses, forming aspects to the same few, sensitive areas of my birth chart. I began to develop a sense that eclipses forecasted scary, prickly moments of truth, turning points, when something important is changing and the landscape of your life suddenly looks unfamiliar, even alien.

June 1970

I was watching *Captain Kangaroo* with my sister the morning they came to tell us our father was dead. It was the first day of June 1970, a morning of clear and dazzling light, and a sky washed clean from the previous night's rainstorm.

A knock at the back door. The sound of muffled voices; I recognize one as my uncle's. I step cautiously to the door of the kitchen; I can make out a few words. "Jim Lewis . . . " "through the windshield . . ." And my mother begins to cry, to sob. I gather something has happened to "Uncle Jim," a family friend. What does it have to do with us? My aunt is moving toward me through the kitchen, a stricken look on her face; she reaches me at the precise moment I hear my mother's voice screaming into the phone, jagged as cut glass, "Where is my husband? What have you done with my husband?"

My aunt gathers me up and holds on tight, and that's when I realize it wasn't Uncle Jim who went through the windshield of his car that rainy night. It was my father. I hide my face in the comforting familiarity of my aunt's calico housedress, and I begin to cry; I barely stop for three months.

Carlos Castaneda writes of Don Juan's teachings about the "assemblage point," one's innate sense of balance, which can suddenly shift in response to an unexpected event. Likewise, an eclipse signals that something in you has shifted, as surely as an earthquake shifts the foundation of a house. Sometimes, the shift is subtle; a crack in the plaster, a picture that falls off a wall. Other times, when the eclipse point makes a close aspect to a difficult planetary combination in your birth chart—as it did for me in 1970, when my father died—your whole house is picked up and shaken.

This year's eclipses, then, resonate with eclipses that happened nine, eighteen, twenty-seven, even thirty-six years ago. What were you doing then? Those years, and the things that happened to you then, are relevant to your life right now. The eclipses that happened then are cosmic cousins of this year's eclipses, whispering across the years, urging you to pick up a dropped thread of your life's narrative.

September 1988

I'm huddled in a phone booth in Sydney, Australia, hysterical, explaining to my mother that the boyfriend I just traveled all the way around the world to visit is completely and utterly out of his mind. Twenty-seven years my senior, he has always been a bit eccentric, and I knew he was probably an alcoholic. But in the two years since I last saw him he has developed full-blown mental illness; last night he woke me up at 2:00 am, checking the overhead light fixtures for hidden cameras. Mom is concerned, but there is nothing she can do for me. I can't even get a flight out for two more days. I am stranded thousands of miles from everyone who knows and loves me, and I am staying with a crazy man. I hang up the phone and stand there for a moment, listening to the monorail train pass overhead. I've never felt more alone in my life.

Mark Twain once wrote, "History doesn't repeat itself, but it rhymes." Losing my father, being stranded far from home with an unreliable man—these are separate acts in a long-running play whose central plot centers around the wisdom of relying on men for my security. Not surprisingly, eclipses in both of these years made difficult aspects to the Moon (symbolizing security) and Pluto (symbolizing threatening forces beyond our control) in my birth chart. And each year marked a turning point in my ongoing Moon-Pluto struggle to acquire emotional self-reliance.

The Way Eclipses Work

We think of eclipses as rare, but in fact, solar eclipses occur every six months at the New Moon, within a few days of the Sun's conjunction with the North and South Lunar Nodes. Solar eclipses are usually, but not always, accompanied by a lunar eclipse at the Full Moon before or after the solar eclipse.

Some astrologers argue that there is a difference between solar eclipses and lunar ones, associating them, respectively, with external and internal events. Personally, I've never gotten much insight from this distinction. After all, solar and lunar eclipses occur within a mere two weeks of each other. Likewise, outer events and inner ones tend to happen close together. One may happen slightly ahead of the other, but for all practical purposes they happen in tandem. For me, the fascination of eclipses, be they solar or lunar, is the change they portend, and, almost always, we change on the inside and the outside, all at the same time.

Eclipses in Houses

As they move through the houses of the horoscope, eclipses reveal the landscape that is being altered, the areas where you are changing, growing, muddling through unfamiliar territory. In short, they describe where you are currently most interesting.

Eclipses move clockwise through your chart (unlike normal transits, which move counter-clockwise), falling in the six house axes (teams of two houses that are directly opposite one another) of the chart approximately every nine years, like so:

> First house / Seventh house
> Twelfth house / Sixth house
> Eleventh house / Fifth house
> Tenth house / Fourth house
> Ninth house / Third house
> Eighth house / Second house

The sizes of these house axes vary, depending upon which house system you're using, and where you were born. For instance, people born extremely north or south of the equator will have one or two houses that are extremely large, while the rest of the houses are very small. Obviously, as eclipses move through your chart, they will pass more quickly through a very small house axis than through a very large one. On average, though, each house axis of your chart will be sensitized by eclipses for one to two years at a time.

Eclipses in Aspect to Natal Planets

Eclipses tend to be more keenly felt when they form close aspects to planets in your birth chart—especially by conjunction (0 degrees), square (90 degrees), or opposition (180 degrees). And when an eclipse makes an aspect to one natal planet, which in turn aspects other natal planets, all of them feel the reverberations. When this matrix of interconnected planets receives an aspect from an eclipse, a narrative emerges that, like my Moon-Pluto eclipse story of loss and insecurity, gets repeated over and over throughout your lifetime. Eventually, it becomes as familiar as the plot of a movie you've seen many times before.

Look to the personal planets (Sun, Moon, Mercury, Venus, Mars) in aspect to the outer planets (Jupiter, Saturn, Uranus, Neptune, Pluto) to find the most sensitive planetary combinations in your birth chart. Unless an eclipse triggers these high-tension aspects in your natal chart, or falls very close to the cusps of the first, fourth, seventh, or tenth houses, you are likely to experience it as a relatively subtle influence, the flutter of a leaf in a chilling breeze. But each time one of the high-tension planets is aspected by a wandering eclipse, you are given another opportunity to face down one of your fundamental fears, perhaps a fear of anonymity (the Sun), of sexuality (Mars), of authoring your own life (Saturn), or of reality (Neptune).

It's Not All Bad

Not all eclipses are associated with what we think of as unhappy events. Many coincide with joyous moments, such as a marriage, or the birth of a child. But because we don't expect to be frightened or disoriented by positive events, and receive little support from others for our feelings ("For heaven's sake, can't you even enjoy it when something good happens to you?"), these positive eclipse turning points are in some ways more traumatic than tragic ones. The truth is: even choosing something good for yourself can shake up your life and call forth old fears.

May 1993

In a couple of weeks I'm getting married to the kindest man I've ever known. Ever since my father died I've been wary of depending on others; but now I'm choosing to become completely interdependent—and I'm absolutely terrified. What if he suddenly dies? What if he takes me away, someday, to his native New Zealand and then something happens to him, and I'm stranded there, far from home?

One day, as we chat about wedding plans, he accidentally calls me by his ex-girlfriend's name. Already stretched to the breaking point by the tension of the wedding plans, I shatter like glass, and run from the room. I fall on the guest room bed, weeping. How can I marry someone who calls me by another woman's name?

Almost immediately, I know how silly I'm being, and how much of my reaction is about all those deeper, older fears of intimacy. I know, now, about eclipses, and those old wounds to the lunar and Plutonian parts of me. "So what if all those things happen, the things you fear?" whispers the steely, eclipse-tested part of my psyche. "They've happened before and you lived through them. Be happy now." My poor, abashed beloved hurries into the guest room to apologize and to comfort me, but I'm already feeling much better.

The Latitudes of Home

Because it is painful to remember the scary moments of the past or contemplate the uncertainty of the future, we tend to go through life ignoring the reality that our entire lives can be irrevocably changed in an instant. Every now and then, when someone close to us dies, a terrorist attack wounds our country, or some other personal crisis shakes us up, we are startled awake for a moment and behold a landscape we scarcely recognize. Our instinct, then, is to turn away as quickly as possible and return to the latitudes of home.

But even after life returns to normal, the shadowy image of the eclipse remains emblazoned on the psyche. Each time the eclipse's shadow falls across one of our guiding lights, we awaken to old fears and, hopefully, get a bit better at facing them. But the eclipse-touched places in us remain a little ajar, just below the surface. They are as rich as freshly plowed earth and ready to receive the seeds of startling change—even after we've returned to our everyday lives, and have gone back to pretending that the Sun and Moon will never disappear again.

2006 Eclipses

3/14/06	Lunar	24° Virgo 15'
3/29/06	Solar	8° Aries 35'
9/7/06	Lunar	15° Pisces 06'
9/22/06	Solar	29° Virgo 20'

Note: "The latitudes of home" is a phrase borrowed from Annie Dillard's essay, "Total Eclipse," in *The Annie Dillard Reader*, Harper Collins, 1994.

April Elliott Kent, a professional astrologer since 1990, is a member of NCGR and ISAR and a graduate of San Diego State University, with a degree in communication. April's astrological writing has appeared in the Mountain Astrologer *(USA) and* Wholistic Astrologer *(Australia) magazines, the online magazine* MoonCircles, *and Llewellyn's 2005 Moon Sign Book. She specializes in the astrology of choosing wedding dates and the study of eclipses, and has authored a self-published report called "Followed by a Moonshadow," based on her work with eclipse cycles. Her Web site is: http://www.bigskyastrology.com.*

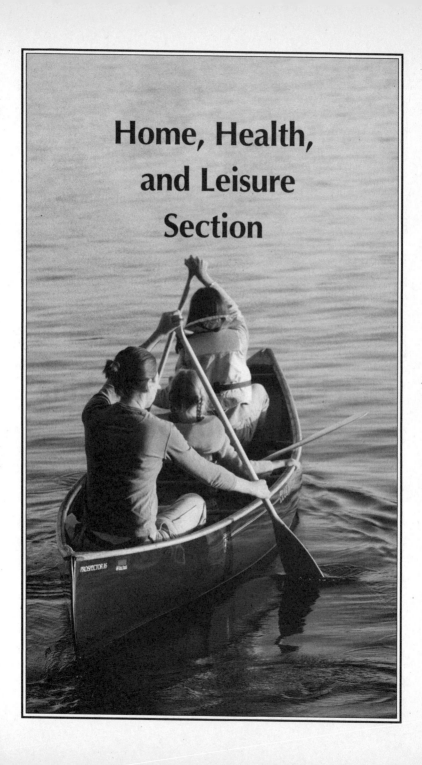

Home, Health,
and Leisure
Section

Quickie Gourmet Cooking Guide for Men

by Daniel B. Brawner

M oms seem to know instinctively how to cook regular meals and know just what they'd make in case Martha Stewart dropped in unexpectedly. But men, especially bachelors, are at a social and biological disadvantage in the kitchen. Everybody expects us to be incompetent. They think the only recipes we know are things like cheese sandwiches grilled on a steam iron. Okay, guys are impatient. We aren't going to spend all day on a chocolate Napoleon with twenty-seven layers of puff pastry and a sauce made with raspberries carved to look like Jacques Chirac. If we cook anything it has to be quick and easy. For most men I know, a quick breakfast means swallowing some Crest while brushing their teeth. So how could we come up with a gourmet meal that would impress guests?

All bachelors have lots of recipes we've received from well-meaning relatives and married friends—as if we're supposed to know whether to make orecchiette with spicy duck ragu for the girlfriend's parents or for the Super Bowl party. To take the guesswork out of selecting the perfect menu, the answer is to choose recipes by the phases of the Moon.

In the fifth century, the Greek philosopher Empedocles wrote that everything could be classified under four basic elements: earth, air, fire and water. Using this as a guide, choose a recipe corresponding to the astrological sign (i.e., Aries: fire, Taurus: earth, Gemini: air, etc.) of your principal guest (the one most likely to help with the dishes). Okay, it's not the way they do it at the Ritz. But hey, it beats playing "scissors, paper, rock."

Let's say your guest is an earth sign. A Taurus is grounded, steady, practical, not overly philosophical. It might be best to stay away from complicated recipes with a lot of stuff mixed together. Capricorns also like to stick to the facts. They are here-and-now, meat-and-potatoes people. A Virgo, the other earth sign, will probably be picky no matter what you feed him or her. Don't worry about trying to satisfy Virgos. Try shocking them with something they wouldn't ordinarily eat on a bet. It will be a memorable experience and they'll be secretly grateful. Or if you're feeling particularly wicked, serve your Virgos alphabet soup and see if they can resist arranging the letters in alphabetical order.

Earth—Taurus, Virgo, and Capricorn

For earth signs, a roast pig is the ideal bachelor recipe. Dig a big hole in the yard (ideally, somebody else's yard), throw in tree limbs and anything else that will burn, set it on fire, toss in a pig, cover and wait for about six hours. It will be a dream come true for the primal streak in a Taurus. Capricorns and Virgos may brood over the imprecise nature of cooking with fire, but if you let them help organize the event, they'll be happy. A pig roast appeals to male cooks for the same reason that fishing does—all that waiting is a perfect excuse to sit around and drink.

Air—Gemini, Libra, and Aquarius

Air sign types tend to be intellectuals, so give them alternatives at the table—like tacos with their choice of exotic cheeses, fresh salsas, and herbs. Serve them foods with startling contrasts like a spicy curry sauce sweetened with peach or crème margot. A sweet, airy meringue with tart strawberry will appeal to Libras who can't make up their minds. Oddball Aquarians might appreciate a meal made entirely of dehydrated foods like jerkys, sun-dried tomatoes, homemade potato chips, and dried apricots, washed down with a very dry red wine. Anybody can grind their own coffee. But innovative Geminis will be intrigued with green coffee beans home-roasted in an air popcorn popper. It works great, but for days afterwards your house smells like Juan Valdez's undershirt.

Fire—Aries, Leo, and Sagittarius

It may not impress women, but if you're having fire-sign guys over for dinner, nothing beats barbeque beer chicken. The ingredients are: chicken, fire, and beer. The Cro-Magnon simplicity will appeal to Leos. Take one whole chicken, open a can of beer and insert it in the chicken's, um, cavity. Place on the grill. The evaporating beer makes the chicken moist and tender. And it also makes it taste like beer, which is good. But I just wonder how the technique was discovered. "Now where did I put my beer? Oh, my gosh! Well, we might as well eat it."

Another good chicken recipe sure to make a hit with the impatient warrior-type Aries is lemon chicken. Take a piece of boneless chicken, beat it violently with a meat tenderizer (or golf shoe) for five minutes. Now, don't you feel better? The rest of the recipe involves wax paper and lemon juice and stuff no guy has in the house anyway, so forget about it. Pop a burrito in the microwave and turn on the Celtics game.

For the extravagant, iconoclastic Sagittarian, you could try roasting a unicorn or a baby seal or one of those spiky, poisonous puff fish (only be sure it's not on a Friday). Otherwise, any recipe will do, as long as it has never been made before.

Water—Cancer, Scorpio, and Pisces

My ancestors in the British Isles learned long ago that anything could be cooked by boiling it. The problem was trying to eat it afterwards. This dilemma made the Irish a restless and warlike race, with a fondness for other people's cooking. So, even for water signs, I can't recommend boiling.

For the nurturing Cancer, serve comfort food like meat loaf or mashed potatoes—foods that rekindle warm memories of a happy childhood. This should also appeal to the compassionate Pisces. But don't serve fondue at a function for Pisces. They are so polite and considerate, they may go hungry before they'd take their turn dipping into the melted cheese. Intense and willful Scorpios are a challenge to cook for. Try a fiery, one-dish Mongolian mutton stew, with leeks and wild onions, that might once have calmed the nomad heart of Kublah Khan. Or maybe a pile of artichokes with melted butter will keep the goal-oriented Scorpio busy with a task he can sink his teeth into.

But who knows what recipe will please which guest? Tastes are as changeable as the phases of the Moon. Let's face it, the most reliable things to make are reservations.

Daniel B. Brawner cooks up peculiar dishes for his guests in Lisbon, Iowa. Dan is the author of the humorous New Age mystery, Employment is Murder.

Emotional Growth

by David Pond

The Moon in your birth chart represents your natural emotional style. Your progressed Moon reveals your evolving emotional self that knows where and how to adapt to life's ever changing circumstances. With the secondary progressions, your Moon advances through each of the signs of the zodiac in a twenty-seven-year cycle. The Moon progresses through your chart at a pace of about 1 degree a month, thus going through each sign and house of your chart for about two to two-and-one-half years. The formula for calculating progressions is one day in the ephemeris equals one year of life. If a person is twenty years old, you go twenty days forward from the birth date in the ephemeris; and the planetary positions for that day are the secondary progressions for the twentieth year of life. Thankfully, modern astrology programs for computers do all of the calculations and can pinpoint your progressed Moon to the degree.

The progressions are the most highly personal and individual of all the timing indicators. The transits are the same for all of us (i.e., Uranus will be in Pisces for the next several years for everyone). The progressions are not based on universal planetary movements, however; they represent movement of your individual and unique birth chart through time. Another important distinction is that the transits tend to be more event-oriented—what is happening to you—while the progressions relate to what is going on within you that the outer world may or may not see, but that you will certainly be aware of.

Of all the progressed planets, the Moon moves the fastest and describes your current emotional needs—basically, what you are in the mood for. However, this does not directly translate into events. For example, I might have been in the mood for a mocha this morning but I made myself a cup of tea. Just because you are in the mood for something doesn't necessarily mean it is going to happen on its own. Thus, it is important to act on your emotional needs and to set up situations that will lead to their fulfillment. The house your progressed Moon is in shows where you will be looking for this emotional fulfillment, but it also shows where you will have to evolve to get your needs met in light of the changing circumstances in this area of your life.

Moon in Aries or First House

Aries is the first sign of the zodiac and you should be feeling the need to start something new. While your Moon is in Aries, you want action and you want it now! Having emerged from the uncertainties of your Pisces period, you are ready to overcome inertia and get things moving in your life. Now is the time to trust your instincts, and if you do your Aries Moon right, friends and family may get a little upset with you. Why? Because, you cannot do Aries by consensus. You've got to focus on you and go for it! When your Moon is in your first house, you may feel a strong sense of urgency about your life and not want to waste a moment of it. This is the time when people get married or divorced, change their names and hair color, or move. Self-actualization and self-development are the name of the game. To help overcome inertia in your life, get moving! Literally, go out and get physical, which will put you in the right mindset; thus, the ideas that come to you while you are out walking are relevant for later that day or into the next day, but not for plans way down the road. The point is to stay spontaneous.

Moon in Taurus or Second House

After all the action and excitement of the last few years, you are ready to settle down and enjoy some comfort and security. Stability becomes important and you would like to develop some routines and a plan rather than flying around by the seat of your pants. You may want to upgrade the quality of your involvement with the material plane, and for many people that means shopping. There is often quite a bit of coming and going of possessions during the Taurus time. Which of your possessions still give you emotional fulfillment, and which of them are you no longer attached to? There are two levels of Taurus. The first is acquisition; you have to acquire the right possessions that give you a sense of meaning. The second level is appreciation, and it doesn't automatically follow. We all know many wealthy people who have all the material wealth in the world but lack the ability to appreciate it. They might as well be broke for all of the good their possessions do them. Taurus likes simple truths, and the phrase that pays for you during this time is: "If you want more fulfillment in life, learn how to spend more time wanting what you already have and less time wanting what you don't have." The progressed Moon through the second house brings a period of highs and lows to your money world, and it is often a time for wanting to develop new skills to add to your security tool bag.

Moon in Gemini or Third House

With your progressed Moon now in Gemini you will feel a need for increased variety and making some changes in your life, and sometimes just for the sake of change itself. You will be hungry for information and you will feel your best if you are learning something everyday. You become bored with routines and start exploring options for spicing your life up with new possibilities. Talking, networking, computers, books, and writing will be important arenas for nourishment for the Gemini's hunger for ideas. You might feel scattered at times—like you can't get anything done—but you will definitely be open to expanding your options. You can feel more light-hearted than usual and when things don't work out exactly as you like them to, you will quickly be able to adapt to an alternative path. With your Moon in your third house, you could find this to be an excellent time for family reunions and reconnecting with brothers and sisters. Communication seems important to you and you want to stay informed.

Moon in Cancer or Fourth House

As your Moon progresses into Cancer, you awaken to strong emotional currents and your personal life calls for attention. Your Gemini period was for expanding your options, and now with Cancer, you want to close the circle and prioritize that which is most meaningful to you. It is important to drop into your emotional body and feel your way through the choices in front of you. Matters concerning home, house, and family become a central theme. Who will you nurture? Who will nurture you? It would be helpful to find ways for self-nurturing as well, such as massages, luxurious baths, and European-style long dinners. You might find yourself feeling quite domestic as the Cancer theme of home beckons, and you will certainly want to trust your homing instincts as to where to live. You will likely find yourself becoming more sentimental and nostalgic than usual. You will want to make choices that fortify your security. With the Moon in your fourth house, you need some quality alone time with your soul, perhaps by gardening and getting to places in nature that nurture you.

Moon in Leo or Fifth House

Cancer was your time for retreat, and with Leo, you are now ready to kick up your heels and have some fun! Leo has three needs before you can become the magnanimous person you are called to be at this time: (1) Leo is ruled by the Sun and just as the Sun is the center of our solar system, you, too, must find your place where the world revolves around you; (2) Leo rules the heart, and you must be with others who you trust are coming from their hearts; (3) Leo rules the fifth house of fun, play, recreation, children, romance, and creative expression. Not bad homework, but without these needs being met, the Leo fire would not be lit. You are meant to be more demanding of attention from others and from life at this time, and as long as you offer as much as you demand, others will love you for it. You are in the mood for romance, but remember, being in the mood doesn't guarantee romance happening. If you are in a long-term relationship, remember when your love was young and the things you did just for the fun of it that banked the embers of your romantic relationship. Be with the friends that keep you laughing. Go out for entertainment. But above all, find outlets for your creative expression. Is it in the arts or lifestyle issues? The key is to put some creative zing into all that you do.

Moon in Virgo or Sixth House

After the Leo party, it is time to clean up. You'll feel it is time to refocus on Virgo's needs: work, health, and daily routines. You will want to go through cupboards, closets, and garages to clean out all that is not useful or beautiful. Above all, Virgo wants to have a manageable life, so simplify, simplify, simplify. Health maintenance becomes an issue during your Virgo season and you would be advised to care for your body as if it were a favorite pet. Diet, nutrition, and exercise are proactive ways to engage health, while a reactive path is to overcome illness. Virgo is ready to get back to work and improve upon work skills. And you might want to have a mentor, or enter into training, because with Virgo you will want to improve on your skills rather than be the all-knowing manager. With the sixth house focus of your progressed Moon, you will need to pay attention to the right use of time and your daily schedule. If you were to die tonight and you reflect back on this past day and week, would you feel like you had a full life? Did you get do everything that is important to you? Whatever you evaluate as missing, that is your homework for the next few years; create a daily schedule as if it were a mini life. Pay attention to the details of your life with the Virgo attitude of: do only a few things and do them well.

Moon in Libra or Seventh House

Now that the work of Virgo is done, you are ready to socialize and move more toward the gracious living that Libra feels as important. Virgo focuses on the practical concerns of daily living and Libra focuses on the aesthetics. It is time to focus on your presentation, hair, make-up, and wardrobe. Are you still attracted to the color and cut of your clothes? It would be helpful to take the clothes out of your closet that you are not wearing and pass them on. Then, refresh your wardrobe with that which reflects your current taste. The same advice applies to where you live; this is an excellent time for redecorating and bringing beauty into your living environment. What does gracious living mean to you? More art, culture, theater, books—what appeals to you? An elegant evening with a special friend or romantic partner could be just right. Relationship issues come to the front with Libra, and you will likely be tested in your ability to negotiate with others. A good Libra and seventh house rule is this: never settle for less than your best interest, and never demand more. You want more fairness, justice, and honor in all of your relationships, but are you willing to do what it takes to bring impeccability into your negotiations and bring all of your agreements into honor?

Moon in Scorpio or Eighth House

Your progressed Moon moving into Scorpio is one of the trickier placements for the Moon. On the one hand, you have an increased hunger for emotional intimacy. On the other hand, Scorpio is where you store the memories of every time you have been hurt, abandoned, betrayed, stepped on, or done wrong. These memories create armor around your emotional nature so as to protect you from getting hurt. But they also block you from experiencing the intimacy you crave; thus the crazy-making energy. Many people get through their Scorpio period more armored up than ever before, and you want to pray that this will not happen to you. The work of this period of time is to keep your heart open. This requires forgiveness of self and others. Even beyond that is the willingness to look at the hidden side of your character revealed through the challenges that present themselves. Ask yourself: "What am I to learn from this situation?" "How can I be a better person by facing something I hadn't seen in my character before?" "What are the lower aspects of my character that are being revealed through this situation?" Although it takes tremendous character strength to face the hidden and darker aspects of your own character, it will keep your heart open.

Moon in Sagittarius or Ninth House

Entering your Sagittarius period after your time in Scorpio often feels like you are leaving a dark tunnel and entering into a wide open sunlit meadow. You are now in the mood to explore, expand beyond existing boundaries, and adventure in life. You will likely have more of a spring in your step and an ability to frame experiences in a positive light. There will be a renewed confidence and optimism about your life as you leave the emotional entanglements of Scorpio and head off into the adventures of your Sagittarius period. With the ninth house you will want to move beyond existing boundaries, one way or another. Keep your bags packed as travel calls and you will likely say "Yes" to all opportunities. Another route for expansion is to go back to college to expand your mental horizons. I call the ninth house the place for the teachers and the teachings. We are so blessed in this era with an abundance of opportunities to engage our higher mind; from bookstores, to the internet, the teachers and teachings are available to help expand your belief systems as to what is possible in life.

Moon in Capricorn or Tenth House

With your progressed Moon now in Capricorn, you are ready to demonstrate that you can be successful in fulfilling the dreams you awakened to during your Sagittarius period. Capricorn is the mountain goat and you will want to climb to the heights of your ambitions, whether they are personal, professional, or creative. You want to shoulder greater responsibility and demonstrate you can handle it, and you feel at your best when you are being productive. It is time to organize your world and become the manager and director of your life. If you were in charge of your life and there was no one to turn to for guidance and advice, how would you go about getting all of your affairs in order and on a successful track? You are not just thinking about the here and now, but are also planning for the long distance future. You are not interested in long shots at this time, preferring the tried and true. You feel the need to buckle down and get to work. What adjustments do you need to make in your career to stay emotionally fulfilled?

Moon in Aquarius or Eleventh House

Now is the time to get radical! Where Capricorn tends to pay attention to protocol and do things as it should, Aquarius wants to break free of conventional thinking and do things in a truly individualistic manner. You are ready to spend some time with your friends and socialize. You may wish to join a group of one type or another, but Aquarius is particularly supportive of humanitarian issues or larger social concerns. You may find yourself re-evaluating your long-term goals and dreams for your future. It is time to entertain what I call your "lesser voices," the parts of your character that never get off the back burner because you are too busy doing what you are supposed to do. Aquarius seems to ask: "If not now, when?" It is a good time for you to look into alternative lifestyles, learning, or health issues—the requisite word being "alternative." With your progressed Moon in your eleventh house, bonding with like-minded souls is enriching and you are looking for "right community." It can be rewarding to spend time volunteering and contributing to social causes and issues that you believe in.

Moon in Pisces or Twelfth House

You will be awakening to your compassionate and romantic side of your character with Pisces. Pisces is the most sensitive sign of the zodiac and feels everything. Most people are overwhelmed by their emotional sensitivity during their time in Pisces, as it is impossible to be thick skinned. Compassion is a wonderful thing, but without skills for releasing your emotions this sensitivity to the suffering of others can lead to two drowning people rather than one. I call one technique for processing other people's emotions: "Laying it on the lap of God." The Buddhist practice of Tonglen, which I describe in the book, *Western Seeker, Eastern Paths*, addresses this issue of discharging the emotions you pick up from others. The point is, you can't stop being sensitive, but you can learn to skillfully deal with your sensitivity. While your Moon is in your twelfth house, you will feel the need for retreat on a regular basis. Quality alone time becomes important and spiritual activities, writing, and walks in nature, can all provide a haven at this time. Dreams seem to be more vivid and it is not unusual to spend more time sleeping than usual.

David Pond has been a practicing professional astrologer since 1975. He holds a master of science degree in experimental metaphysics from Central Washington University, and is the author of several books, including Mapping Your Romantic Relationships *(Llewellyn, 2004). His life-long study of yoga and meditation have given him an in-depth awareness of the field of metaphysics. He has helped individuals find a deeper meaning in life, get in touch with their source of strength, improve relationship skills, and identify and overcome problem areas in their lives. He can be reached via his Web site at http://www.reflectingpond.com.*

Food, Fads, and Nutrition

by Alice DeVille

Giving the old knife and fork a workout is human nature. Much as you would like to live on air and keep your food bills down, your body craves nourishment in the form of regular meals. Visits to the grocer are an absolute necessity. Local stores stock every food group listed on the USDA Food Pyramid, you can order hard-to-find items by phone. Food ranks high in creating and preserving your memories (the Moon at work)—and it is almost impossible to predict just what memory a specific temptation to your palate will yield. Visit any shopping mall and you'll witness serious snackers dining on the guilty pleasure offerings in the food courts. Even the most disciplined among you will occasionally nix the balanced diet routine in favor of the crunchy, munchy treats that satisfy your soul.

Food fads are a fact of life and exhibit common characteristics: they are loaded with sugar, salt, or calories, and tend to be conveniently located in most stores so you can instantly satisfy your hunger tantrums. Food fads require little or no preparation. Most of you associate these foods with sinful indulgence, frivolous feasting, an energy boost, or eating on impulse. On any given day the media bombards your gastronomic subconscious with tempting treats, and just as your waistline begs for a reprieve, headline news, television and radio ads, and the Internet lure you with advertisements about food trends and diets that are guaranteed to keep you healthy, fit, and trim.

Shaping Up

When you are on a mission to drop weight, you probably complain that portions are small and leave you wanting more. What you really want is the magic formula that keeps you feeling full and blocks the constant preoccupation with food. Ever had the thought: Eat more and weigh less? Right! Every dieter on the planet would like to achieve that state of bliss. Is it an impossible dream? Maybe not. Foods with a high water or fiber content add bulk to your meals so you feel satisfied without having to eat more calories than your body needs. You can really appreciate the energy that comes from "wonder" foods like apples, Jell-O, a juicy tomato, broth-based soups, and salads. These foods demand to be eaten slowly to give your stomach time to register feelings of fullness.

Calories really do count when you are committed to reshaping your body. Notice I didn't say losing weight: anything lost can be found again. Those pounds can be hiding under your table, ready to jump back on your hips. Start thinking in terms of what you want your body to look like. Visualize the outcome and even the number of pounds that represent your ideal weight. Jog your memory with a jingle—"I feel great at 108," or "I look nifty at

150." Tune into your higher self and ask to be led to exactly the right food choices for your body and your soul. You were not meant to suffer with unappealing or bland meals or the proverbial "bird-food diet."

The Sixth House

Your astrology chart holds clues about how you indulge in your food fantasies, take care of your body and deal with the subject of wellness. Planets that occupy your sixth house of health and nutrition reveal your habits and attitudes about food. For example, the presence of Uranus often leads to eating on the run; Venus leans toward rich foods and indulges a sweet tooth; Neptune craves seafood and alcohol beverages; Mars eats too quickly and loads up on spicy foods; the Moon raids the pantry and eats everything including a big breakfast; Saturn is into portion control and doesn't mind leftovers; the Sun prefers a juicy steak and other protein; Jupiter enjoys exotic cuisine and a hearty breakfast; Pluto likes a big, thick sandwich, a loaded baked potato or pizza; and Mercury is in heaven with veggies and lots of opportunities to graze throughout the day. How these planets relate to your Moon sign often drives the type of diet or maintenance program you prefer.

As an astrologer, I have long been interested in health and wellness and look for a mind-body connection when questions about a client's health come up in a consultation. I pay particular attention to nutrition and health patterns when I am interpreting individuals' charts. Maybe that is because I am a double Cancer (Sun and Moon) and have the planets Saturn and Mercury in the sixth house. These configurations led to my interest in the healing field in the mid-1980s, and I have been both a Reiki Master and a Seichim Master since 1996. With these disciplines, healing energy flows through my hands and enables me to help clients redirect their pain.

For those of you new to astrology, please note that whatever I discover regarding an individual's health is always subject to the opinion of a medical practitioner. Over the years, medical specialists have consulted me about their own lives or that of patients. As I wrote this section of the article, a client called for help in selecting possible dates for surgery. On any given day the calls revolve around body image, surgical reduction, stomach bypass surgery, joining weight loss and exercise programs, or using fat burners. Many of the developmental workshops I have created over the years revolve around the total health picture and putting one's life in balance.

The Battle of the Sexes

Women rule when it comes to discovering food fads or dieting tips. Most weight loss programs target women. This fact shouldn't surprise you, since most females have monitored their weight all their lives. The fairer sex has a flair for counting calories, weighing foods and measuring portion sizes. Unless they have been hiding under a rock, women have learned to choose the least fattening foods on any given menu. Ask any water-sign woman (Cancer, Scorpio, or Pisces) and she will tell you that inhaling food seems to pack on the pounds or trigger acute water retention.

Often women are process-oriented when they work through weight problems. They have been living with the premise that foods high in fat and calories aren't "diet foods." Women traditionally stuck with programs such as Jenny Craig, Weight Watchers, or the L.A. Weight Loss Diet that opt for slow but steady reduction of weight. Men, on the other hand, have always defined the consumption of meat and fats as masculine tendencies and have had no patience for long-term weight monitoring. Most of what women pushed as healthy eating had little appeal for the men. Then women discovered Sugarbusters, Atkins, and South Beach and shared their secrets with the men. Finally, a note of compatibility where the sexes could share a protein feast without nursing a guilty conscience! Men promptly revered the captains of the low-carb way. Is it any wonder that the primary promoters of carbohydrate-restricted diets have been men?

Low-Carb Diet Mania

This trend caught on so intensely that now it is also a "guy thing" to watch the carb intake. The male of the species thought of dieting as something for the "girlie men" or the women and shied away from talking about it. They didn't want to be caught eating classic diet food: vegetables without butter, skinless chicken, broiled fish, and salads with dressing on the side. Then, along

came Robert Atkins with a regimen that made it politically correct for men to eat liberal portions of he-man food like loaded baked potatoes, thick, juicy cuts of meat, and vegetables in rich butter-based sauces. All the men had to do was cut back on the number of carbohydrates they ate each day to shape their physiques and build those coveted muscles.

Other low-carbohydrate, high-protein eating plans soon followed, with fitness or diet gurus making the rounds to tout their products and books on national or local talk shows. Most of them put the kibosh on pasta, potatoes, and pastry, sending producers and sellers of these foods into a financial tail-spin. By 2004 several restaurant chains catered to carb-conscious taste buds and revised their menus to promote healthy eating with their carb-friendly choices. Food manufacturers followed this trend by stocking supermarket shelves with a growing number of low-carb or reduced-carbohydrate versions of popular main courses, snack foods, and desserts. The bottom line: read the nutrition facts on the label because low-carb is not necessarily low-cal.

Moon Sign Food Fads

The Moon rules your appetite for food and the type of foods, nutrition, and snacks you favor. How you feel emotionally contributes to your cravings for certain food types, your eating patterns, and the type of weight change program you're likely to adopt. What you do is rooted in childhood and relates to whether your parents gave you latitude to make your own choices or encouraged you to eat a variety of nutritional foods.

Regardless of your Moon sign, you'll want to maintain an attractive weight without going hungry. The following passages reflect typical fad diets preferred by your sign, a few of your snack preferences, and a balanced approach to altering your weight. Look over the variety of nutrition programs, food choices, weight-loss plans, and food fads or diets. From the descriptions, you'll know which ones to avoid. You probably favor a combination of two or more eating styles—or you have tried them all. Sample the options and savor the one that is exactly right for you. Bon Appetit!

Aries—Make It Fast and Make It Last

You want results in a hurry. In your fad phase you could go for the three-day-diet that focuses on mixing certain food types to create a reaction in your digestive system. The chemicals boost your metabolism and help you burn fat at a higher than usual rate. Food choices are limited and may leave you at a very low energy level. You'll lose weight because your caloric intake is low. The plan calls for eating restrictively for three days and then taking two days off. Sounds like yo-yo dieting—and you'll gain the weight back because eating habits never have a chance to change.

- Snack Attack: Barbecued chips, garlic-smoked almonds, fried egg rolls.

- The Right Stuff: A combination of exercise, high-energy choices from the major food groups, and eating more slowly goes a long way toward preserving your svelte physique.

Taurus—Cabbage Soup Plan

The "anytime I'm hungry" option is what you desire. Years ago a member of your Moon sign introduced my entire office to the cabbage soup diet. This plan calls for making a specific cabbage soup recipe that can be eaten any time you feel hungry. Now *that* premise greatly appeals to a Taurus Moon's perpetually growling stomach! It also calls for a strict menu cycle repeated every seven days that includes this soup at least once after the first day. You could drop fifteen to twenty pounds in the first month. Once you reach your goal, however, you're tempted to pass on this gas-powered eating style and head for the burger joint to load up on much-missed carbs.

- Snack Attack: Fried zucchini, sausage sub, chocolate fudge sundae.

- Fitness and Fun: Do you have stubborn fat cells that just won't let go? Get out the pedometer and count your daily steps as you walk your way to good health. You'll be amazed at how much ground you cover. At the same time, watch your calorie consumption by eating a wide variety of foods low in saturated fat and cholesterol. Then reward yourself at least once a week with a favorite recreational or entertainment activity.

Gemini—Get Poppin'

You're attracted to the popcorn diet. This plan calls for healthy eating—especially low-fat proteins such as fish and lots of vegetables—and it asks you to limit your snacks to plain popcorn. Since popcorn is high in fiber and low in fat, consuming large quantities of it sounds like an inexpensive way to eliminate hunger pangs. But your Moon sign loves variety, and it would be hard for you to satisfy all your snack cravings with bland popcorn. Sooner or later you will load on the butter and clog up your digestive tract. Nix this idea.

- Snack Attack: Cheese curls, buffalo wings, soft-serve ice cream.

- Surfing for Satisfaction: When you logged on to the eDiets Web site, you found the ideal tool to stimulate your weight management plan. The eDiets weight-loss plan personalizes and customizes a formula that takes into account your individual needs, goals, and preferences. As you progress through the plan's balanced suggestions, you substitute options at any time to provide more variety in foods and fitness regimes. Looking good!

Cancer—Seven Day Diet

The fad that attracts meal-monitoring Cancer Moons is the seven-day-diet. On this diet you can eat all you want of prescribed foods as follows: Monday, all fruit except for bananas; Tuesday, all vegetables but seasoned only with soy sauce, vinegar, or mustard; Wednesday, all fruits and vegetables; Thursday, five bananas and five glasses of milk; Friday, four three-ounce beef, chicken, or fish portions with fresh vegetables; Saturday, four three-ounce beef steaks with fresh vegetables; and Sunday, four three-ounce beef steaks with fresh vegetables. No cheating!

- Snack Attack: Mozzarella sticks, toffee, hot buttered popcorn.

- Healthy Alternatives: Eat fish, poultry without skin, and leaner cuts of meat instead of fatty ones. Six or more servings of cereals, breads, pasta, and other whole-grain products balance out your nutrition needs much more than bizarre quantities of only one food or food type. Workouts with the balance ball trim your waist, while using hand weights improves your cardiovascular system. Nothing says loving like a nod of approval from your loved ones when they see your astonishing new figure.

Leo—Remembering Julia

When you want to veer from your lean and mean cuisine, you are likely to enjoy a Julia Child-inspired meal consisting of hearty meat choices with a rich wine sauce and elegant hollandaise vegetables. You may have been among the first to adopt the Atkins Diet and dropped significant weight. Give your digestive system a break: when you aren't counting calories, it is groaning from absorbing too many artery-clogging fats from bacon, processed cheeses, and an overload of protein.

- Snack Attack: Philly cheesesteak, Frappucino, chocolate chip cookies.

- Heart Smart: Your Moon sign stays trim when you follow an eating plan that works to prevent heart disease and lower cholesterol. The key is to keep the total calories consumed each day under control while eating more fruits and vegetables, avoiding too much saturated fat, replacing refined carbohydrates with whole-grain fiber foods, and increasing your physical activity.

Virgo—Apple-Cider Vinegar Diet

An attention-grabber for Virgo Moons is the apple-cider vinegar diet. This fad primarily appeals to you because of the fat-burning effects contained in the acidic vinegar solution comprised of fermenting apples and pectin. The directions call for taking one to three teaspoons of apple-cider vinegar before each meal. That's a load of acid for most stomachs, but after a few days you get used to it. It's not clear whether vinegar has properties that help you lose weight but if you eat moderate portions, watch food types, and exercise, you're on your way to a leaner physique.

- Snack Attack: Corn fritters, frozen yogurt, macadamia nuts.

- The Balanced Approach: You take to the ZonePerfect diet because it urges followers to view food as the body's medicine rather than as a pleasure trip or a means to alleviate hunger. Your practical and analytical mind relates to the diet's formula: 40-30-30—the ideal ratio of carbohydrates, proteins, and fats. The body resides within a hormonally controlled "zone," which divides carbohydrates into favorable and unfavorable categories. Although pasta, potatoes, and bread fall into the unfavorable group, your body easily adjusts to the prescribed level and you feel good about keeping your commitment to maintaining a healthy weight.

Libra—Sweet Treats

That's what you'll have every day when you follow the chocolate diet, one of the tastiest fad diets on the scene. Chocolate acts as a vitamin replacement, fighting high blood pressure and preventing heart disease. The chocolate you get in this diet is mostly liquid. You blend a powder or supplement with water or milk. These "shakes" are not meant to replace meals; they are intended as healthy snacks but you may be inclined to consume several each day. There is no real proof that chocolate stimulates your metabolism and helps the fat burning process. While chocolate does contain anti-oxidants that prevent arteries from clogging, too much of anything can be bad.

- Snack Attack: Soft pretzels, pistachios, chocolate cream pie.

- Liquid Assets: Since you like to sip and snack your way to good health, a better option for you may be the Slim-Fast plan. This weight-management program combines its Slim-Fast brand products with a single sensible meal to achieve long-term weight loss results. The plan's flexible system and personal support help you stick to a lifestyle that includes healthy food and exercise. The bottom line: you burn more calories than you consume and your clothing never looked so good.

Scorpio—Media Exposure

Like Jared Fogle, the famous promoter of the Subway diet who lost 245 pounds, you have the determination to start your day with a lone cup of coffee, eat your low-fat six-inch sub and baked chips for lunch, and polish off a twelve-inch veggie sub for dinner. This plan drastically changes your eating habits, yet it is not the best route to weight loss. If you are serious about whittling away the fat deposits, you have the will power to take a more balanced approach by reducing your caloric intake and pumping iron.

- Snack Attack: Seven-layer dip and chips, onion rings, Pop Tarts.

- The Long and Short of It: Your Moon type is more successful with a long-term lifestyle change. Bob Greene's "Get With the Program" diet offers valuable advice and an eating plan that focuses on sensible choices and dining habits instead of restricting food types. Buy his book and learn about emotional and haphazard eating patterns that lead to overeating. Then hit the treadmill and find your metabolic burn rate.

Sagittarius—Random Sampler

Members of your Moon sign tend to snack all day long and lose track of calories and quantity. You're just plain grouchy when your blood sugar drops, and night eating is your downfall. You crave an energy surge and rely on soda and crunchy snacks to keep you going way past your bedtime. When your belt gets too tight you follow a plan that allows grazing or many meals. The five-day caveman diet is one such fad that gives you the latitude to consume large quantities of specific foods—but it lacks the energy-balancing breads that carbohydrates provide.

- Snack Attack: Fried calamari, salt and vinegar chips, pecan pie.

- Traveling Light: Lay off the colas and you will lose the cellulite layers that cling to your hips and thighs. Then follow a hypoglycemia or low-sugar diet to help you stabilize your blood sugar. Make a conscious effort to watch your daily calorie, fat, and sugar intake. Replace your erratic eating patterns and time on the couch with a healthy eating and fitness lifestyle. Your svelte new figure will be the talk of the town.

Capricorn—Carbophobic Catastrophe

Convinced that carbs must be the culprit behind your sluggishness, you select a plan that guarantees quick results. Although the grapefruit diet lasts only twelve days, it promises rapid weight loss. No wonder! Most of what you eat is water-based. The premise is that grapefruit has fat-burning properties, so each meal includes half a grapefruit. Participants avoid most complex carbs and increase the number of vegetables. Snacks are taboo, so you'll have to fill those hunger gaps with at least eight glasses of water per day. This plan is extremely low in calories, resulting in lack of energy and light-headedness. That thing going bump in the night could be you stumbling down the dark staircase in search of a stale bagel.

- Snack Attack: Cheese fries, deli hot dog, fudge brownies.

- Keep Things Moving: With your tendency to clog up with mucous and bouts with constipation, the high fiber diet fills you up without making you gain weight. This plan stabilizes your blood sugar, lowers cancer risk, and controls your appetite. By drinking more water, you soften the food in your stomach. The plan offers many delicious recipes that include the major food groups. Making these choices balances your metabolism, improves the irritation in your gastrointestinal tract and lowers elevated cholesterol levels.

Aquarius—Smooth or Crunchy

Provided you aren't hypoglycemic, the peanut butter diet not only helps you lose weight, but it is easier to stick to than most of the fads. If you can handle four to six tablespoons of peanut butter daily, you are on your way to steady weight loss. The reduced-calorie menu calls for cereal, milk, and banana at breakfast, a peanut-butter-and-jelly sandwich at lunch, and the remaining tablespoons of peanut butter between lunch and dinner to ward off hunger. Surprise! Dinner is peanut butter free. You still have to exercise and watch portions and calories to drop the pounds. This fad has less food restrictions than others, but it can get boring if your only guilty pleasure is a dab of Peter Pan.

- Snack Attack: Honey roast peanuts, thick-crust pizza, chicken quesadillas.

- Energy Rocks: You prefer a fitness regimen, and you gain weight when you don't get enough exercise. Although you can be a picky eater on occasion, you understand your body's nutritional needs more than most. You're proactive about experimenting with eating programs such as South Beach, Atkins, raw foods, or detox plans when you feel the need to shape up. You won't stay with a program that discounts exercise. Many Aquarian Moons tend to be lactose intolerant and shy away from dairy products and sugar. To supply your body with vital nutrients, select other calcium-rich foods to prevent brittle bones. Then visit the gym and work on the shapeliest ankles or firmest calves in the universe.

Pisces—Look Out Hollywood

The Hollywood diet originated in its namesake city. Followers typically lose between five and fifteen pounds in forty-eight hours. You mix certain juices to stimulate your metabolism and burn fat, while avoiding alcohol, tobacco, and caffeine. Since juice is the only thing you consume for a few days you'll drop weight, but expect to be weak and a bit cranky from caloric withdrawal.

- Snack Attack: Pumpkin pie, coconut shrimp, cotton candy.

- Get In Touch With Your Feelings: If you're not in touch with them you could be eating your way to obesity. One way to do this is to take the advice of Dr. Phil and follow his "Shape Up Plan." It emphasizes key points: (1) right thinking for self control; (2) healing feelings, the key to emotional control; (3) no fail environment, mastery over food and impulse eating; (4) high-yield nutrition; (5) intentional exercise; and (6) your circle of support.

Effective weight control is a slow and steady process.

Alice DeVille is an internationally known astrologer, writer, and metaphysical consultant. In her busy northern Virginia practice, she specializes in relationships, real estate, government affairs, career and change management, and spiritual development. The StarIQ Web site and numerous other Web sites and publications feature her articles.

Your Nurturing Parent

by Stephanie Jean Clement Ph.D.

Some years ago, it was pretty much a given that your mother was your nurturing parent, while your father was the bread-winner and the more authoritarian parent. That meant that astrologers could look to the Moon in your chart to interpret your relationship to your Mom, and Saturn to interpret life with Dad. This convenient division of responsibilities is no longer true in a vast majority of U.S. households.

One reason is the number of single parent homes. In 1900 divorce was extremely rare. At that time there were as few as one thousand divorces per year. Now the number is more in the range of one million each year.

Another reason is the increase in two-income families, which points to the necessity for a division of parental responsibilities between Mom and Dad. Day care means that children are in the hands of other caregivers for many hours each day. The nurturing of children is shared by necessity, as well as desire on the part of both parents to participate in their children's lives. The disciplinary role can no longer be delegated to one parent either.

Astrologers still look at the Moon to determine your potential relationships with your nurturing parent, and they look to Saturn to identify the disciplinarian. The blurring of parental roles means that both the Moon and Saturn reflect qualities of father and mother. As you read about your own Moon sign, think about your parents. Did their roles change during your childhood and young adult years? How did illness, injury, and other major events affect their nurturing roles? Which of your parents had a greater impact on your beliefs about nurturing style and responsibilities?

The parent represented by the Moon in your birth chart has the main responsibility for nurturing other family members. Traditionally this parent accepted a secondary position in terms of leadership outside the home. In contrast, the Moon parent takes on most of the responsibility in matters that relate solely to home and family. The Moon parent may be endowed with natural parenting skills, or develops these skills through experience. The rhythms of daily life tend to flow according to the Moon parent's tempo. Clothing and decorating trends, dance fads, the condition of the stock market or the weather—anything that has a rhythmic pattern of behavior fits within this parent's perspective.

The signs modify the qualities of the Moon and indicate how nurturing takes place. A general description of your parent who is most closely related to the Moon follows.

The Moon Through the Signs
Aries
The Aries Moon parent is a study in contradictions. Impulsive tendencies cause this parent to make rash purchases, change plans at the last minute, and take the path less traveled if the

mood strikes. All this makes for lively, exciting times. It is not the stuff of comfortable, stable daily life. These qualities in a parent come across as quick to anger and quick to forgive.

Because of the inconsistent behavior, you may have feared this parent's anger that came seemingly out of nowhere. Even if physical punishment was never part of the picture, you probably developed a cautious approach in your relationship. At the same time you experienced this parent as taking a secondary role to the other parent much of the time. The contradiction between awesome power and willingness to follow a leader may have confused you at times

This is the parent to go shopping with. He or she understands individuality and is able to furnish your room or buy clothes that suit you well. You will never look like a carbon copy of your siblings, unless you are wearing costumes or uniforms. You each get your own hairstyles too. The Aries Moon parent allows you to express your individuality, as long as you don't harm yourself in the process. He or she may even encourage you to try things that are edgy or futuristic.

Taurus

Consistency could be your Moon in Taurus parent's middle name. You sometimes feel that this parent was predictable to the point of being dull. You could guess what supper would be by the day of the week, and you could count on having the house cleaning and laundry done on schedule.

Just when you were sure you had this parent figured out, he or she would throw you a curve, forcing you to rethink your relationship. The rules that seemed comfortable and flexible suddenly became rigid when you crossed the line. The Taurus Moon person didn't intentionally spring new things on you, far from it. You knew the rules all along. You just didn't know that your normally appreciative parent would crack down so hard.

Your Taurus Moon parent appreciates value. This means that clothing had to be durable first, then attractive. You were not encouraged to wear frills, and probably everything tended to coordinate—except for dress-up attire, which may have been distinguished.

Whether father or mother, your Taurus Moon parent helped you through the toughest crises, and still does. This parent may experience serious ups and downs in life, not only financial, but also regarding career, health, or other matters. He or she knows how to handle difficult turns of events, and can teach you a lot about managing your life.

Gemini

Your Gemini Moon parent shares some of the qualities usually associated with siblings. You get frequent flashes of a younger person living in this parent's body. There is a lively curiosity that takes you along on adventures into new, exciting territory, either in the physical world or in the realm of imagination. You may take day trips to explore the area surrounding your home, explore antique shops or the mall together, or share an interest in a particular author's work. You also enjoy the same games, television programs, and classroom subjects.

The Gemini Moon indicates a rather moody emotional life for your nurturing parent. Sadness will sometimes be apparent, yet he or she carries through to take care of business in spite of difficult emotions. The sudden expression of ideas and feelings convinces you that this parent has deeper, stronger undercurrents of feeling and imagination than you can see on the surface. Develop a close relationship and you get to share in that depth of mind.

The Gemini Moon indicates a life full of dreams that may never come to fruition. Your parent may feel sad about opportunities not taken, or events that caused a change in direction away from an important goal. You sometimes find yourself cast in the role of fulfilling your parent's dreams—dreams that you do not share.

Cancer

The parent represented by your Cancer Moon is adept at identifying the emotional content of any family situation. This parent consistently balances the needs and desires of each family member, creating a sense of fulfillment for each person individually and for the family as a whole. You discover that if this parent is fulfilled and happy, then so is every member of the family. You learn to go along in situations where you are not sure what to do because this parent has turned out to be right so many times where feelings are concerned.

Comfort is a foundational principle in this parent's approach to life. Home is a place where you should feel comfortable, and this parent makes that comfort their #1 job. Understanding the physical environment as well as the emotional ambiance, this parent arranges the rooms, the furniture, and the decor to suit each person. The house doesn't have to have a consistent look from one room to the next. Instead, each area reflects the emotional flow associated with that room's activities.

Life has not been easy for this parent. There have been dramatic highs, matched by equally dramatic low points. As an adult this parent benefits from every effort to maintain balance. At the same time he or she appreciates the rhythmic movement of life and knows that everything cannot be static; that balance is a constant flow of energies. You probably tested this parent's sense of balance on more than one occasion, and you experienced the inevitable emotional response.

Leo

Leader or drill sergeant? Your Leo Moon parent sometimes acts like king or queen of the world, demonstrating very little interest in your perceptions or desires. While this attitude can feel harsh at times, you develop a sense of trust in the security of knowing that there is a plan for each day. You don't have to create the plan so much as execute your role competently. Eventually, you seek independence, and the Leo Moon parent may try to hold on a bit longer than you want.

The Leo Moon parent desires comfortable, even luxurious surroundings. Significant amounts of money are spent on furnishings and other possessions. However, you also learn the value of quality from this parent. For example, you only have to purchase the oriental rug for the living room once every hundred years or so if you buy high quality in the first place. (Of course, you want to get the rug that you will still like twenty years from now.) This parent can decorate an entire room around one or two heirlooms.

The Leo Moon parent can teach you a lot about leadership style. You may not feel as confident as this parent, but you can emulate the appearance of style and confidence in your actions. You also learn how to make and keep friends.

Virgo

Your Virgo Moon parent is mentally thorough and methodical. You get the sense that he or she has given substantial thought to any project before ever making the first move. When you ask a question, this parent doesn't just toss back an instant response. Instead, you may hear several questions to clarify and explore the situation. In the process, you often come to your own conclusion. This parent teaches you how to approach problem solving by helping you to develop choices and make decisions.

Sometimes it seems like this parent misses good opportunities by holding back a bit too long. You may want to jump in, metaphorically speaking, whereas your parent explores the depth and temperature of the water first. Generally, you discover that your parent has been ahead of the curve all along. He or she has held back to allow a situation to play out before committing to a specific course of action, not because of hesitation, but because foresight suggests that shifts will occur in the playing field. While this approach may not work for you, this parent pulls it off time and time again.

You sometimes feel that this parent is super critical of your behavior. You may feel that your schoolwork brings nothing but criticism, or your appearance is scrutinized constantly. Even your feeling life is open to criticism. Unfortunately, this kind of criticism is remembered long after any praise is forgotten.

Your Virgo Moon parent has the capacity to study any subject deeply. If you share an interest, expect to delve deeply into the subject. Years later, your parent may continue to come up with adaptations or considerations relating to the subject. From this person you learn how to get a broad overview and then gather data to flesh out every area of the subject.

Libra

Your Moon parent began to treat you as an equal when you were quite young. At first this alternated with parent-child interactions, but as you grew up, the two of you eased into a more balanced relationship.

This balance is not consistent. For one thing, your parent has the heart of an army general, and you may play many roles during your life—lowly private, trusted lieutenant, or major in charge of just about everything. To keep the relationship running smoothly, you must remember that your parent is the general in this army. You may not like it, but it's true. Follow orders. Provide information that you think is necessary to making good decisions, and relieve this parent of duties little by little as aging demands.

At some point you may have to take a stand. Do you resign from the Moon parent's army and go your own direction? That may be necessary. However, you may also find that the general can listen to reason. You could get things your way if you are prepared for the fight.

Your Moon parent is the one who taught you about consistency, and about the benefits of harmonious relationships. You learned by example of how to and how not to accomplish balance.

Scorpio

Your Moon parent probably had a secret emotional life that was rarely shared with anyone. The emotional undercurrent was probably always present, but you didn't know the reasons behind any emotional responses. This parent could hide in a corner, waiting to see what might happen, or there could be aggressive outbursts that may have been frightening to you as a child. In fact, you still may be a bit timid around this parent.

If you had a secret, you could always tell this parent. Once you got past the initial reaction, hot as it might have been, you knew this parent would not only keep your secret, but would also do everything possible to help you solve the problem.

This parent had a way of getting what he or she wanted. Not enough money? A way would be found, or a bargain located. There was always a sense of wanting to look the very best, perhaps just a step above the income available. Your parent gave keeping up with the Joneses a whole new meaning.

The truth is a central part of this parent's core beliefs. The frame for the truth, however, might not have matched up with the real world. For example, all those secrets add up to a way of withholding useful, even vital information. In addition, you were supposed to tell the whole truth and nothing but the truth, whereas your parent would sort and filter the truth to suit the specific situation. Or the truth might come out in the most awkward moments.

Both fearless and tenacious, this parent may have clawed his or her way to success, dragging you along for the ride. You learned how to go after what you want, and more importantly, how to decide if something is really worth the effort.

Sagittarius

Your Moon parent has a whole life that goes on inside the mind. You sometimes know when he or she is far away, thinking about something else. You may have to address this person by name to

get through, as Mom and Dad are relatively new titles compared to John or Marsha. This parent is definitely moody, whether you can tell it or not. You sometimes only find out when you have pushed way too far at a time when your parent needs personal space.

This parent is the one who is always planning for the future. As a child you may have thought he or she was omniscient, as you were told so often how things would turn out, and then they did. Your parent may not understand why you can't divine the future for yourself. If that is not your strong suit, you can at least learn how to think about the future as part of your planning process.

From this parent you learned values and ideals that you have carried with you for years. You may have changed your thinking, but you probably still value the mental training you received.

Capricorn

Your Moon parent is a hard-working individual. Family and financial security are driving forces, with the focus on personal effort to attain high goals. It may seem there is little time for you in this personal process because career interests are so important to him or her. This parent is likely to push you to achieve as much as you can, and to pursue a career that holds the promise of financial and social success.

This parent may soften with age. Once you enter adulthood, your parent may become more of a friend or mentor, or even your personal cheerleader. This parent may enjoy life more after age sixty. This happens because career issues are no longer the main concern. Family matters assume a larger share of the attention, and he or she becomes more patient, especially with grandchildren and other young people.From this parent you learn to assess realities and cultivate a practical, goal-oriented approach to life.

Aquarius

The Aquarius Moon parent is a good observer of the human condition. He or she is able to consider the facts in a situation and arrive at logical conclusions. Always a champion of something, this parent can be your most ardent fan. Because of a deep understanding of human nature, this parent may identify your weaknesses and focus on them in order to help you gain balance and power. Sometimes you will feel that he or she only sees the weaknesses. Just when you feel sorriest for yourself, there will be a surprise that shows exactly how much this parent really cares for you.

Later on you may discover areas in which this parent rebelled against authority. He or she appreciates the unusual and the new, and is willing to study a new subject or undertake the development of new skills.

From this parent you learn the importance of helping others with no expectation of direct return on the investment.

Pisces

Your Pisces parent is reserved and rather quiet. Seldom the first person to jump into a conversation or argument, this parent often is the one who comes up with the ultimate solution to a problem. He or she can demonstrate great patience in working through most difficulties.

This parents keeps secrets. This can be a source of great irritation, as the information may be essential to family unity and calm. You become skilled in anticipating when information has been withheld, and may develop great investigative and logical skills in an effort to compensate for the lack of essential information. By holding back, this parent can seem negligent or ignorant in some situations.

From this parent you learn the value of reserving information that does not show you in your best light or suit the immediate situation.

Stephanie Jean Clement, Ph.D., is the author of Mapping Your Family Relationships *(Llewellyn, 2004). This book comes with a CD-ROM program so you can print out birth charts and interpretations for anyone in your family. She resides in Florida.*

A Mediterranean Travelogue

by Sally Cragin

Baseball fans have Cooperstown, movie fans have Los Angeles, but astrologers have the whole of the ancient world to explore, and feel affectionately about their craft. Of course, some of us have Vedic influence (and should go to India), others imbue our work with far-eastern overtones, but if you want to get back to basics, spend time in Greece.

Last year, my husband, my year-old son Christopher Tigran, and I spent a very busy week on Crete and in Athens, and it renewed my enthusiasm for astrology in ways I couldn't possibly have predicted.

Crete

If Italy is a boot, and Greece is a hand reaching into the Mediterranean, Crete is the jewel just beyond the reach of the "fingertips." This long, mountainous island has five Minoan Palaces, including the Grand Palace of Knossos. But let's go back even earlier, as Crete is said to have been the birthplace of Zeus. (He is also known as Jove, or Jupiter, the ruler of Sagittarius. Yes, there are numerous names for these deities, but for simplicity's sake, I'll stick to the ones we know from astrology.)

According to one fable, Saturn promised his brother Titan that Titan would ascend the throne and rule the gods after Saturn's death. Titan made his brother promise to destroy all his male children, and so Saturn devoured them after birth. However, Saturn's wife Rhea hid Jupiter and then sent him secretly to Crete. There, he was suckled by goats on Mt. Ida, a spectacularly perfect peak at the heart of the island. He was educated by the nymphs, and the goat that suckled him was later placed among the constellations. It is no small irony that Saturn, which rules Capricorn and is symbolized by the goat, should have provided both hazard and salvation for Jupiter. If it sometimes seems that harsh lessons come along with Saturn transits, the common wisdom is that "we're the better for it."

Mt. Ida dominates one of the three central plateaus on the island, but you can see (and hear) goats anywhere in the hills. We stayed in the southeastern corner of the island, which had glorious hiking in some spectacular gorges but extremely long drives to the interesting ruins. There are very good highways along the edges of the island, but because of the mountainous terrain, what looks like a short hop on the map and is marked a relatively short distance in kilometers on the road signs turns out to be "as the crow flies"—with innumerable hairpin turns in between.

Hiking in the Gorges

Sturdy boots and a walking stick are recommended. Really detailed maps are hard to find unless you're on the island, but go when the stifling heat and the tourists are elsewhere—in early spring when everything is in bloom (March), or early fall when the heat breaks, the pomegranates ripen, and the herbal aroma everywhere is intoxicating (October).

In the east, where we stayed, the climate is similar to southern California, although much of the landscape is a cross between the desert outside Los Angeles and the Ares Vallis flood plain on the planet Mars: lots of red earth (sedimentary) and frequent gray rocks. These are usually volcanic—many of them literally hurled many miles onto the island from the explosion of Santorini that wiped out the Minoan civilization about 1700 BC.

Once we had a good map in hand, and the recommendation of locals on where to walk, we'd pack a picnic lunch (sausage, bread, olives, yogurt) along with the diapers and wipes in the knapsack and set off. Since short journeys are ruled by Mercury, which can be a capricious little planet, we often overshot our destination, "just to be sure" we knew where we wanted to go. But you can't get lost on Crete if you're driving—at least not for long.

Once the car was parked (well, heaved into a ditch or a clearing off the road), we headed into the hills. There, we usually found a gentle path at the base of a very sharp-sloping V-shaped valley. It is extraordinary and humbling to be beyond amplified, mechanical sound. No planes drone overhead, no cars are heard.

When we turned around after a few minutes walk, we saw what Homer described as the "wine-dark" Mediterranean Sea in the notch of the valley. I counted at least three separate varieties of thyme—very pungent with tiny leaves—and almost as many species of sage. The combined aroma was invigorating as we walked along.

Hippocrates (the father of medicine) recommended a trip to Crete for anyone recovering from sickness, and Theophrastos (the father of botany) called Crete "rich in medicines" because of the variety of flora found there. In fact, many of the gorges on Crete have indigenous species found nowhere else. Ancient herbal lore holds that two of the herbs ruling Taurus (the bull) are thyme and sage. Ada Muir's *The Healing Herbs of the Zodiac* (Llewellyn, 1986) explains that thyme is considered good for courage and sage tea is good for sore throats (Taurus rules the throat).

More Taurus Influence

And speaking of the bull—now we come to the most famous myth about Crete: the Minotaur, who lived at the center of the labyrinth. This is a very odd story, but connects several mythical strands.

All the kings of the Minoan era (2600 to 1100 BC) were called Minos. The last of the line had a very amorous wife who was romantically obsessed with a gorgeous white bull. Daedalus, an Athenian carpenter/craftsman, built a hollow wooden cow to conceal her so that she could safely have her assignation. Lo and behold, she gives birth to the Minotaur (he had the head of a bull on a human body). Minos was appalled, but summoned Daedalus to build a labyrinth to contain the monstrous creature.

Every year, seven youths and maids from Athens were brought to the maze and sent into its intricate turnings to their certain death. Finally, Prince Theseus, appalled at the yearly tribute, offered himself as a victim. Armed with a spool of thread from Ariadne, Minos' human daughter, he penetrated to the center, killed the monster, and returned unharmed.

From here, the story turns to the fate of Daedalus, who with his son Icarus, was incarcerated in the center of the maze. Using only wax and feathers, the father built wings for both, to soar upward. And we all know what happened next.

The Man Who Fell to Earth

The most famous ruin on Crete is Knossos, the Grand Palace. This is just south of Heraklion, the largest city on the island, and worth a long day's visit—especially if you also go to the Archaeological Museum in Heraklion to see the artifacts unearthed from the archaeological digs throughout Crete. (Sadly, all that remains of the great Minoan palaces are walls, floors, and amphorae too large to move. At the time of the major archaeological excavations, the prevailing philosophy was to put all the precious objects in one place, rather than keeping them near their place of origin.) The Minoans actually predate the Achaen and Classical period which has given astrology so many wonderful gods and goddesses. But there is a "Temple of Rhea" on the premises—at least that's the presumption, because the language used by the Minoans in this era, Linear A, is *still* untranslated. We would heartily recommend a walking tour within the compound, as the sprawling size and endless (labyrinthine!) "rooms" make it very difficult to stay oriented, even with a guidebook in hand. This is Daedalus's greatest work—1,500 rooms. The original frescoes have been removed to the Heraklion Museum, but brightly colored reproductions can be seen, including a pair of griffins, athletic youths, maidens, dolphins, tropical flora, beasts, and birds (the climate was much wetter then!).

There are no depictions of warfare, as the Minoans maintained peaceable trade with all their neighbors, especially the Egyptians. The Minoans had running water, as demonstrated by tiled drainage ditches, with separate systems for drinking water, washing water and sewage. They also held regular athletic contests, with sports we still enjoy (boxing, wrestling, sprinting), and some that have passed into antiquity, like a game played in a bull ring where a young man (or woman!) would face off with a bull. As the giant beast lowered its head, they'd attempt to somersault off the horns, over its back.

What is it like walking among ruins many thousands of years old? Humbling and fascinating, especially when one considers that the entire multi-acre area was once covered by a mound, only discovered in the late ninteenth century by archaeologist Arthur Evans. He and his Cretan crew had to dig nearly twenty feet down to uncover a vast, forgotten kingdom. And, just to bring the story full circle, Jupiter (Zeus) died on one of the mountains opposite Knossos.

We also visited Xerocambus, a rare series of sandy pocket-beaches with sculptural rock formations and worn coral-heads, a small Minoan ruin and a tiny church. The drive is breathtaking—a series of switchbacks on a gentle hill, and there's a gorge there, too. No matter how you spend your day, have the evening meal at Taverna Kostas, where we enjoyed an amazing dinner served by chef Vera Theodorakis, who invited us into the kitchen to select what we wanted. (This practice is actually quite common on the island, even among people who speak English.) Her taramasalata (fish roe) was sublime—sweetly salty. Her roasted aubergine appetizer was so good we had it again as an entrée along with the exquisite catch-of-the-day. Vera and husband Kostas also run Villa Petrino, where rooms for two on the beach will run $40 to $50 a night (plus $6 for air-conditioning if you want it). You can find them at www.xerokampos.com.

The signage for archaeological sites is terrific, and this was a stately home surrounded by stucco-walled storage rooms, and a deserted Byzantine village, all quite recently used as sheep folds. The tiny spring that the village was built around has nevertheless cut a deep ditch around an orange tree, which blooms and blooms—its fruit unreachable.

As for the Moon's influence on this magical island—well, we journeyed there during the New Moon-to-first-quarter phase. With each passing day, we felt more drawn toward seeing more places. And this is a place with numerous layers representing many transitional, invading cultures including multiple Minoan eras, later Greek settlement, the Byzantine invasion, and the Venetian and then Turkish occupations. There are many fine Renaissance-era Venetian palazzos on the island, usually on headlands or promontories—elegant villas that whisper not a breath of the pain and religious persecution that invariably accompanied occupation.

Crete definitely seems a "Moon-ruled" place. We were travelling with a one-year-old, which prompted vociferous nurturing instincts in the inhabitants. On Crete and in Greece, it was like traveling with a celebrity. People ooh'd and aah'd, and wanted to tickle and kiss him, and he was given more lollipops than most children get on Halloween. The Moon's influence can bring out the "intense mother" in us all, and, faced with a smiling, laughing child, the Cretans we met were instantly besotted.

More Mercurial Thoughts

Since this island is dominated by the Jupiterian influence that rules Sagittarius, which counts "long journeys" among its themes, we were impressed by how quickly short trips turned into very long hauls. Fortunately, the paved roads up and down the mountains and ravines and plateaus are spectacularly smooth, well-engineered, and well-built. Because the weather is so moderate, potholes are few and roads look freshly-paved for years. Since there's no need to leave the roads unbanked for snow-plowing (as in the Alps) the corners are far easier to navigate, no matter how vertigo-inducing the scenery. Take some of the money you'll save on lodging and food and splurge on a sports car!

Athens

Remember the labyrinth and the Minotaur? For us, leaving was the challenge. I note with interest that our final two days on the island coincided with the Moon in Aquarius, which is usually associated with exploring the new, making friends, and using new technology. Our day of departure coincided with a (planned) air-traffic controllers' strike, and so we missed a connection. What to do with a day in Athens?

Where to begin, is the more accurate question. In short order, we rented another car, found a hotel not too far from the airport and drove into the city. And yes, everything you heard about the positive effect of the 2004 Olympics is true. The subway is new, clean, and very inexpensive (.70 euro; less than a dollar), and took us straight to the Acropolis. The Athens subway stop is astounding, as there were several vitrines in the waiting area which held various fifth-century artifacts that had been dug up during the construction. Toys, drinking vessels, figurines, amphorae—so many, they were stacked two deep. Just the construction debris from this one site compared favorably with the entire collection at Fitchburg (Massachusetts) Art Museum where I work.

If you spend any time at all in Athens, make sure you have comfortable shoes, because you can walk to numerous places. We started at the top—the Acropolis. This is the city's famed largest hill, which offers a lookout on all directions. Reaching the Acropolis requires a healthy little climb, and it's fascinating to see the huge white columns of the Parthenon emerge once you pass through the grand Propylaea (portal). The Parthenon has served multiple functions as a temple/treasury/civic building. It's the centerpiece of an enormous area that includes the Erechtheion (a smaller, more elegant temple to Athena), and two theaters, which are visible on the west side of the hill.

The steps of the Parthenon are literally hewn out of the bedrock, so the building seems to rise naturally out of the Acropolis. Even with plenty of tourists, you'll be able to feel you have this place to yourself, and once you look around, you'll see a smug population of calico cats, sunbathing on the warm stones.

If the Parthenon is a pinnacle, descending the Acropolis on the east side takes you past the Areopagus, the "hill of Ares," where the god of war was once on trial for killing one of Poseidon's sons. From there, you can descend into the very narrow winding streets of Plaka, the oldest part of the city of Athens. Around nearly every corner there's a discreet Byzantine chapel or Classical outbuilding. And the restaurants are plentiful.

Vegetarians and meat-eaters alike will be well-fed here. Gyros sandwiches (marinated pressed meat) can be had on every corner, and salads are usually enormous, with a heavy emphasis on cucumbers, tomatoes, and feta cheese. For those with a sweet tooth, baklava (parchment pastry with honey and nuts) is delicate and filling. Well, the Moon *does* rule the stomach!

Travel Tips

Some hints on getting to Greece and Crete. Most commercial airlines will have a connection that goes straight to Athens, and
after considering many possibilities, we finally booked ourselves
straight through with Lufthansa and Aegean Airlines through Or-
bitz. We flew from Boston to Frankfurt (a very smoky, and, yes,
labyrinthine airport), Frankfurt to Athens, and then got a pud-
dle-jumper flight on Aegean Air to Iraklion where our luggage
was first off the plane (less the baby's suitcase that we'd left by
his changing table back home. Can you say "dark-of-the-Moon?").
From there, it was a two-hour drive to our lodging, but were we
to go again, we'd definitely stay more centrally and expand our
explorations to parts of the island we didn't see. On the island,
it's easy to stay for $60 to $75 a night, but the euro is only getting stronger. In Athens, the subways are cheap and fast, and a
good meal for two in the city costs between $25 and $40 (including wine). Even if you're not "a museum person," the museums in Athens are not to be missed. This is the cradle of our
civilization and craft.

Sally Cragin writes "Moon Signs," an astrology column for the Boston Phoenix
*newspaper in New England. She also writes theater- and arts-related topics for
the* Boston Globe. *Her Web site is www.moonsigns.net.*

Here Comes the Bride!

by Leeda Alleyn Pacotti

In the last few years, talk of marriage has centered around legal definitions of what it is. We have a biblical construct, generally evolved in western societies as sanctioned religious and civil unions between a man and a woman. Eastern societies, too, authorize this obvious meld between the sexes, although marriages may extend to enfold other relationships that round out the needs of the married partners. Without concern for the appropriateness of one approach toward marriage over the other, each attempts to recognize a fulfillment of the individual within what is presumed to be an enduring commitment of time, resources, and personal energies.

Although the topic of quality in a marriage has taken a back-seat to its definition, meeting socially or legally approved parameters does not guarantee a nurturing, loving relationship. The job of seeking answers to understand a partner's requirements and satisfactions in a well-rounded relationship usually falls to the woman. If she is fortunate, her prospective or existing mate willingly states what he wants. If she isn't so fortunate, he probably signals his needs and preferences through actions and nonverbal responses. Being a woman and wanting to please, she investigates a wider range of sources for desirable information, such as his friends, his family, or guidelines from a religious text. Usually the more intuitive of the two, the prospective bride finds it easy to turn to astrology.

Because marriage or some form of life-long commitment is one of the more established institutions, astrology has found its place historically as a tool for finding fulfillment within a relationship. After all, astrology, either eastern or western, was and still is used in dynasties and kingdoms to find just the right match among royals. Consulting the divinatory art eventually seeped into noble and common relationships, presenting itself as composite, comparative, and synastric astrological studies.

Yet, the most compelling disclosure about a man's approach toward and expectations within marriage comes from his natal chart. Exploring the nativity, a woman finds clues as to whether he will marry, if his circumstance for marriage will be early or late in life, whether he will seek union once or many times, and what his prospects are for children and livelihood. All these circumstantial ingredients are interesting, but they follow what usually are only the acceptable social definitions or mores of the moment.

The Fourth of the Fourth

An enlightening technique in astrological interpretation is derivative houses, in which the natal house under question is taken as if it were the first house of the horoscope. In this respect, it becomes the personal image or foundation for all matters of that house.

Another important concept in astrology is the "end of the matter," specifically attributed to the fourth house, the Moon's domain. Frequently, in natal astrology, the fourth house suggests the circumstances at the end of life, or how an image has been put into practice or application and what is likely to occur. In part, this philosophy reflects the forward progressed movement of the Ascendant, which reaches the fourth house cusp in about ninety years—a reasonable human life span.

Used often in horary astrology, the end of the matter is sought from every originating house, suggesting interesting correlations. Application of personal earnings or resources from the second house eventually culminates in the recreational expressions, loves, and progeny shown by the fifth house. The broadening ninth house of higher education, philosophy, and philanthropy produces the sensitive consciousness, sympathy, and provision for the less fortunate depicted by the cosmic twelfth house.

Using derivative houses, with the fourth house of nurture portraying an image from a first house conceptualization of needs and wants, its future actuality unfolds in a shared relationship or marriage described by the seventh house, which is the fourth house's end of the matter. How we are nurtured, what gives us comfort, what makes us feel loved, what represents safety—these strongly impressed experiences become the foundations of communication, emotional contexts, and activities we believe are right in a marital relationship.

As children, our experiences are totally absorbent. Not until we are older do we understand that what seems so good is not necessarily expressed or provided by both parents. In early years, we are the recipients of all good things, which seem to flow from all people in precisely the same way. By the time we are old enough to distinguish that the wonderful gifts from our parents are intermittent or simply not available from them both, the foundation of what we believe is a good emotional and interactive environment has been well established. Wanting all those good feelings again is what propels us toward the search for a desirable mate, who complements us by approving our particular expressions and activities.

With the fourth house defining the preferred circumstances and possibilities of the seventh house of marriage, the Moon in a horoscope is the natural significator of what a person believes is best.

Lunar Influences of the Marrying Man

For the woman with serious interest in joining her life to another, an examination of her prospective mate's natal Moon gives her a strong idea of what he expects to be and do within marriage. Even when he cannot express himself well, she uncovers an understanding of how his nature lends itself toward supportiveness, his expectations of behavior from his mate, and his basic emotional construction.

The interpretations that follow describe the overall marital attitude of a man based on the position of his natal Moon by sign or house. These explanations can also be combined when sign and house positions are not the same, showing complements or contradictions that have remained undiscovered during courtship.

Aries or First House

This man grew up in a competitive household. He may not have been the first-born and had to vie for his rightful recognition. What he has gained is an ability to move skillfully through turbulence, and he anticipates a strategy for any form of confrontation. With a pugilistic nature, he is argumentative. Most of this need to fight is only a cover for intense feelings and a desire for unobstructed movement. Because he is physically and mentally able, he needs to experiment with activities, emotions, and situations. The Aries Moon makes him self-involved, but his curiosity and sense of adventure frequently alter the landscape and circumstances of the marital life. His wife will never experience a dull moment.

Taurus or Second House

Taurus borrows the eye of the eagle from Scorpio in finding his mate. Once he sees beauty, he's drawn like a moth to a flame. Direct and certain, his relationship is simple, long lasting, and emotionally supportive. As much as he treasures his wife, he must feel treasured in return. This man has a memory for grievances, which must be resolved for the relationship to develop. He is always at the core of his being and refuses to be cajoled with gifts and promises to solve problems. The woman who digs in and wades through the mire of mutual difficulties reaps the rewards of enduring emotional and financial support.

Gemini or Third House

Expect Gemini to talk, call, and write. His is a chummy relationship with an informal tone, although he does dress up well for social events. His mate should be able to stand on her own, emotionally, financially, and socially, because Gemini is not inclined to possessiveness. He's adaptable to a woman's preferences and open about problems. The breeziness of Gemini's nature deflates when his partner is cryptic, despondent, or uncommunicative. His activities are always changing, including the way he makes his money. For the woman who enjoys a charged home life, a constantly changing pace, and a varying palette of activities, Gemini is the perfect complement.

Cancer or Fourth House

Cancer presents a bundle of quandaries, not unlike his ever-changing ruler, the Moon. This man needs someone close by him twenty-four hours a day, although he is drained by the emotional problems of others. Not surprisingly, he wants a faithful companion, although he never really releases his old loves. Because Cancer recognizes the security and safety of a comfortable home—his retreat—he'll work any hours necessary to create a nest for himself and his beloved. Unfortunately, he mistakenly believes that all he gives wards away the needs of others. A woman who benefits from Cancer's preferences is one who is secure without a recognizable profession or social stature of her own, and derives a deep satisfaction from shared activities and home life.

Leo or Fifth House

To remain at the top of his game, Leo needs social gatherings, and he'll use them to spread his abundant love around until he finds the right woman. This man is gentle, generous, and wholehearted in his approach to life, feelings, and love. Once he settles on his life mate, she becomes the inspiration for all his self-expression. For Leo, marriage only begins the fun of lavishing enjoyable pastimes, social gatherings, food, status, and wealth on his mate for life. The woman for Leo needs a high energy level, unquenchable curiosity, and an unending sense of adventure. She'll never be left out.

Virgo or Sixth House

Conformity creates security for Virgo, and he only accepts a structured relationship. Very cautious in his life selection, this man often and unpredictably ends up teaching or raising a less experienced mate. His fussiness shows in his need for familiar surroundings and intricate expectations in the relationship. Although an initial shock gives way quickly to problem-solving, Virgo doesn't tolerate surprise well. Virgo's income is unlikely to be extravagant. An excellent wife is something of a waif, who appreciates direction and guidance. This woman must also be willing to deal with rules, constructs, and frameworks, which will permeate the flow of discussions, emotional interactions, household chores, and social activities.

Libra or Seventh House

Libra provides an equal partnership, which others might see as melded. So resonant with his spouse, the Libra man often risks forgetting her boundaries. Although he is full of advice and wants to solve problems, his enthusiasm can get in the way of his mate's self-expression and independence. First to show his helpfulness, Libra shifts the environment inside and outside the home for the sake of preserving balance in his relationship, which can become an escape from confrontation. Libra's mate needs to be certain of her own identity and not given to precipitous behavior or heated altercations. Expect Libra's marriage to be one of the most harmonious and genteel.

Scorpio or Eighth House

A little frivolity goes a long way toward uplifting Scorpio's serious nature. His sexual propensity is renowned; his mate gains from the legacy of his ample experience. Generally, this man lives life on a grand scale that nearly rivals Sagittarius. Any activity, feeling, or interest that speaks to depth quickly grabs his interest. However, his need to be dazzled by mystery gets in the way of resolution to disagreements, and Scorpio has to learn to let minor mysteries unfold to disclose greater ones. His lifelong wife is worldly, not easily shocked, mature, experienced, and educated. She charms his interest with one simple statement: "That's my little secret."

Sagittarius or Ninth House

Sagittarius doesn't stay in one place, one line of work, or one marriage. For him, more is better, and that includes his approach to spending. This man cultivates humor, positivity, and adventure with his money of the moment. He's a happy companion, unfazed by problems or entanglements. His easy-going manner lets him talk out problems, but only if these come to a swift resolution. He has plenty of dreams, fantasies, and vaporous pursuits when he can't be footloose. Sagittarius is satisfied by a woman with a stable life experience, independence, and a rising level of income. She can expect to share the living and playing expenses after his money well has run dry.

Capricorn or Tenth House

Although Capricorn is the sign of status, he will not participate in a marriage of convenience. Give him true-blue love and throw in some volatility. For him, circumstances shape his destiny and chart his career; his safe haven is his wife. When he makes the right choice, his marriage and fidelity is long-lasting. This is the man who moves heaven and earth to be supportive and reassuring of his wife in every area of her endeavors. Because Capricorn gets depressed when he muddles for too long in the environment of the moment, his mate must show a sense of future orientation, which lifts his spirits. Although she can exhibit some flair, Capricorn operates best around measured emotions and considerate conversation.

Aquarius or Eleventh House

While Libra strives for the equal partnership, Aquarius is the equal partner, wanting his wife to find and activate her best expression. He takes a long time to commit to a relationship, usually marrying a woman whose status is upper crust, compared to his own. Congenial and attractive in all social relationships, Aquarius appreciates a challenge and is swayed by witty, intelligent conversation. Ruling friendships, Aquarius does not dispose of past loves completely and maintains contact with these old flames. Not to worry: once committed, he is entirely faithful. No matter how well off or how high her social level, his wife is helped toward any success she chooses. She is likely to make more money than he, but Aquarius maintains the lead in his own life.

Pisces or Twelfth House

Pisces delves into the psychological, tenuous ties of relationships, wanting to understand the delicate bonds. All of this sign's relationships are deep, bringing anything to the surface that might subvert a good marriage. He is a sensitive man who experiences many emotional changes that help him relate to his wife and her needs. Unless that sensitivity is appreciated and reciprocated, Pisces willingly takes a long development time to tie the knot. This sign's many emotional changes affect his perspective while making employment or business decisions. Ever supportive, he must know his wife stands by him. A woman who marries a Pisces needs a solid, independent income to cover financial obligations through life changes. Despite his ready emotional support for her needs and aims, her own emotional constitution has to be sturdy.

The Astrological Wife

When considering married life, the new bride benefits from the old saying, "It's no bed of roses!" As the descriptions above demonstrate, a man (or a woman) contributes both positives and negatives to the relationship. When these qualities are carefully examined, a woman learns what a man is seeking as a supply to his needs, a balance to his emotions, and an avenue for his efforts. The best astrological approach is a full study of both horoscopes for abilities to turn weaknesses into strengths.

Short of that, a woman has an astrological step up on the ladder of marital success when her Sun sign is the same as her prospective husband's Moon sign. While some astrologers consider this a karmic or fated attraction, this match of signs between the lights of the two horoscopes shows that beaming qualities from the woman's Sun help stabilize and mature emotional needs, projected by her husband's Moon.

Adapting to Marry

Although some women read astrological possibilities and decide they can live with peculiarities and oddities, a woman finds it a fruitless endeavor to reinvent her own emotional life to appear perfect for the chosen man. She, too, has emotional demands and insecurities, which have probably already made their appearance. If she has attempted to suppress them, those appetites will demand their due when the marriage suffers some rocky moments.

As long as she keeps a level head and a mature attitude, astrological indications can flower into the satisfaction and pleasure of a shared life fulfilled.

Leeda Alleyn Pacotti specializes in dream language, health astrology, and mind-body communication.

Need Meets Desire

by Lisa Finander

The need to be safe, the need to be loved, the need to nurture, the need to be nourished, the need to be known, the need for self-expression, the need to have a place in the world—versus all the desires impersonating those needs.

A veiled woman visible on certain nights follows a predestined path. Her power does not depend on being seen. She speaks a secret language heard by the inner ear and translated by the heart. Every month she revisits the same twelve houses of our birth charts, circling again and again and tirelessly imbuing each of our natal planets with her sentiments. Transmitting and receiving information, spilling out and refilling as she journeys, she serves as an emotional compass in our lives. Our moods fluctuate as she moves around our chart whispering the intrinsic needs of our true selves while at the same time never fully revealing herself to us.

Sometimes she is gentle and compassionate, encouraging us, telling us we are nurtured and well cared for, making it easy for us to welcome her presence. Other times she is unwelcome, and we feel vulnerable to her messiness as she spills over the edges of our lives, collapsing walls, and rebelling against the container we have created for her. Demanding at the same time to be emptied and filled, she is both untouchable and hungry for our attention.

Still, we do not banish her from our lives forever because the fear of becoming numb and impassive is stronger. Ignore her and every goal, every victory, and every success will feel meaningless. Minimize the importance of her emotional approval, and she will hold your heart hostage in a way most punishing to your natal Moon sign until you honor her wisdom. Intuitively we know we need her and yearn for her blessings. Her frequent travels allow her more intimacy with our birth charts than any of the other planets. Follow her and she will reveal the hidden pathways to emotional grace. Tune in to her rhythmic undulating through the signs, and you will feel her heartbeat instinctively driving your life and chart along. This veiled lady promises a lot, but left un-balanced she can lull you into a half-life of illusion and self-in-dulgence until you crash against something real.

She entranced me as I wrote this article. I went on fantastic journeys and followed her images deeper and deeper. My desires filled my mind there in her land of pictures, the things I longed for and the person I wished to be. A seductive perfection that my waking life could not emulate displayed itself in my mind's movie. Anything difficult or undesirable could be re-imagined. I could edit the story, changing characters and plots in the most appealing ways. These images would reappear in my dreams consuming as much of my thoughts and energy as I would allow. The "battle" ensued when I tried to detangle myself from her web. Why would I placate myself with desires that would fill the "hole" but not fulfill the "whole?"

Writer's block and resistance were what arose. I was sure I would have nothing to say at the end of my journey. I struggled repeatedly, trying to focus my consciousness and move through the visionary desires to something profound. After all, I like to write, I like the journey, so what was wrong? It had something to do with the word "battle." I chose this title without giving it much forethought, and this year's journey was guided by it. Working with the energies of the Moon is not a linear path. Deadlines, goals, and to-do lists do not influence her revelation. Vacillating between feelings of tranquility and distress, some small part of me had faith. I knew I was not alone. Everywhere around me, I saw people battling with themselves trying to find out what makes them happy, while also placating themselves with superficial desires. My hope is that some of the things I found true for me will be of help to you.

Before going further, let me explain what I mean when I use the words "need" and "desire" in the context of this article. I use the word "need" to describe a necessity, something essential, fundamental that is required in the psyche's search for wholeness. I picture needs as the center of a great nautilus. Their strength is potent, but unavailable to us until known. The chambers around the nautilus are layers of desire. Desires possess and consume energy, time, and/or money. Desires have superficial power that is hard to maintain physically They are the familiar fixes we reach for when we are frustrated in trying to acquire our imagined ideal. When left unconscious and unexamined, they keep us stuck and move us away from our needs. But each time we release a desire we get closer to our needs.

For example, a person might need to develop his or her capacity for self-love. A desire masking that need would occur when the person tries to obtain a certain physical appearance believing it will attract love thereby proving that she or he is loveable. Working on the beliefs and values that promote self-love will have a healing effect on the psyche. Trying to manipulate the body through desires will cause inner and outer struggles and often weaken it. Marketing and sales ads create more layers of desire by producing images meant to entice us into believing they are "needs." We deplete ourselves by remaining unaware of what we are searching for, and when we are disappointed in what we have. Instead of recognizing our desires as clues to underlying needs, we use desires to extinguish the impetus of the need. Desires are used merely as tools to squelch, shut up, indulge, and fake out an unmet need. Ultimately, it is our Moon that fakes us out by providing only a brief high, a brief happiness, and then replacing that feeling with one of endless longing.

Unaided, this alluring woman cannot achieve her goal in making our needs known to us. She spins in circles, negated. That fact became clear to me when I stopped wandering in her land of enchanted images and started looking for a pattern. The Moon, the powerful, beautiful woman in my mind, always had an equally powerful consort. The female vision was never without a male. These images were conveying an important message to me, and I was perceiving them as a form of escapism. When watching a movie or looking at a piece of art, you do not try to live inside the image. You step back and try to interpret it based on your own perceptions. I stepped back and realized a large piece of my battle: I kept the feminine and masculine parts of myself separate. When I engage myself in the world of endless commitments and to-do lists, I use only my conscious abilities. I become a high-energy doer while my intuitive, feminine abilities are not accessed. As I burn myself out from the intense pace, I rebound over to the feminine part of myself and just "be" for a while. I do not have enough energy for much else. Once there, I admonish male supremacy and my Sun-god society, while resting and replenishing myself.

I hide there as long as I can, banishing the male gods from my sanctuary. But dissatisfaction creeps in there, too. I alternate between blaming the masculine and the feminine polarities in my psyche for causing such discontent in my life. When I was younger, I valued my consciousness and my masculine, solar side, until my repressed feminine had had enough. She overthrew the gods and replaced them with the goddesses. Exalting the feminine image, after many years of exclusively revering the male, gave me two admirable forces and I could no longer choose one over the other. I "needed" both parts of myself to move toward the center of the nautilus.

I had finally grasped what she was showing me. Going back through my writings during this process, I found the Moon was in

Pisces opposing my Sun when I had my "aha" moment. I flipped back further in my notes looking for subtle clues, wondering if I could locate the first place a glimmer of that idea might have formed. The first traces recorded in my journal occurred twenty-eight days earlier when the Moon was also in Pisces! It took one full cycle around my birth chart for me to understand what she had reflected back to me.

Ready to greet her again with my newfound wisdom, I traveled to her shore carrying just enough of my conscious light to navigate the path. The veiled woman appeared and reached into the sand. I held out my hands eager to receive my nautilus. I was surprised to find her holding two. She placed one in each hand. One was slivery-white, and the details of it were difficult to see until I cast my light upon it. The other was golden, and shining so brightly that I had to pull my light away from it in order to examine it more closely. It appeared the Sun had cast his needs and desires into the sand along with the Moon. Why did I bring him along again?

Stop for a moment and imagine your perfect mate. Ask the conscious part of yourself what he needs. Make a list. Those are the needs of your Sun sign. What kind of lover will satisfy the needs of your emotional self? Make another list. Those are the needs of your Moon sign. Compare the lists. How well have you been able to gratify the needs of both parts of yourself? Which one is the source of most of your desires? Is a battle emerging over whose needs are more important? If you are like me, all is not well in your divine marriage. There is the battle. The needs of both have to be met without collapsing into an endless spiral of filling desires.

But there is hope. Just as the Moon's images cannot be decoded without conscious awareness, the Sun's expression is meaningless unless it is rooted in genuine feeling. They interpret for each other, each of them holding half of the message. You do not have double the needs and desires, unless you keep them divided. The needs of the two nautiluses will overlap, and so will their desires.

The following questions may help you distinguish your desires from your needs.

Moon

I long for/to be _____, (desire) so I can feel _____. (need)

If I was or had _____, (desire) then I would be _____. (need)

When I desire _____, it _____ my need to be/feel _____.

Sun

I feel good about myself when I _____. (need)

I am disappointed in myself when I _____. (desire)

If I could do anything I want in my life, it would be to _____. (need)

A personal goal is to _____. (need) I keep myself from obtaining this goal by _____. (desire)

The symbols of astrology can also help us with this process. You have a personal connection to the Sun and Moon based on your time of birth. Most people know what their Sun sign is. You will need a copy of your birth chart to find out your Moon sign. There are many places on the Internet where you can cast your chart, or order one. It will come in handy if you want to explore their relationship beyond their astrological signs. But for now, let's simplify things. Each of the twelve zodiac signs has a corresponding element. I have listed a brief description of each element's needs and desires. Compare the needs and desires of each based on their element. Do their elemental needs have a natural affinity towards one another or is it going to take some work to unite them? What needs are being emphasized, long to be acknowledged? What desires are entrapping you because they are just so easy to continue?

Fire Signs—Aries, Leo, and Sagittarius

Their needs are met through distinctiveness, creativity, feeling special, being playful, emotional warmth, recognition, passion, activity, inspiration, excitement, vitality, personal growth, and taking risks.

Their desires are fueled by control, dominance, superiority, consumption, lawlessness, selfishness, aggressiveness, impulsiveness, and false hope.

Earth Signs—Taurus, Virgo, and Capricorn

Their needs are met through physical manifestation, practical pursuits, the body, material sustenance, the earth, problem solving, trustworthiness, groundedness, and loyalty.

Their desires are fueled by fear of change, narrow mindedness, criticism, materialism, stubbornness, misuse of the body, and inflexibility.

Air Signs—Gemini, Libra, and Aquarius

Their needs are met through the exchange of ideas, relationships, inventiveness, communication, socializing, curiosity, intellectual pursuits, and justice.

Their desires are fueled by immaturity, daydreams, gossip, inconsistency, indecision, detachment, superficialness, and over-analyzing.

Water Signs—Cancer, Scorpio, and Pisces

Their needs are met through nurturing, protecting, feelings, sensitivity, merging, receptivity, intuition, psychic pursuits, mystery, and empathy.

Their desires are fueled by fear, dependency, insecurity, helplessness, victimization, manipulation, dishonesty, martyrdom, and chaos.

The veiled woman's familiar footsteps continue to encircle my chart, but now her tread feels lighter. She has one less image to carry and she has the support of her consort to help convey future messages. No longer standing between them, the energy I expended to keep them separate was returned to me. I can put it to better use. We decide whether her adventures will be purposeful or purposeless. Either way, she will not rest until she can inhabit our hearts and illuminate our psyches. Her presence is constant. She will show us the same image repeatedly until we fall in love with it. She tells us it is our duty to feel the deepest parts of ourselves in a way the mind cannot defend. The Moon teaches us to feel failure, fear, disappointment, and unhappiness long enough to face it, transform it, and release it back to her allowing her to increase and mature. When your consciousness has mastered one set of her symbols, she will change the game so that a new level of expertise and sophistication is required.

I invite you to step off the Sun's path for a while and onto hers. See what images emerge. Learn her language. Let her inspire you, replenish you, and cleanse what has become stagnate. Remember that one-twelfth of her reflection is contained in your Moon sign. Share your special part with the world, for the Moon seeks wholeness, too.

Lisa Finander is a writer, teacher, and consultant who works with symbolism, including the symbolism of astrology, tarot, and dreams. In her work, Lisa uses symbols to bring richness and meaning into the lives of others and herself. She enjoys working with and among nature. She receives much support and inspiration from her husband Brian, along with their cats Toby and Yule. Lisa is currently working on her first novel where she will bring these teachings to life.

Doing Your Life Laundry

by Terry Lamb

Doreen's house was out of control. She could barely open the front door. Boxes lay under piles of clothes and toys. But the biggest problem was books. Books everywhere! She loved books, and she had passed that joy on to her two young children. She had one bedroom filled with boxes of books, while she and her children were squeezed into the other bedroom. The house was so bad, she was embarrassed to have visitors. Even though she was divorced, young, and attractive, she rarely went out because she was reluctant to have a boyfriend see how she lived. Her children also lived by the same constraints, playing outside with neighborhood friends or going to their houses instead.

In these modern times, physical objects are readily available to us. We move infrequently, and there's always something more to buy; yet we don't always clear out what we don't need. The result is clutter, sometimes life-choking, as in Doreen's case. Our homes and how we manage them are ruled by the Moon. The sign the Moon is in shows what type of clutter we are likely to collect, while the aspects to the Moon from the other planets pinpoint why we collect it. Doreen's Moon is in Gemini. Her mother loved books, and Doreen learned to love them from her. Her mother signed her up for several book clubs when she was a child, and she'd been collecting ever since.

Often there is a deep-seated emotional issue behind our unhealthy habits, and the amount of clutter we collect can be a measure of this. Doreen's clutter became unmanageable when her mother died, leaving her large library and the rest of her belongings to Doreen. Somehow, Doreen couldn't bear to part with her mother's things—even to look through them. It was too painful for her.

For most of us, our clutter is not that extreme, and it may not stop us from living our lives to the fullest. Every time a bill gets lost under a pile of papers or looking for our keys critically delays our departure, we may resolve to clean up only to push the notion aside indefinitely. To overcome this pattern, we can go to our Moon, decipher its code by looking at its sign and aspects, and act on what we learn.

Your Moon Sign and Clutter

Aries Moon

Your clutter consists of all the unfinished projects that are the fruits of your enthusiasm for new ideas and activities. These could range from sports equipment to the paraphernalia of discarded hobbies and household DIY undertakings. Your reasons for collecting clutter tie into unprocessed emotions, because you prefer to fill your life with action rather than take the time for the pensive moments that resolve emotional experiences. You simply would rather be doing something proactive. You may even avoid being at home as a way to avoid thinking about it all. To motivate yourself, plan a special weekend away once the work is done, or have friends over for a post-clean-up celebratory bash. Or make it a competition with another friend to see who can complete their clear-out first. Once you're in the flow, it will be easy to discard unnecessary items, because you are not nostalgic. Rather, you may be tempted to throw away valuable items such as important documents, so resist the urge to toss stacks of paper wholesale. If emotional issues that have been stuffed or avoided come up, allow yourself your moment of truth—it will pass soon enough with your optimistic take on life.

Taurus Moon

You surround yourself with objects d'art, collectibles, silk clothing, and a myriad of practical objects, from that dusty waffle iron to embroidery supplies. Your reasons for collecting are based on the need for physical security. When you are surrounded by beauty and finery, you feel better about yourself, more secure. Unbalancing events may tempt you to buy something—hence the mounting pile of things you just couldn't do without. However, a cluttered home is not beautiful, and it drags you down. If it's hard to part with your treasures, give them to friends, or sell collectibles to someone who will cherish them. Plan to spend your proceeds in a high-value way (which could be an experience rather than a thing), then take a picture of your "friend," and sell it at auction. As you clear out, memories will arise that you associate with each item. It's harder to let go of things that represent pleasant memories if you're afraid you'll forget. The

photo and a paragraph in a scrapbook will make releasing them easier. For objects that symbolize painful moments, letting go of them lets you also let go of the pain.

Gemini Moon

Geminis collect paper, from books, magazines, and journals to unread mail. You surround yourself with stacks of partially read materials because of your endless curiosity about the unknown. But clutter reduces your ability to focus, and your lack of focus increases clutter—where does it end?! You can start by realizing that you don't have to read every word written down. It's okay to pass on a book you didn't finish—evidently you've read what was meaningful to you. Donate those books to your local library, or give them to a school. Recycle magazines more than a month old. Any resistance is related to your fears of not being sufficient in yourself and an urge to avoid buried experiences. You prefer not to resurrect the ghosts of past experiences, even though you can learn as much from those as from printed words. Simplify your life by canceling unwanted subscriptions and refusing junk mail. Place a bill holder at your desk, a magazine rack by the couch. Keep only as many books as fit on your shelves, giving away one when you acquire a new one. The important knowledge is carried in that sharp mind of yours, and the rest is recoverable.

Cancer Moon

Cancers collect everything—memorabilia, photographs, heirlooms, anything that needs a home. People often donate their clutter to you, because they know you will take care of it, even if you don't want it and don't have room. How can you bring yourself to let go of these treasures? You hang on to things because they hold emotions and memories for you or because they would be abandoned without you. Like Taurus, a photograph and scrapbook entry will help you preserve what you really want to keep. Organize your things into groups, and keep only the most cherished member of each group, passing the others along through auction, gift, or the junk heap. Think in terms of the useful life of an object, not all the service it has given you. Finding the right place to recycle or discard it will also help. Limit your memorabilia to only the most meaningful items and no more than you can attractively display. Then, organize what's left, and just say no when others want to give their discards to you. If you have difficulty getting perspective on what you own, get someone to help you.

Leo Moon

Leo is the entertainment king, and you are likely to have a storehouse of videotapes, CDs, and DVDs that prove it! Your home may also be a repository for objects d'art, and your own sporting equipment squeezed in around that big-screen HDTV. Your wardrobe could also be an area of retention, as you strive to keep up with the latest fashion trends. Your closets are the saga of all your unfulfilled or past-fulfilled glories, your claims to fame.

They hold you back by keeping your gaze fixed on the past rather than the future, where your next glory lies. Deep inside, you may fear that your past successes are better than anything you can achieve now. Realizing that these extra belongings curb your success should be sufficient motivation to clear out, but if not, set up a competition with another sporty friend or throw a "clear-out party." Pass the old clothes and dormant equipment on to charity and pat yourself

on the back for a deed well done. Then let your inner hero out and invite some friends over to party and drool over your posh new look.

Virgo Moon

Don't let anyone tell you that Virgos don't clutter. It's not true—they just know where everything is in their mess! You collect books, vitamins, yoga tapes, and the right tool for the right job, reflecting your multiple interests and desire to become competent at every task known to man. Your resistance to decluttering comes from your fears that you are not good enough to handle life's challenges, so you hyper-prepare by collecting the tools to cope. The trouble is, you get buried under all those things and feel no more ready than with nothing. To let go, think in terms of calling on other people to help you. Sell those tools at a garage sale or on-line and save the money for that rainy day if you must—or spend it on a pleasure cruise. Keep the best how-to books, and get rid of the outdated health foods and supplements. Discard those extra cleaning supplies and hire a maid to do the scrubbing. Then apply the organizing skills you so easily express in other's lives within your own domain. Remember that your strength lies in interdependence with others, and you'll unleash a sleeker, cleaner look in your home.

Libra Moon

Whether it's closets full of clothes, drawers overflowing with make-up and skin creams, or the latest original painting, beauty is what matters to you. You love those accessories—that pile of purses and shoes everywhere! Your extra belongings consist of the ways you've tried to create harmony and beauty in your life. Your clutter results from your need to always be perfectly coordinated, to satisfy your secret need to have others' approval. It's tempting to think that if you look appealing, you'll attract the love you need. Plus, it's just hard to let go of something that holds beauty for you. Soon you have so much stuff, you can't find what goes together anymore—you forget what you have. So, haul everything out of those closets and give away anything you haven't worn or used in a year. There are plenty of charities willing to accept clothing, especially women's and homeless shelters. Give away all those relationship books and invite some friends over for high tea. Have confidence in yourself, and your new glow will attract the love you need. Remember that beauty is a radiance that emanates from within, so let it shine through with a simpler approach.

Scorpio Moon

You've got what it takes to survive—flashlights galore, the tent, the hoist to work on your car, even that extra pantry of canned food and the shed full of tools and workout equipment. Your interest in hidden things may result in stores of tarot decks, occult books, murder mysteries, and treatises on Jungian archetypes. You've prepared yourself for threats both physical and psychological, but you collect these items through your secret need to connect with others. However, they actually isolate you, you feel less secure, and they seem all the more necessary because of it. The more you acquire, the less you feel prepared to face the challenges of life. The key is to disentangle yourself from the tools and to reach out to develop relationships of trust. From the neighborhood auto mechanic to the friends who can help you feel more linked with the world, they are the key to ending your isolation. It takes faith to let go of things which represent a way of life for you, but once you commit yourself you'll use your natural transformative gifts to see you through. What awaits you is a world of warmth and mutual support.

Sagittarius Moon

You are not a tremendous collector, unless it is all the latest gadgets to meet your travel needs. You would prefer to go through life lightly, but your high interest in everything foreign to you keeps you from fulfilling that ideal. Whether it's the perfect suitcase, ten guidebooks to Ulan Bator, or the stacks of *National Geographic* going back to 1952, you want to know what goes on in our world. Your interests may extend to athletics or the ethereal realms of abstract thought, resulting in rooms full of books and journals. Your motto could be: only too much is enough, reflecting your ever-readiness for the next adventure. Your clutter builds up because you can't be bothered to finish things, so busy are you in advancing to the next conquest. Deep inside though, you harbor a fear of being confined, so you move too quickly to avoid being trapped. Taking the time to look behind should be a sobering experience, but one from which you will learn quickly. All that detritus holds you back—it can't just be ignored out of existence. Stopping long enough to clear it from your world will create true freedom in your life.

Capricorn Moon

If you collect anything, it's out of fear of lack, so your clutter can run the gamut. You could throw away that twist tie, but what if you need it again? Your stuff is comprised of the potentially useful things you might need in the coming times of want—rubber bands, old clothes that just need a little mending, and back-up items to the hilt—just in case. Your collection may reflect your enthusiasm for history, from books to family documents. To your credit, you are usually prepared to handle any contingency, and people know they can depend on you. However, placing more trust in others will draw you closer to them. Realizing how capable you are will help you let go of all the objects that keep you from accomplishing what you want—an orderly universe where you can manage your needs and help others out too. Everything that allows you to be self-reliant prevents you from reaching out to others, and it's exhausting. Too much results in isolation. You don't have to change your own oil. A wide world of humanness awaits you if you will ask for support in exchange for all that you give.

Aquarius Moon

Your drive toward intellectualism and individuality dictates the nature of the things you collect, from political magazines and the latest progressive pamphlet to the green tint you used on your hair last week. Even if you're more conservative, you've got the ideological symbols scattered around your abode to prove it. And you love gadgets, especially electronic ones—how many computers and PDAs do you have? Your paraphernalia may extend to labradorite crystals, tachyon belts, magnetic mattress pads, and aromatherapy diffusers. What makes you tick is the need to break through the mold of the old and create waves that take us into the future. However, you are hindered if you have so many possessions. Too many remedies scatter your healing energies and muddy the waters of your intentions. Clarity comes from simplicity, and simplifying your surroundings boosts your ability to meet your objectives. It will be easy to see which items stand out in your life once you apply your famous objectivity to the task. Recycle any magazine older than a month, and use yesterday's newspapers to wrap today's fish. As you lighten your load, you empower your ability to focus and create what you want in life.

Pisces Moon

You are blessed with the ability to let go of feelings as easily as you shed your clothes at night, but you have to be aware of them first. This is your key to those excess possessions. You hold onto things not because of memories you can't let go of, but because they hold feelings you haven't yet become aware of. Without processing your feelings, your life slips into chaos, and your unprocessed possessions reflect and add to it. Mostly, you have trouble sticking with something long enough to complete it, especially when life throws stimuli at you too quickly to digest. Your detritus is more likely to be unread (or unshredded) mail than it is to be items of value, unless it is spiritual objects that won't fit on your altar or stuff you forgot to put away. You are capable of incredible clarity and vision, but you can't go there unless your life is cleared of debris. Get help from someone who can be objective, and take a break when you feel discouraged or confused. The goal is a clear and focused mind and highly attuned perception of your world—and it can be accomplished.

Letting Go of Painful Memories

Although she didn't realize it, Doreen held onto her possessions because of the pain surrounding her mother's death. When our possessions are way out of control, it is usually because there are painful memories associated with them, and we don't know how to let go. With the help of an organizing team, she got to the root of what was bothering her and learned how to clear out her belongings as well as how to keep them organized. Doreen is now better adjusted and happier in her life. Here are some guidelines:

- Journal about unpleasant memories or share them with someone else
- If the memories are traumatic, get someone to help you as you declutter
- Feel free to employ others to help you with the challenge, from a therapist to a clear-out team

How to Do Your Life Laundry

Cleaning up and clearing out is laundry that improves your life, your health, your feng shui, and your personal power. Here's how to do it:

1. Prepare ahead of time by getting boxes, trash bags, and the phone numbers of local recycling centers; find out what discard services are available through your local trash collection agency; rent a roll-out bin if needed, and buy at least one tarp on which to place your belongings.
2. Pick a sunny day, lay the tarps on the lawn, and put everything on the tarps.
3. Sort into either a "keep" from a "toss" pile, and keep in mind that objects hold pain as well as memories. It is possible to let go of the objects without betraying the memories.
4. Permit yourself to keep one memento of the important people and milestones in your life. Take photos, build scrapbooks (digital ones are extra compact), and set up a small area in your house where memorabilia can be displayed.
5. Sell what is valuable through auction, garage sale, or private ad; recycle what you can; give away what may be truly valued by someone you know; throw away the rest. Use your proceeds to reward yourself for a job well done.
6. Set up systems to help keep things like bills and paperwork organized.

7. Establish rules to manage the parts of your life that were unmanageable before, like "give away one piece of clothing for every one I buy."

Get Ready for a New Life!

In addition to your Moon's sign, its aspects and house placement tell why you collect what you do. They also tell when milestone events occurred which are key to your habits.

Terry Lamb specializes in electional astrology (choosing the right day for an event according to planetary influences), as well as family and relationship matters. She currently resides in Spring Valley, California.

Business
and
Legal
Section

Economic Watch 2006

by Dorothy J. Kovach

Do you feel like you are just running to stay in place? You are not alone. Take a deep breath: 2006 may try the collective patience of all of us. Simply put, the pantry is bare. As deficits soar, we are saddled with a rising tide of expenses and little in the way of new business opportunities. The United States might be the mightiest military nation in the world, but it is also up to its ears in debt. As long as so much of our money goes out and so little comes back in, as a nation we risk becoming economic share-croppers, picking away at a mountain of debt. In such a climate, the market can only go up so much before meeting resistance.

Why worry about the market? Even if you don't own one single stock, so much of the fiber of this country is tied up in Wall Street that when it is up, we all feel happy and secure. We have faith in the future. When it is down we worry about our jobs, our health insurance, and just about everything else.

Bulls and Bears, Jupiter and Saturn

When it comes to markets, we talk about the dynamic between two opposing factions: Jupiter and Saturn. Depending upon the duet these two sing, there is want or plenty in global markets. Business is comprised of two basic themes: expansion and contraction. We call the various markets representing these two principles bull or bear markets, respectively.

Jupiter will rule the bull or expanding markets, when everybody gets rich and we all have the Midas touch. Saturn, on the other hand, rules the down-and-dark bear markets. Where these mega business planets meet and how they interact will tell us what will happen in the coming cycle. Investors are interested in expansion, so we begin with Jupiter.

Jupiter in Scorpio

Jupiter is just about as good as it gets. He furnishes our every fantasy. When Jupiter dominates the marketplace, all of our wishes turn to gold: we get easy raises and all is right in our world.

Jupiter spends approximately one year in each of the twelve signs. Smart investors always know what sign Jupiter is in, because whatever sector is symbolized by the sign Jupiter traverses will tend to go up. In 2006 Jupiter will spend most of his time in Scorpio. Businesses that value security and pragmatism will do well.

Companies like Symantec and McAffe, which deal with the ever-increasing problem of computer viruses, and those businesses working on biological identification will do well in 2006.

Scorpio rules over vermin, like bugs, so when this energy is applied to the technology sector, the result is even more viruses in our computer networks. Companies like Symantec and

McAffe, which deal with this ever increasing problem, and those businesses working on biological identification, will do well in a world where business is increasingly done online. Scorpio is also connected to secrets and taboos: Big Brother is watching you. Watch for expansion of the secret government investigative bodies and techniques. We will watch expansion in all detective and surveillance businesses.

Scorpio is connected to surgery and transformation. We may see some miraculous breakthroughs in surgery. Artificial body parts and medical devices continue to be positioned well for the first quarter of the year. Companies working on the problems facing an aging population will also do well.

Scorpio is the night sign of Mars, the planet of war. Watch for more buildup in the defense industry. However, those defense contractors that have been overcharging the government might have to account for their actions later in the year when Jupiter and Saturn cross paths. We can expect a good deal of business to take place behind closed doors. When Jupiter is in Scorpio, all that is dark expands. With government funding down, the underworld becomes a growth industry as people turn to private contractors instead of the local government to protect them. Translated: all secret organizations, including mob activity, flourish. Jupiter in Scorpio will expand all energy companies, including oil, coal, and natural gas. Those companies employed by the military will continue to see a bump up for the time being. Keeping corporate secrets will mean keeping corporate profits. Watch for a surge in hacking activities as the war on terrorism shifts to computer banking. A word to the wise: business people who can keep confidences and a low profile will succeed where the brash and showy will be shown the door.

Saturn

In the realm of what goes up must come down, Saturn is the down. Saturn rules decline and depression. It is a sign of shortages and want. Above all, Saturn demands that we pay our dues. It is the principle of "what goes around comes around." For the past five years this country has run up enormous deficits. The problem with a national debt in the trillions is that we bankrupt our future. As competition becomes more intense for the world's resources, Americans will wind up paying more for goods and services but get far less in return.

As we know, Saturn's function is to deteriorate; therefore, whatever is represented by the sign Saturn is in will become scarce. When we have less of a product, it becomes more valuable. Leo rules that which is fiery and shiny. We may see gold continue to rise, and along with it silver, copper, iron, bauxite, and nickel. Since Leo is fiery, Saturn in Leo will promote another round of shortages in the oil supply. We may see this greatly impact many areas of the U.S. economy because, at present, oil is the blood of this nation. When oil goes up, inflation is on the horizon. When inflation goes up, the economy stagnates.

Because of Leo's royal connotation, Saturn is hardest on people at the top. Since the U.S. is the most powerful country in the world, Saturn placed in Leo might present some very real obstacles for President Bush. Even though he has control of both houses of the legislature, Saturn will have a way of holding him back. Look for the end of July and early August to be especially difficult for him and the rest of this country. At the top of the economic food chain, there is a good possibility that American economic power may be challenged in some way. If history does repeat itself, we might liken this time to thirty years ago, during the Carter administration. Look for all those nations born during Saturn in Leo to have growing pains. Look for both China and Iran to join neighboring Iraq in the news in 2006.

Saturn rules all things old. The ancients felt that when Saturn was in Leo, old people suffer. At the edge of retirement, baby boomers have to face some ugly realities. When Alan Greenspan

says, "We need to recalibrate the system," that translates to: there isn't enough money left for baby boomers to have anywhere close to the kind of retirement benefits their parents enjoyed.

To complicate matters, Jupiter, the planet of luck and profit, will be sitting in a hard angle to Saturn, the planet of business. Restrictions, red tape, and regulations abound under this dynamic. To make matters worse, venture capital dries up. When business tries to expand it is met with insurmountable obstacles. In short, booms go bust. Every seven years, Jupiter and Saturn make a hard aspect to each other, taking the steam out of the marketplace.

Saturn and Jupiter will square off in fixed signs. This indicates that business and people in general will hold tight to their ideas, and will not give up easily. On the one hand that's good for being tenacious, but when it comes to labor and management, disputes are not easily solved as neither side is willing to compromise. Investors will need to steel themselves for some difficult business days ahead for businesses involved in theater and movies. Watch for some peaking in the mining industry under this aspect. Some might use any serious peak in the market to clean up their portfolios and clear out any unproductive issues. The days ahead on the market will test the stamina of even the heartiest. In this climate, if you cannot afford to lose, don't play. Seventy percent of the market goes with the trend. Saturn is the dominant trend in 2006. In other words, there will be a price to be paid for the frivolity.

Spring Equinox

Amongst the main predictive tools that financial astrologers have is the Spring Equinox. This chart is set for the exact nanosecond that the Sun enters the sign Aries.

The Spring Equinox takes place on March 20, 2006, at 18:27 G.M.T. (5:27 pm EST). We locate our chart at New York City, because this was where George Washington's inauguration took place and, thus, where we officially became a nation.

The most poignant feature of this year's spring chart is the placement of Saturn in Leo right on the cusp of the eastern horizon. Saturn so placed warns us that there are no short cuts; Saturn forces us to pay our dues and make amends for what we break. Like it or lump it, in the end, the universe will always seek to balance. Now placed in fiery Leo, Saturn could tend to make all items related to energy and metals more precious, so we may see oil go up. But when we pay more at the pump, we have less to spend on other things. When we have less to spend on other things, business everywhere suffers. Saturn's medicine is like chemotherapy: poisonous and painful. But it will tend to bring balance back to the marketplace.

In the past few years, the government printing office has been working overtime giving money away in the form of low interest loans and tax breaks, while conducting some rather expensive operations abroad. Meanwhile, many baby boomers are getting ever closer to retirement. Just printing dollars can't solve real economic problems, though, because running enormous deficits does matter. Money has been pouring out like water from a faucet, and in a few short years, the value of the U.S. dollar has plummeted.

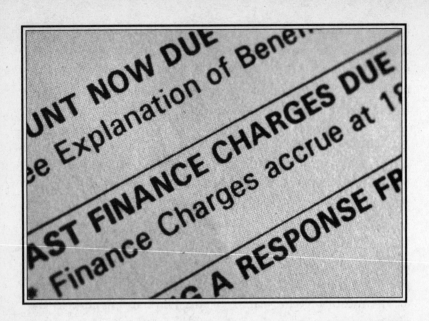

Making money readily available did lift the stock market, temporarily, but it did so at a price: the U.S. treasury was gutted, and an enormous debt has accrued. In fiscal terms, Saturn warns us that it is time to pay up.

And on top of this, the natives, especially in the cities, are restless. The combination of diminished social services, fewer jobs, and a politically alienated populace is a recipe for social unrest. The "have-nots" are looking up at the "haves" with a kind of envy bordering on contempt. In this climate, security companies, bodyguards, and surveillance businesses thrive as the rich seek protection from an ever-more-uncertain world.

The first house of the chart represents the common folk in any given country. When Saturn is there, there can be little harmony between management and the workforce. Negotiations are nixed and strikes are on the increase. Expect people in urban areas to be most frustrated in the year ahead.

The ancients believed that the Moon's placement at the equinox will describe the mood of the people. With the Moon in pious Sagittarius, we might look for the religious right to use their might against the loose morals in the entertainment industry. This could mean trouble for companies, like Viacom, that like to push the sexual envelope on television. The Moon in Sagittarius is good for those in religious and spiritual businesses, especially those that are closest to ancient tradition. Does this mean Latin is coming back into style? No, but we may see trouble for royalty—be it the queen of England or the pontiff. 2006 will be most difficult on both.

Fire in abundance is inspirational and, unfortunately, inflationary. The number one cause of inflation will be rising gas prices. As we know, when gas goes up, everything else follows, from food to clothing. We pay more for what we need and get less for our money. Venture capital dries up and new ideas do not lead to great businesses. There could be an increase in immigration as restrictions are eased.

On the bright side, those who were worried about some sort of real estate meltdown can breathe a little easier while Bush is president. This is due to the makeup of Bush's own chart. However, these are not the rosy days of yesteryear. The real estate market is cooling. It becomes a buyer's market as money tightens.

There may be trouble lurking on our roads and in our ports in the coming year. Over 10,000 ships make more than 68,000 port calls in the U.S. each year, but fewer than 5 percent of them get inspected. This is a recipe for disaster. Those in the shipping industry and those in charge of our ports should take every measure possible to tighten up security in 2006.

Many will feel depressed and frustrated, especially in the population centers. In this climate, there will be a rise in alcohol and antidepressant sales.

The North Node in Aries spells good times for metals, but it's not so good for home beauty aids. Hold off on that face-lift or other expensive cosmetic treatments until mid-June, when the

North Node finally leaves Libra, and the potential for serious complications.

The Total Eclipse in Aries

On March 29, 2006, at 10:10 am UT (Universal Time), a total eclipse of the Sun will envelope all under it, all the way from Brazil to Outer Mongolia. At its peak, the eclipse shadow will cover much of the Middle East, including Saudi Arabia, Israel, and Iraq.

Unlike modern folk, who rush to film total eclipses, the ancients feared eclipses, and connected them to upheavals for leaders and nations. They examined eclipses closely, paying attention to the sign in which the eclipse would take place, because the things ruled by that sign would become unbalanced in the year ahead. This March 29 total eclipse takes place in Aries. Because Aries was prominent when the first king of England ascended the throne, eclipses falling in Aries have always been linked to the United Kingdom. With this in mind, we may see the war on terrorism highlight Great Britain in some manner.

Although the eclipse will not be seen in the U.S., its effects will be very noticeable here because it takes place in the first house of the people. This is a warning to those in the U.S. to be on their guard. The ancients felt that an eclipse in the eastern skies had great power for trouble.

This eclipse falls in the constellation Andromeda. According to ancient myth, Andromeda's mother bragged about her beauty so much that she brought down the wrath of the god Neptune, who sent a storm to destroy her homeland. To stop the destruction, Andromeda was to be sacrificed to Neptune.

This myth has to do with the consequences of pride. The ancients said that when an eclipse took place in this region, the countries of the world would be prone to anger. This infers that we may see the war on terrorism take a bloodier turn. Andromeda's deity is Ahir-Budhnya, meaning the "bottom snake." Snakes are noted for their sneakiness, and this could imply that terrorism will rear its ugly head again in the coming year.

Eclipses have special meanings for heads of state because of their symbolic connection to the Sun. Falling in President Bush's ninth house, this eclipse may darken his goals in foreign relations. He and his people will need to use special caution this year, because the ruler of both the president and his people (the Moon) is in the section of the eclipse chart that represents crisis, death, and debt. It appears that there will be much opposition to American policies in the coming year. There are indications that President Bush and his government will have to make some real adjustments.

In general, this eclipse does not bode well for new ventures abroad. It favors businesses having to do with exploration, energy, and war. Because Aries is a headstrong sign, the March eclipse threatens economic hardship due to moving without giving enough thought to the consequences of our actions.

Market Watch!

December 2005

There's a lot of uncertainty about the future as the spending season officially begins, and shoppers do not buy when they are worried. Saturn has cast his pall on the market, and all is not jolly. Despite a post-Thanksgiving bump, bad news around December 5 can send ripples through the tech-laden NASDAQ. With Saturn perched at the pivot between

Best bets are in research and development and in surveillance companies.

Mars and Jupiter, putting a wet blanket on our urge to shop and provoking dark memories of our not-so-distant past, the potential exists for more terrorism fears to surface. There might be some increase in the military. Perhaps we will see a return to the draft. Best bets are in research and development and surveillance companies.

January 2006

The market is in a jovial mood as we start the new year. Look for some surprises at the end of the first week and again around January 13 to produce good news for stocks. However, the cost of fuel is high, fencing in our profits in the second week. Focus continues to be on the war. Companies that cater to the troops overseas profit in this environment. Energy and utilities increase due to various strains on demand, with gas and heating oil following suit. Look for rising interest rates to spook the real estate market. As home heating expenses rise, folks not do not have cash for other things, and commerce slows to a snail's pace near the end of the month. Smart retailers will discount to lure nervous customers into their stores.

February

Tech takes some punishing the first week. There are still some positive signs in pharmaceuticals, but they may be overpriced at this time. If you hold a goodly amount of oil stocks, you are smiling, but if you are the average person, you are continuing to watch your purchasing power decline. Even so, there are still positive signs in the market for firms involved in research and development. Remember: all that glitters is not gold. We may see the market drop around the second and third week despite positive discoveries in medical research. Be prepared to take profits or sell short at the end of the month. Sign all important documents by the last week, or you'll pay the price for months to come as Mercury retrograde will spoil all agreements.

March

Mercury is retrograde almost all month. Hold back on major purchases and don't sign important documents until March 25. The hard aspect from Jupiter to Neptune favors neither shipping nor

earnings. We might expect some volatile trading in the second week as Mars squares Uranus. There is potential trouble on the high seas as the shipping and travel industry may be in for a shock. Business is slow as stagnation descends. Secret dealings could cause trouble. Wise business owners know that this is not the time to spend on purchases. March may prove to be a volatile month, so position yourself accordingly. There may be some recovery around March 18, but this continues to be a very wild market: it is hard to make money under Saturn's frigid gaze. For the most part business is slow, with both Mercury and Saturn trudging backward. Secret dealings could cause trouble.

April

Expect volatile markets as business wrestles with the meaning of brute force. Keep business on the up and up; secret dealings could cause trouble. The wise will keep their heads about them while all around them lose theirs. War uncertainties threaten to subdue any momentum in the market, especially around April 18 and 19. In this climate, unless you own copious amounts of gold or oil, it is hard to find much to smile about. As interest rates rise the housing market slows and inflation worries nag at the market as energy prices hit new highs while equities sag. Gold and oil could be nearing peaks right now. Some potential mismanagement in the pharmaceutical industry might surface in the market. We will need to rein in our desires or the markets will do it for us.

May

Holders of oil and banking stocks smile and report good earnings due to rising interest rates. Oil may be testing some highs right about now. The month is dominated by bad news from abroad. With so much of our tax dollar going to foreign causes and the deficit, real profits become frighteningly elusive. Overall, a sense of uncertainty continues to drain away consumer confidence. The market tests some bottoms the first week as Saturn freezes the real estate market. The high cost of energy and the war on terror have left an indelible mark on the economy. Higher interest rates are hard on the market, but a necessary evil. It seems as though everything is conspiring against those who want to make money. Some troubling news in techs appears during the last week as Mercury squares Uranus. Higher interest rates continue to scare away would-be buyers.

June

The month opens with gas edging higher as the driving season begins. Look for some kind of adjustment in the tech and communication sectors. Uncertainty leaves investors jittery early in the first week, but they are able to shrug it off the next. This could signal a short recovery beginning in techs. Get ready to profit the second and third week of June as the great bull smiles on the tech market, and the market opens on a positive note. Biotech and medical stocks do especially well at this time with Mercury's trine to Uranus. Technology stocks are on the move as communications bring smiles back to the NASDAQ. Summer begins at 9:05 am on June 21, and we are in a fighting spirit, which is good for markets but not good for our own profits. Take some profits at peaks.

July

Worry seems to stick to this market like gum to an old shoe. Despite a bump up after the long holiday, on the whole, markets are jittery. Do not sign on the dotted line! Avoid signing any important papers, unless you thrive on regret. Mercury is retrograde as we head back to work after July 4, so wait until August before committing to contracts. Don't be fooled into any get-rich-quick schemes this month, with Jupiter so positioned against Saturn and Neptune. The odds are that what you see will certainly not be what you get! Hold off on all major purchases until August—that includes stocks. Those invested in HMOs are smiling. Keep your ears open for news of breakthroughs in the biotech and medical sectors. New development in treatments could boost stocks. Flooding may be a real factor right now, so those in low-lying regions, especially in the Midwest, should be prepared to move to higher ground. Position yourself carefully: the last week of July could see some terrorism bring markets down.

August

A sense of uncertainty continues to drain away consumer confidence. Troubling times trickle down to the street. When people are fearful, they hang on to their wallets. Business is having a "don't fix it if it ain't broke" attitude toward purchases, and new hiring is at a minimum. People just do not spend when they are afraid, and the market responds in kind. The bearish cycle finally breaks on NASDAQ around August 10, as some solid earnings are finally reported. Bad news in the war abroad hurts the market and helps would-be terrorists. In this climate it is hard to make money unless you are already well positioned. Those who have turned to the safety of gold might consider taking profits at the beginning of the month as Saturn's influence deepens. Troubled times for retail and tech appear during the last week.

September

Finally, some relief—and the market responds in kind. Look for rises in pharmaceuticals. While the worst seems to be over, there are lingering fears. We receive some good news in the communications sector this month, and there may be some bargains in tech—especially those companies that serve the military. If only gas prices would go down, we would see a real recovery. In the meantime, we must accept what we get, which is a nice rally in techs during the third week. Everybody loves tech that week, but look for some adjustments, too. Though smiles abound in the communication sector, that is not the case in retail: people are not spending on back-to-school clothes. There are still some troubling developments abroad at month's end, but the market overall is optimistic.

October

The market continues in a positive mode, with some bargains in tech remaining, but troubling news brings the market down to reality at the end of the first week. Wise speculators know when to hold and when to fold. The trine between Saturn and Pluto reminds us that despite our best efforts, it is still too easy for terrorists. Business is in a very tenuous place right now. There are those whose only purpose is to separate you from your hard-earned capital. Invest only for the long term. New development in treatments could boost stocks; however, any secret dealings will be exposed, and could cause much future trouble. It may be wise to take some profits midmonth, as some indications are for a reverse as Jupiter heads out to perfect a square to Saturn. Look for gold to be on the rise at the end of the second week. Make certain to sign all important documents by October 29, when Mercury turns retrograde.

November

Put off important purchases until the end of the month. Trouble may lurk in unexpected places this month, but smart investors will know how to keep on their toes. War and nuclear issues abroad have the focus of the market. Troublesome times in the war on terrorism brings a market adjustment. Drug makers may have reason to smile the first week, but there are numerous enemies to business right now.

Even to the untrained eye, five planets in the deadly sign of Scorpio is an ominous sign for investors. Position yourself accordingly.

December

Business traumas ease, and we finally can get down to some business as Mercury turns direct on December 17. Those invested in foreign markets are all smiles now. The New Moon in Scorpio turns our attention to the war on terrorism. Biotech pharmaceuticals all look good this week, as researchers make new discoveries. Position yourself accordingly. Nuclear energy and banking are highlighted.

Dorothy J. Kovach is a traditional astrologer, writer, and timing expert based in northern California. She acts as a consultant to individuals and business people who desire to start their projects at the optimum time for success. Her specialty is horary, the branch of astrology that answers specific questions, and she uses the wisdom of the ancients of both western and eastern astrology. Her articles have appeared in www.stariq.com, www.msnbc.com, and the Astrological Association of Great Britain. She was a contributing editor to the Horary Practitioner. *In recent years, Dorothy has turned her attention to the financial markets. She can be reached through her Web site at www.worldastrology.net.*

New Moon Beginnings

by April Elliott Kent

I was about seven years old when I made my initial foray into the world of business. Intrigued by an advertisement in my *Archie* comic book, I sent off for packets of seeds that the ad strongly suggested could be parlayed into significant wealth. In due time, the seeds arrived, in packets decorated with beautiful sketches of the lush flowers and vegetables that these seeds would someday become. Enthused, I immediately began trying to sell them to friends and family; who could resist, I figured?

But in my youthful enthusiasm, I had overlooked one important point: I lived in a farm community, and seeds were not exactly in short supply. So, my career in horticultural commerce was short-lived. The seed of the idea—sell an appealing, inexpensive product to lots of people—was a fine one. But the soil and growing conditions were not hospitable, and so the "seed" of my youthful entrepreneurism withered without bearing fruit.

Any gardening book will tell you how to produce the best results with a given seed—what kind of soil to plant it in, how much light and water it needs. But there is no guarantee that what is planted and nourished in a particular way will flower as expected. Even nature cannot make solid predictions that a plant will end up looking like the picture on the seed packet. As scholar Edith Hamilton once put it, "The seed never explains the flower." Two gardeners plant seeds from the same zucchini, and tend them with care; one ends up with a garden full of green, the other with a shriveled vine. What made the difference? Neither can say.

And then there are those mysterious plants that thrive despite harsh conditions. My husband tells the story of a rose bush that once flourished on his property. He didn't want a rose bush; he understood them to be "high maintenance," needing lots of water, food, and attention that he didn't have time to give. So he systematically deprived the shrub of all water and ran over it repeatedly with a lawn mower. It responded by growing stronger and healthier, producing beautiful, fragrant flowers. Some ideas, like hardy plants, have the strength of the zeitgeist on their side. In the words of Victor Hugo, "An invasion of armies can be resisted, but not an idea whose time has come."

As in gardening, making predictions based on beginnings is what astrology is all about. The whole system, from charts of people to charts of countries, marriages, business ventures, buying a car—is based on moments of beginning. Astrology works, we reason, because moments in time, like seeds, contain the prescription for what they will become. But even gardeners and farmers, with a wisdom borne of years of negotiating with nature, acknowledge that at some point, all the planning and care and preparation in the world won't ensure the outcome of their crops. Nature and life have a way of surprising us; but the lore of both gardening and astrology can serve as guides to supervise our humble efforts to undertake new beginnings.

The New Moon Seed

Each month, the New Moon's longitudinal point falls in one of twelve houses of your chart. Think of this point as a seed that wants to be planted, an idea for a new venture, the picture on your seed packet. The house of your chart where the New Moon falls describes the "soil" you have available for planting. Is it sandy, rocky, heavy, or light? How can you make the soil ready to receive the seed of a new beginning and give it the best chance to grow? And is this the right moment to plant this particular seed —or might your yield be increased if you planted during a different month?

At each New Moon, a new seed is given to you with instructions to plant it in a particular area of your chart. Two weeks later, in the light of the Full Moon, the decision to plant this seed is reevaluated. How is it faring in the place where it's planted— does it need more light, more air, more water? This quick, Full-Moon glance over your shoulder will help you evaluate whether you're on the right track, and whether you need to adjust or change your direction. But you won't know for sure whether your planting has been successful until six months from now, when the New Moon falls in the opposite house of your chart. Then, from the other side of the garden, you can get a good view of the first buds of new growth.

2006 New Moon Chart

Date	Longitude
January 29, 2006	09° Aquarius 32'
February 28, 2006	09° Pisces 16'
March 29, 2006	08° Aries 35'
April 27, 2006	07° Taurus 24'
May 27, 2006	05° Gemini 48'
June 25, 2006	03° Cancer 58'
July 25, 2006	02° Leo 07'
August 23, 2006	00° Virgo 31'
September 22, 2006	29° Virgo 20'
October 22, 2006	28° Libra 40'
November 20, 2006	28° Scorpio 27'
December 20, 2006	28° Sagittarius 32'

New Moon in the First House

When the New Moon energizes the first house of your chart, you will not lack enthusiasm for new undertakings. But like my seed-packet adventure, begun with a child's naive enthusiasm, your latest scheme may prove less than fully developed when viewed in the light of the Full Moon. You have much work to do this month simply plowing your soil, which is still a bit hard from winter's frost. New seeds planted this month won't take root easily unless they are especially hardy. But like my husband's scrappy rosebush, you are ready for the bite of the plow's blade; and whether it is a change of job, appearance, or address, this is probably the best month all year to undertake a radical new beginning in your life.

New Moon in the Second House

If you spent all your energy last month in one furious sprint, you may have to overcome considerable inertia now. But if you can, whatever you begin this month will have real staying power—so as much as possible, avoid filling your days with joyless obligations. Plant seeds of enjoyment, filling your days with people and activities that give you pleasure. In the light of the Full Moon, consider whether you are planting enough to cushion you against life's inevitable lean times. You may have fewer options for growth when the New Moon falls in your eighth house, six months from now. So plant a few extra seeds—more friends, a job with more money—as a cosmic insurance policy.

New Moon in the Third House

So many ideas interest you now; how to commit to just one? Don't: rather, scatter your seeds like wildflowers, and leave pollination to the birds and bees. Your job this month is to explore as many new ideas you can. Talk to people, read books, get in your car and drive; you need a crazy quilt of ideas, opinions, and scenery this month. At the Full Moon, others may urge you to commit to a single idea, but your garden is not really ready for careful planting. Later you will need to do some weeding, but don't worry about that now. There will be plenty of time, when the New Moon falls in your ninth house, to choose a favorite from among the many ideas and seedlings that you germinated this month.

New Moon in the Fourth House

It is time to irrigate your garden, and you must dig deep in search of water. Perhaps the hidden wellspring that nourishes you is conviction, or creativity, or kindness; almost certainly it includes sensitivity to your environment. What are the things you notice that nobody else seems to? Your particular sensitivity to the world is what you will carry into the fifth house next month and turn into art. So this month, tap into those inner reserves and drink at the well. Meditate. Sleep. Chant. Get centered. The emotional authenticity you cultivate this month will carry forward, six months from now, into the tenth-house world at large.

New Moon in the Fifth House

This month, you begin to parlay your fourth-house nourishment into a creative act. But the fifth-house act of creation requires some element of courage and risk. Fifth-house soil is the sand on the beach, damp from the waves of the fourth house and perfect for forming into sandcastles. At the Full Moon, a crowd gathers to look at your handiwork. Some are dazzled, and spur you on to even greater heights. Others are indifferent; why, they wonder, would you spend so much time and effort building something that a wave will wash away tomorrow? But their opinions, which will prove valuable when the New Moon falls in your eleventh house, are not as important just now as the joy you invested in building that sandcastle.

New Moon in the Sixth House

Building sandcastles may be creatively fulfilling, but of what practical use are they? Even as a creative act, the medium is too temporal to be of long-term inspiration. With the New Moon in your sixth house, your creative efforts are pressed into the service of some higher good, urging you toward a practical use for your creativity. No seed can flourish in sixth-house soil unless it serves humanity or the planet. Perhaps the skills you used to build sandcastles can be used to help build houses for people with low incomes. Or, you could take underprivileged kids to the beach to build sandcastles of their own. If you find a way to make your art useful, if you can combine work and love, then in six months, with the New Moon in your twelfth house, you will have found nirvana.

New Moon in the Seventh House

Standing in a gown, in front of an altar and a group of loved ones, the bride fulfills the promise of the New Moon in the seventh house: she begins a new life with another person. Life, death, parenthood, marriage—these are common transitions that mark you as significantly changed, initiates in a sorority or fraternity previously closed to you. As the New Moon falls in your seventh house, you join one of these groups, sowing the seed of a new way of relating with the world. What you learned about yourself with the New Moon in your first house is parlayed now into a better understanding of who you are in relation to others. Through careful companion planting—making room in your life for others—you become stronger.

New Moon in the Eighth House

Eighth-house soil has been heaped with compost, and when the New Moon falls in this house you must turn that compost into the soil. It's unpleasant work, because the smell of the fertilizer is not enjoyable. But it is necessary work—to turn what has died and decayed into food for something yet to come. With the New

Moon in your eighth house, you are planting seeds of investment in the future. It takes faith to spend time turning your compost heap when others around you are scattering seeds or enjoying the fruits of their harvest. Your faith is in the invisible, the vision waiting to be fulfilled. Your faith is that the uncomfortable work of this month will contribute to a bountiful return, when the New Moon next falls in your second house.

New Moon in the Ninth House

Weed through what you have sown in the past nine months, and choose just one kind of plant you can commit to. It may not be the tallest flower or the juiciest tomato, but whatever you choose will have the best chance to succeed because it has the full measure of your enthusiasm behind it. This is the month to begin actively believing in something. Six months ago, when the New Moon fell in your third house, you had a lot of interesting ideas; which of them still sounds interesting to you today? It's time to take a leap of faith toward the path with heart. Sow the seeds of hope this New Moon, and at the Full Moon you will find even more ideas to fuel your enthusiasm.

New Moon in the Tenth House

When the New Moon is in the tenth house, it is time to take authority over your life. Last month you took a risk and hitched your star to some person, idea, belief, or course of action; this month, you are called to stand up for that idea. Your level of success will depend on your ability to draw from the well that you dug when the New Moon was in your fourth house, and present yourself as a voice of credibility and integrity. It is one of the hardest months for sowing seeds, because the tenth house craves what is already fully-grown. But if this month you are not yet in a position to be the boss, sow the seed of ambition to someday hold that honor.

New Moon in the Eleventh House

A few years ago I was reunited with a friend from high school. She is an artist now, and the first time I visited her home, I was overwhelmed by the ravishing color and whimsy of her décor. Over the years I have borrowed shamelessly from her treasure trove of ideas, painting my living room in bold colors and hanging my windows with valances of fairy lights. Of course, I've brought my own ideas and preferences, but my friend provided the inspiration. The eleventh is a house of friends, of politics and groups, of joining together with like-minded people. When the New Moon is here, borrow seeds of inspiration from these friendly souls. They will round out your garden of ideas, especially the seeds of creativity sown when the New Moon fell in your fifth house—in unexpected and delightful ways.

New Moon in the Twelfth House

A couple of years ago, a friend gave us a shy little plant in a small, blue enamel pot: a moonflower, which only blooms at night. When the New Moon is in your twelfth house, plant seeds that bloom in private, in the dark. They can be seeds of spiritual awakening, whose flowers only bloom when you meditate. They might be seeds that you plant and tend for others as a loving gift, behind the scenes, without seeking honor for doing so. This month, you are a quiet farmer in a secret garden, behind high walls covered in morning glories and hibiscus. This is no time for practical planting of roots and vegetables; instead, sow moonflower seeds of beauty and inspiration.

Seeds of Change

At each New Moon, we feel the urge to begin something new. But just as in gardening, New Moon beginnings have an element of brave guesswork and trust about them. It is worth remembering that the New Moon is a dark time; wander around outdoors on the night of a New Moon, and you'd better bring a flashlight with you. Otherwise, the light of the Full Moon might reveal that you've traveled quite far afield of your original destination. Fortunately, astrology can be just the flashlight you need, shedding light on the symbolism of the New Moon as it germinates seeds of change in your chart, and in your life.

April Elliott Kent, a professional astrologer since 1990, is a member of NCGR and ISAR and a graduate of San Diego State University with a degree in communication. April's astrological writing has appeared in the Mountain Astrologer *(USA) and* Wholistic Astrologer *(Australia) magazines, the online magazine MoonCircles, and Llewellyn's 2005 Moon Sign Book. She specializes in the astrology of choosing wedding dates and the study of eclipses, and has authored a self-published report called "Followed by a Moonshadow," based on her work with eclipse cycles. Her Web site is: http://www.bigskyastrology.com.*

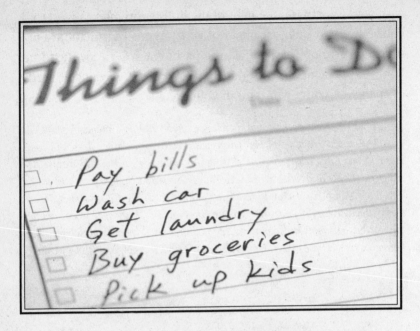

Conquer Your To-Do List

by Lynn Gordon Sellon

Surely you know people who seem to be ultra-organized and able to accomplish more than seems humanly possible. Well, you too can conquer a to-do list in record time by understanding how your Moon sign influences your daily routine. Tuning into your "lunar style" is like having a personal organizer to help you determine what you need to accomplish in a day, and how to organize your tasks so you can be ultra-productive.

Tapping Into Your Lunar Style

The Moon in your birth chart represents how you respond to your environment and how you integrate past experiences into daily life. Your Moon sign also influences how you establish routines. Being sensitive to how you live your life from day to day offers clues that will help you to define your organizational style.

The first step toward tapping into your personal "lunar organizer" is to think back over projects you completed successfully with ease and identify why. Did you start the project without a plan? Did you accomplish it carefully and slowly? Or did you work on it a little at a time? The key is to design your to-do list so that you can repeat the process that brought you success in the past. Honoring your personal style enhances your ability to accomplish more than you ever thought possible.

Take a look at the organizational style of your Moon sign, and then think about how you manage your time. Consider making adjustments in your planning process that are compatible with your natural habits. Even small changes can have a powerful impact.

Aries Moon or Moon in the First House

Focus your attention on what needs to get done and you can tackle anything with courage and determination. Empower your strong need to work independently. You may find that energy spent planning never holds. Maybe you impulsively pull everything out of the closet and once the contents are on the floor you can't imagine why you pulled it all out in the first place. Next time you are driven to-do something, conquer one area at a time. You are still working with your need to just get in and do it, but you may not run out of steam before you finish.

A typical to-do list should be brief. Use bullet points to outline a task rather than listing every detail. Keep your list within sight and write it on brightly colored or exotic-looking paper. In fact, it is very important to keep your ultimate goal in mind at all times. Start each task with the intention of finding new ways to perform it and see how quickly you get those dull tasks completed.

Consider starting new projects when the Moon is in Aries, Leo, or Sagittarius.

Taurus Moon or Moon in the Second House

Take your time and take pleasure in the world around you. Emulating the work of others at what appears to be lighting speed is very frustrating. Working at a slow, steady pace is your most efficient method of operation. Approaching everything in logical steps honors your need to attain the highest quality in all aspects of your life. Surrounding yourself with things you value (working with a beautiful pen or a well-crafted tool) can help you enjoy any process more fully.

At least one item on your daily to-do list should include personal priorities and fulfill a need to take care of yourself. Sooth your inner senses while you work by burning a scented candle, having a snack, or playing quiet music. Purchase a beautiful note book to track your accomplishments. Create an interactive list which requires you to check off each task completed and build in rewards for accomplishments. Find value in your routines and your routines will flow with ease.

Begin new projects or finish up tiresome projects comfortably when the Moon is in Taurus, Virgo, or Capricorn.

Gemini Moon or Moon in the Third House

Do you work on too many projects at the same time? Do you start one thing, move to another and never finish things the way you would like? Embrace your need to flit from one project to the next. Work with your ability to accomplish two tasks simultaneously. Next time you are planning a grocery list, clean out the refrigerator at the same time, or when collecting the dry cleaning, organize the closet. On the other hand, doing too much can lead to overcommitment. Try following a simple rule: finish one project before adding another.

Computerize your to-do list or discuss your plans with someone else. Capture your ideas by filling your list with every detail possible. Keep one main list which you can add to continuously and pull daily goals from the main list. Most importantly have a little fun, use whimsical paper or color code your short-term projects. If you find yourself losing interest in the task at hand, you may want to keep a humorous calendar or a book of interest-

ing facts nearby to indulge your need for a change in venue. Allowing yourself flexibility within your own routines increases productivity.

You'll excel at multitasking when the Moon is in Gemini, Libra, or Aquarius.

Cancer Moon or Moon in the Fourth House

Recognize your need to connect on an emotional level to the world around you. Reveling in memories evoked by every step in a process is almost unavoidable. The most efficient path to reaching your goals may not be a direct path. If you find an overdue library book while cleaning out the car, you may decide to flip through the pages, remember when you checked it out, and return it before continuing to clean the car. In anticipation of your need to collect and connect, keep a memory box nearby at all times so that you can deposit important memorabilia to savor later.

Find a comfortable place, preferably at home, to organize your to-do list. Your planner or calendar should be filled with photos of family and friends. Consider collecting articles about innovative planning solutions to consult at times when you are feeling un-organized. You thrive when you are comfortable in your routines, so take time to think about your habits and make adjustments. Small changes to your schedule at home effect larger changes in other areas of your life.

Make adjustments in routines with a sense of security when the Moon is in Cancer, Scorpio, and Pisces.

Leo Moon or Moon in the Fifth House

Rewards, self expression, and recognition are key motivating factors. If there is a football game or movie you would like to see, use your interest in these activities as rewards for a job well done. Your warmth and inner personality must shine through in everything you do. Building time into your schedule to teach one of your skills to others can be very energizing. Sharing your time and talents creates enthusiasm that spreads to all areas of your life.

Create a flashy to-do list. Post a large wall calendar where you can see it and try notating goals by using colorful pens in red, orange, or yellow. Make sure your personal interests or talents are clearly noticeable in your office or work area. If you are a sports fan or an animal lover, for example, make sure those interests are obvious. When the time comes to accomplish routine tasks, draw from personal experience and utilize your innate creativity to break old unnecessary patterns.

You can utilize your creativity most effectively when the Moon is in Aries, Leo, or Sagittarius.

Virgo Moon or Moon in the Sixth House

Embrace your nature to serve others while also finding value in any process. You can take any task, identify what is beneficial, and remove anything no longer appropriate. If old routines are tiresome, re-evaluate them. You can quickly discern which of your routines no longer work. What was optimal and necessary yesterday may not work today. Remind yourself daily how your attention to detail benefits others, and your daily routines will take on a new level of importance.

Enjoy a lined notebook to jot down your never-ending to-do list. Make sure that you leave space between each task on your list to add more because you will inevitably add to the list. Create two columns: one that highlights how each item relates to an overall goal, and the other to show how a task serves others. Your productivity improves when your need to serve others is interwoven throughout your routine.

When the Moon is in Taurus, Virgo, or Capricorn you can quickly deal with details while accomplishing your goals.

Libra Moon or Moon in the Seventh House

Cooperation helps accomplish your goals and soothes your inner need for balance. Simply sharing ideas can inspire you to move ahead and help you make decisions. When you find that despite how hard you try, you just cannot get through that stack of unopened mail or a mundane chore, getting out to see other people can help motivate you to finish the task when you return. Just be sure to finish what you started.

In addition to the importance of involving others in your routines, the arts can have a very energizing effect. An attractive planner will give you a sense of pleasure and help to set you in a productive frame of mind. Next time you are in a museum check out the gift shop for notepaper or planner pages that are filled with art, or listen to music while going about your daily tasks. Try modifying your to-do list through conversations with others. In fact, you may be able to delegate some items right off the list. Maintain a sense of balance between yourself and the world around you, and daily routines will flow effortlessly.

Let the transiting Moon help enhance productivity: you can find balance and move through routines more easily when the Moon is in Gemini, Libra, and Aquarius.

Scorpio Moon or Moon in the Eighth House

Working intensely to complete one project at a time is a great way to manage your time. Set your schedule so that you can immerse yourself in a task. Rather than doing a little filing, you may find that you pull all the files out and overhaul the entire filing system. Plan a whole day to work on one thing, and focus only on that project rather than working on one task in the morning and another in the afternoon. You will be surprised at what you accomplish by tailoring your projects to meet your intense work ethic.

Categorize your to-do list by subject, and leave room to continually revise it. Investigate the latest planning methods before choosing what works best for you. Keep in mind that you may only use an organizational process until you find a new way to keep yourself on task. Total transformation should be your goal when starting anything new. Research all the facts, then roll up your sleeves and get started.

Make transformative changes when the Moon is in Cancer, Scorpio, or Pisces.

Sagittarius Moon or Moon in the Ninth House

Discover great joy in learning new approaches toward ordinary life. The most difficult tasks become easier when you maintain a sense of humor. If you always take on more than you can handle, or find yourself always saying yes, try taking a class that teaches how to outline your priorities. Gaining a new perspective can help guide you through the details and assist you in determining which tasks to say "Yes" to, and which ones to tackle first.

Find a calendar that has cultural overtones, cartoon characters, or even historic facts. It's important to have a to-do planner that you enjoy looking at, and that offers new information each day. Make sure your personal priorities are highlighted clearly, and let these priorities guide your decision-making process. Finally, build some fun into your work. If you start projects knowing that you can look forward to a fun break, you will be more motivated to complete all of the items on your list.

Find new ways to apply old principles when the Moon is in Aries, Leo, or Sagittarius.

Capricorn Moon or Moon in the Tenth House

Ready, willing, and highly competent best describes your inner drive. Thoroughly completing a project and gaining respect from others inspires you. It is easy for you to start a little project on the weekend, and before you know it you have worked the entire weekend without a break. Find a way to relax while working because taking a break is not your style. You are more likely to build in down time as long as it is purposeful. Taking a seminar or a work-related trip can help you find some deserved relaxation.

A simple to-the-point to-do list complements your practical nature. Keep it where you can access it at any time to jot down your thoughts. Make sure to include the ultimate goal behind each item on your list. Find additional motivation by explaining a task to others, and take a hard look at all of the things that you expect of yourself and figure out what you can delegate and what you can simply let go of.

You are most efficient when the Moon is in Taurus, Virgo, or Capricorn.

Aquarius Moon or Moon in the Eleventh House

Spontaneity and serving a larger purpose are your keys to improved productivity. Being mindful of the needs of others while working on your own projects can be very energizing. Next time you are out shopping for groceries pick up some extra canned goods for the local food pantry. Weaving your own values into your daily routines not only helps complete tasks, but meets your need to consider the world at large.

Each day brings many unscheduled interruptions, so try to be flexible and avoid frustration by keeping a to-do list that outlines tasks to be accomplished in a week rather than in a day. This way you can respond to urgent projects while keeping sight of tasks still needing completion. Use a calendar that reflects your concern for a particular cause or social organization. Spend some time collaborating with friends and colleagues when planning, and always keep a notebook at hand to jot down those unexpected moments of brilliance. Keep the big picture in mind and the little things will be accomplished with ease.

Review and pursue your goals when the Moon is in Gemini, Libra, or Aquarius.

Pisces Moon or Moon in the Twelfth House

You can work on your own, or teach others with the greatest efficiency, if you have faith in yourself. Clearly defining your own values is a great way to keep on task. Responding to the needs and concerns of everyone else comes naturally to you, and you might find yourself in a situation where you help others with a project and, as a result, end up missing a personal deadline. Taking on a cause that directly connects with or relates to your own goals can work as a powerful organizational skill.

Maintain calm and focus by daily reviewing your priorities. While organizing your schedule try listening to quiet music or sounds of nature, and keep your to-do list organized in a soft colored planner, or in one that features peaceful scenes. Use your planner as a reminder of your important projects. Keep it near at all times so you can check it before agreeing to something that is not in keeping with your own goals. Believe in what you are doing and tasks are easily prioritized and completed.

Connecting with your personal beliefs and values is best done when the Moon is in Cancer, Scorpio, or Pisces.

Conclusion

Organizational advice is easy to find, but not always easy to follow. Unless you recognize your innate methods first, benefiting from expert advice can be almost impossible. Once you identify your own approach to routines you can seek professional guidance that complements your style.

Your Moon sign is one of many factors in your birth chart that influences your personal routine. It is an intimate daily influence that can help you define personalized efficient habits if you take the time to recognize them. Making subtle changes in schedules can have a major effect on your life. So consider making some minor adjustments in your organizational style if they will help bring you in line with the needs of your Moon sign, and see how ultra-effective you can be.

Lynn Gordon Sellon has studied astrology since childhood and has degrees in sociology and education. She is a professional member of the American Federation of Astrologers (PMAFA), and a Level IV consulting astrologer through the National Council for Geocosmic Research (NCGR). Lynn is the coauthor of Simply Math: A Comprehensive Guide to Easy & Accurate Chart Calculation. *In addition to writing she maintains a professional astrological practice in Connecticut.*

Finding Money by the Moon

by Natori Moore

Moon cycles can make it easier to find money. Okay, so you may be thinking you're really not inclined to take a metal detector out under a Full Moon and make a erazed hunt for subterranean valuables. I understand. Unearthing coins and such via said method, while not a bad idea, is not the only way to take advantage of lunar periods to find money. Like the train we know will arrive at a specific time, we can use the Moon to determine when we're likely to receive an expected check in the mail, a deposit to our account, a work offer, a new client, a bonus, or any satisfying milestone in financial matters. We may also be seen by the public as more valuable on these favorable lunar days, worth what we're charging and capable of marshaling resources to get the job done. Knowing these days are ahead, we can effectively plan important meetings, avoid wasting time on special trips or phone calls, reduce stress, and get an edge on the competition. It's good business sense to use these days to conduct any dealings with banks or financial institutions as well.

Second House Rulers

So what are these special favorable days? For starters, everyone has at least three of them each month. These are: (1) the day the transiting Moon conjuncts your natal second house ruler; (2) the day the transiting Moon makes a waxing trine (120 degree aspect) to the second house ruler; and (3) the day the transiting Moon makes a waning trine to the second house ruler. A person with Venus ruling the second house and Venus in Capricorn will find these fortunate days when the Moon is in Capricorn conjunct natal Venus, when the Moon is in Taurus making a waxing trine to natal Venus, and when the Moon is in Virgo making a waning trine to natal Venus. The conjunction and waxing trine to the second house ruler tend to be stronger in providing favorable conditions than the waning trine, but the humble waning trine can bring benefits, too. Even charts that have Neptune or the Moon as the second house ruler, which might be considered not very "earthy" signatures, will find financial flow and receptivity enhanced on these favorable days.

Second House Planets

After looking to the natal second house ruler, we can look at planets located in the natal second house itself for additional auspicious times. If you don't have a planet in the second house, don't worry. Use your natal second-house ruler as outlined above. If you do have a planet in the second house, consider yourself doubly blessed, as you're likely to have six rather than three favorable days each month. Conjunctions of the transiting Moon to a second house planet, waxing trines to that planet, and waning trines to that planet may be added to your stable of favorable money or business days. If you have natal Mars in Virgo in the second house, your additional favorable money days will be when the Moon is in Virgo conjunct natal Mars, when the Moon is in Capricorn making a waxing trine to natal Mars, and when the Moon is in Taurus making a waning trine to natal Mars. If you have more than one planet in the second house, I'll let you do the math, but you've definitely got one additional set of lunar trines for every additional second-house planet you have, and thus more days per month to angle yourself for financial and business benefits. If you happen to have the ruler of the second house in the second house (say Saturn in Capricorn in the second), you'll get fewer transiting lunar conjunctions and trines and thus fewer favorable days each month, but chances are they'll be doubly potent with this double second-house emphasis.

Use the handy table shown below to know what transiting Moon signs to plan for as favorable money and business days.

If your natal second-house ruler or second-house planets are in the left column, your favorable money days (when the transiting Moon is in the signs) are listed in the right column:

Aries	Aries, Leo, or Sagittarius
Taurus	Taurus, Virgo, or Capricorn
Gemini	Gemini, Libra, or Aquarius
Cancer	Cancer, Scorpio, or Pisces
Leo	Leo, Sagittarius, or Aries
Virgo	Virgo, Capricorn, or Taurus
Libra	Libra, Aquarius, or Gemini
Scorpio	Scorpio, Pisces, or Cancer
Sagittarius	Sagittarius, Aries, or Leo
Capricorn	Capricorn, Taurus, or Virgo
Aquarius	Aquarius, Gemini, or Libra
Pisces	Pisces, Cancer, or Scorpio

The Moon Makes Money Stick

The Moon coming into harmonious alignment with second house indicators can bring good fortune our way on favorable days, but it's not only the timing factor. Due to its rulership of the receptive and water sign of Cancer, symbolized by the crab, the Moon also has marvelous retentive power that can enable us to not only attract but to grasp and hold on to what we receive. The Moon functions the way an egg does when it binds a recipe together: it induces coagulation, culmination, and completion, which make us better able to retain the goodies that may come our way at these favorable times. We can think of these days as days our personal tide is "in." Working with the waves coming our way will bring best results.

Signs, Signs, Everywhere Signs

The astrological sign that your second house ruler (or planets) is in, as well as the sign of the transiting Moon on your favorable days, may give clues to how you can make plans that may lead to receiving money or advantages on your favorable days.

Use days the Moon is in an air sign (or contacting a natal air-sign planet) to focus on networking, social connections, intellectual property and ideas, speaking, writing, diplomatic efforts, computer-based work, and group meetings—especially with the Moon in Aquarius. The down side of these days is that people may be somewhat superficial.

Use days the Moon is in an earth sign (or contacting a natal earth-sign planet) to get finances in order, buy and sell, construct new facilities, organize or streamline, establish structures and foundations, and for earth-related activities such as gardening and horticulture. The down side of these days is that people may lack imagination.

Use days when the Moon is in a water sign (or contacting a natal water-sign planet) to look beneath the surface, make emotional connections, work at home, make domestic improvements, or to use counseling or psychology skills to be effective with others. Investments made on these days may tend to grow (as they are watered well). The downside of these days is that people may be overly sensitive and read too much into matters.

Use days the Moon is in a fire sign (or contacting a natal fire-sign planet) for sales and promotional endeavors, presentations, and to lay out bold future visions. Business travel is often most enjoyable on these days. The downside of fire-sign days is many ideas may be generated, but there may not be much inclination for practicality or follow-through.

Enhancements (or Other Things to Look For)

Additional items to look for that can enhance or amplify the favorable day effect include noting whether any transiting planets (especially Venus, Jupiter, Saturn, Uranus, Neptune, or Pluto) are moving near or in trine to your second-house planets or your second-house ruler, and paying attention to the day(s) the transiting Moon crosses these transiting planets. The transiting benefics (Venus and Jupiter), as well as the outer planets, can act as amplifiers. When the Moon crosses these planets in proximity to your natal second-house ruler or planets, it can act as a trigger that brings days when things go very right! (Do take into consideration the nature of the particular transiting planets involved.) New and Full Moons that conjoin your second-house ruler or planets, as well as progressed Moon aspects to your natal second-house ruler or planets, can have amplifying effects.

Now They See It, Now You See It, But They Don't

Another nuance of these favorable lunar day transits is whether or not they occur above or below the horizon in your birth chart. In the example of Venus in Capricorn ruling the second house of a chart, let's suppose Venus is located above the horizon in the ninth house. When the Moon conjoins this ninth-house planet each month, the advantage of the day may relate to a far-away place or an overseas contact, a connection with a university or a publishing house. Chances are this will be a public and rather far-reaching, future-oriented contact. On the other hand, if Venus is located below the horizon in the sixth house, a lunar conjunction may relate more to the routine underpinnings of a business or household, such as office schedules, office or home organization, employee relations, or steady but not flashy sources of income. The transiting Moon's waxing and waning trines to the second-house ruler (or planet positions) will fall either above or below the horizon as well. This will "flavor" the particular fortunate day slightly and let you know whether or not to plan for or expect a relatively public, far-reaching kind of favorable day (especially when the transiting Moon falls in the natal ninth, tenth, or eleventh house) or a more private and routine but nevertheless significant money or business advantage. This is especially true when the transiting Moon falls in houses two through six. Use your astrological knowledge to determine, based on the natal house the Moon transits on your favorable day, how you might use the particular favorable day's energy to your advantage.

Flying Without a Net (or a Birth Time)

A less precise version of the favorable money and business days can be used even if you don't know your time of birth. Follow the natural chart wheel for your Sun sign, and see which days the Moon moves through your second house of money (Fortunate Day 1 in the table below), or forms a waxing trine to your second house, to find days that can be generally favorable for you. Without a birth time, the waning trine is not particularly favorable, thus it is not included here.

Natal Sun or Rising Sign	Fortunate Day 1 (Moon in)	Fortunate Day 2 (Moon in)
Aries	Taurus	Virgo
Taurus	Gemini	Libra
Gemini	Cancer	Scorpio
Cancer	Leo	Sagittarius
Leo	Virgo	Capricorn
Virgo	Libra	Aquarius
Libra	Scorpio	Pisces
Scorpio	Sagittarius	Aries
Sagittarius	Capricorn	Taurus
Capricorn	Aquarius	Gemini
Aquarius	Pisces	Cancer
Pisces	Aries	Leo

Overall, this technique works more reliably with a timed birth chart, so by all means try to track down a time of birth or have your chart rectified for a workable time of birth if you can.

Putting it to Use

Let's use a practical example. If you have a job interview or a proposal to make to a potential client, it's advantageous to schedule this for a favorable money and business day if you can. Even more to the point, when you get called back for, or want to schedule a second meeting, it's worth the effort to try to schedule it on an approaching favorable day if you can. Energy builds within the lunar cycle and you can leverage this energy each time you use a favorable day to make the whole cycle turn out to your advantage. Sometimes, it just can't be helped and the gods of bureaucracy will want you to meet on a day they've pre-established. At the very least, avoid (like the plague) scheduling important meetings under a void-of-course Moon (when the Moon will make no more major aspects to other planets before it leaves its current sign). The best laid plans of mice and men come to dust under void Moons. Meeting on a day the Moon is void suggests nothing is likely to come of your endeavor, negotiations may dissolve, and you may not even get a thank you note for having suited up three times for the interview process (true story from my client files!).

You've Got Mail

If you get your mail at some distance from your house in a rural area or at an address different from your home address, wait until favorable days to collect it to maximize your time. If you collect your mail prematurely, the check or letter you've been waiting for might not be there yet anyway. If your second-house ruler is Jupiter, and you're thinking one afternoon of going to get your mail to get a check you're expecting, but the Moon will not conjoin or trine your Jupiter until the next morning, consider waiting until the next day for best results. Not only will your check likely have arrived by then, but additional items may arrive that enable you to get caught up with projects more efficiently than you expect. The Moon's consolidating energy is at work here, attracting items you may need to complete a particular phase of an endeavor at the right time. If you desire more days where you feel, at least for the moment, that you're on top of things and not too many details are hanging over your head (and what homemaker or business person doesn't!), wait until

your favorable days to collect your mail and messages, when things will tend to fall into line more readily.

The Eighth House Works, Too

The above information regarding the second house applies primarily to individual business and financial endeavors such as generating personal income, keeping solo checking accounts, or buying and selling individual personal property. For financial matters that involve other persons or other people's money, harmonious lunar aspects to the eighth house should also be considered. Favorable days in this case would be the transiting Moon's conjunction to the natal eighth-house ruler, the waxing trine to the eighth-house ruler, and the waning trine to the eighth-house ruler. Matters that might be a fruitful focus on these days include taxes, investments, loans, insurance, wills and trusts, large gifts, inheritances, and conferring with a mate or business partner for financial discussions. Use the table on page 256 and substitute the sign of your eighth-house ruler or planets for second-house ruler or planets and your favorable lunar days should read appropriately.

Why Trine?

You advanced Moon followers may wonder why only lunar conjunctions and trines to second- or eighth-house rulers and planets indicate favorable days. Why not sextiles (60 degree separations)? To use a domestic analogy the Moon can appreciate, as far as lunar transits to the natal chart are concerned, a sextile is a little like laundry getting stuck halfway down the laundry chute, a trine is like having it drop all the way to the basement and into the washroom. Cha-ching! Lunar sextiles to second- or eighth-house rulers or planets aren't likely to be bad days, but they may not provide quite enough cosmic flow to make business benefits noticeable.

Go Forth and Find

Though it may take a little effort at first, learning to follow the transiting Moon to capitalize on your favorable money and business days can become as easy as watching the Moon move from New to Full and back again in the sky (or as easy as using the table on page 256.) I've found that these favorable lunar aspects to the second- or eighth-house rulers and planets increase the likelihood of making sales, receiving money in the mail, attracting new business, getting raises or bonuses, receiving favorable loan terms, handling taxes and investments efficiently, effectively reviewing finances with a mate, and more. It may not always be cold hard cash that arrives on these days, but it's usually an advantage, edge, or resource that can work to one's benefit. Enjoy finding money by the Moon! And feel free to e-mail me with any successes you have using these techniques.

Natori Moore is a counseling astrologer practicing in Encinitas, California. She has written for Dell Horoscope *and the* Mountain Astrologer, *published film criticism in San Diego area publications, including* SLAMM Music and Arts Magazine *and the* Light Connection. *Natori specializes in individual astrological forecasts as well as family and relationship compatibility counseling by telephone. You can contact her through her Web site at www.soulfoodastrology.com.*

Farm, Garden, and Weather Section

Gardening by the Moon

Today, people often reject the notion of gardening according to the Moon's phase and sign. The usual nonbeliever is not a scientist but the city dweller who has never had any real contact with nature and little experience of natural rhythms.

Camille Flammarian, the French astronomer, testifies to the success of Moon planting, though:

"Cucumbers increase at Full Moon, as well as radishes, turnips, leeks, lilies, horseradish, and saffron; onions, on the contrary, are much larger and better nourished during the decline and old age of the Moon than at its increase, during its youth and fullness, which is the reason the Egyptians abstained from onions, on account of their antipathy to the Moon. Herbs gathered while the Moon increases are of great efficiency. If the vines are trimmed at night when the Moon is in the sign of the Lion, Sagittarius, the Scorpion, or the Bull, it will save them from field rats, moles, snails, flies, and other animals."

Dr. Clark Timmins is one of the few modern scientists to have conducted tests in Moon planting. Following is a summary of his experiments:

Beets: When sown with the Moon in Scorpio, the germination rate was 71 percent; when sown in Sagittarius, the germination rate was 58 percent.

Scotch marigold: When sown with the Moon in Cancer, the germination rate was 90 percent; when sown in Leo, the rate was 32 percent.

Carrots: When sown with the Moon in Scorpio, the germination rate was 64 percent; when sown in Sagittarius, the germination rate was 47 percent.

Tomatoes: When sown with the Moon in Cancer, the germination rate was 90 percent; but when sown with the Moon in Leo, the germination rate was 58 percent.

Two things should be emphasized. First, remember that this is only a summary of the results of the experiments; the experiments themselves were conducted in a scientific manner to eliminate any variation in soil, temperature, moisture, and so on, so that only the Moon sign is varied. Second, note that these astonishing results were obtained without regard to the phase of the Moon—the other factor we use in Moon planting, and which presumably would have increased the differential in germination rates.

Dr. Timmins also tried transplanting Cancer- and Leo-planted tomato seedlings while the Cancer Moon was waxing. The result was 100 percent survival. When transplanting was done with the waning Sagittarius Moon, there was 0 percent survival. Dr. Timmins' tests show that the Cancer-planted tomatoes had blossoms twelve days earlier than those planted under Leo; the Cancer-planted tomatoes had an average height of twenty inches at that time compared to fifteen inches for the Leo-planted; the first ripe tomatoes were gathered from the Cancer plantings eleven days ahead of the Leo plantings; and a count of the hanging fruit and its size and weight shows an advantage to the Cancer plants over the Leo plants of 45 percent.

Dr. Timmins also observed that there have been similar tests that did not indicate results favorable to the Moon planting theory. As a scientist, he asked why one set of experiments indicated a positive verification of Moon planting, and others did not. He checked these other tests and found that the experimenters had not followed the geocentric system for determining the Moon sign positions, but the heliocentric. When the times used in these other tests were converted to the geocentric system, the dates chosen often were found to be in barren, rather than fertile, signs. Without going into a technical explanation, it is sufficient to point out that geocentric and heliocentric positions often vary by as much as four days. This is a large enough differential to place the Moon in Cancer, for example, in the heliocentric system, and at the same time in Leo by the geocentric system.

Most almanacs and calendars show the Moon's signs heliocentrically—and thus incorrectly for Moon planting—while the *Moon Sign Book* is calculated correctly for planting purposes, using the geocentric system. Some readers are confused because the *Moon Sign Book* talks about first, second, third, and fourth quarters, while other almanacs refer to these same divisions as New Moon, first quarter, Full Moon, and fourth quarter. Thus the almanacs say first quarter when the *Moon Sign Book* says second quarter.

There is nothing complicated about using astrology in agriculture and horticulture in order to increase both pleasure and profit, but there is one very important rule that is often neglected—use common sense! Of course this is one rule that should be remembered in every activity we undertake, but in the case of gardening and farming by the Moon, if it is not possible to use the best dates for planting or harvesting, we must select the next best and just try to do the best we can.

This brings up the matter of the other factors to consider in your gardening work. The dates we give as best for a certain activity apply to the entire country (with slight time correction), but in your section of the country you may be buried under three feet of snow on a date we say is good to plant your flowers. So we have factors of weather, season, temperature and moisture variations, soil conditions, your own available time and opportunity, and so forth. Some astrologers like to think it is all a matter of science, but gardening is also an art. In art, you develop an instinctive identification with your work and influence it with your feelings and wishes.

The *Moon Sign Book* gives you the place of the Moon for every day of the year so that you can select the best times once you have become familiar with the rules and practices of lunar agriculture. We give you specific, easy-to-follow directions so that you can get right down to work.

We give you the best dates for planting, and also for various related activities, including cultivation, fertilizing, harvesting, irrigation, and getting rid of weeds and pests. But we cannot tell you exactly when it's good to plant. Many of these rules were learned by observation and experience; as the body of experience grew we could see various patterns emerging that allowed us to make judgments about new things. That's what you should do, too. After you have worked with lunar agriculture for a while and have gained a working knowledge, you will probably begin to try new things—and we hope you will share your experiments and findings with us. That's how the science grows.

Here's an example of what we mean. Years ago Llewellyn George suggested that we try to combine our bits of knowledge about what to expect in planting under each of the Moon signs in order to gain benefit from several lunar factors in one plant. From this came our rule for developing "thoroughbred seed." To develop thoroughbred seed, save the seed for three successive years from plants grown by the correct Moon sign and phase. You can plant in the first quarter phase and in the sign of Cancer for fruitfulness; the second year, plant seeds from the first year plants in Libra for beauty; and in the third year, plant the seeds from the second year plants in Taurus to produce hardiness. In a similar manner you can combine the fruitfulness of Cancer, the good root growth of Pisces, and the sturdiness and good vine growth of Scorpio. And don't forget the characteristics of Capricorn: hardy like Taurus, but drier and perhaps more resistant to drought and disease.

Unlike common almanacs, we consider both the Moon's phase and the Moon's sign in making our calculations for the proper timing of our work. It is perhaps a little easier to understand this if we remind you that we are all living in the center of a vast electromagnetic field that is the Earth and its environment in space. Everything that occurs within this electromagnetic field has an effect on everything else within the field. The Moon and the Sun are the most important of the factors affecting the life of the Earth, and it is their relative positions to the Earth that we project for each day of the year.

Many people claim that not only do they achieve larger crops gardening by the Moon, but that their fruits and vegetables are much tastier. A number of organic gardeners have also become lunar gardeners using the natural rhythm of life forces that we experience through the relative movements of the Sun and Moon. We provide a few basic rules and then give you day-by-day guidance for your gardening work. You will be able to choose the best dates to meet your own needs and opportunities.

Planting by the Moon's Phases

During the increasing or waxing light—from New Moon to Full Moon—plant annuals that produce their yield above the ground. An annual is a plant that completes its entire life cycle within one growing season and has to be seeded each year. During the decreasing or waning light—from Full Moon to New Moon—plant biennials, perennials, and bulb and root plants. Biennials include crops that are planted one season to winter over and produce crops the next, such as winter wheat. Perennials and bulb and root plants include all plants that grow from the same root each year.

A simpler, less-accurate rule is to plant crops that produce above the ground during the waxing Moon, and to plant crops that produce below the ground during the waning Moon. Thus the old adage, "Plant potatoes during the dark of the Moon." Llewellyn George's system divided the lunar month into quarters. The first two from New Moon to Full Moon are the first and second quarters, and the last two from Full Moon to New Moon the third and fourth quarters. Using these divisions, we can increase our accuracy in timing our efforts to coincide with natural forces.

First Quarter

Plant annuals producing their yield above the ground, which are generally of the leafy kind that produce their seed outside the fruit. Some examples are asparagus, broccoli, brussels sprouts, cabbage, cauliflower, celery, cress, endive, kohlrabi, lettuce, parsley, and spinach. Cucumbers are an exception, as they do best in the first quarter rather than the second, even though the seeds are inside the fruit. Also plant cereals and grains.

Second Quarter

Plant annuals producing their yield above the ground, which are generally of the viney kind that produce their seed inside the fruit. Some examples include beans, eggplant, melons, peas, peppers, pumpkins, squash, tomatoes, etc. These are not hard-and-fast divisions. If you can't plant during the first quarter, plant during the second, and vice versa. There are many plants that seem to do equally well planted in either quarter, such as watermelon, hay, and cereals and grains.

Third Quarter

Plant biennials, perennials, bulbs, root plants, trees, shrubs, berries, grapes, strawberries, beets, carrots, onions, parsnips, rutabagas, potatoes, radishes, peanuts, rhubarb, turnips, winter wheat, etc.

Fourth Quarter

This is the best time to cultivate, turn sod, pull weeds, and destroy pests of all kinds, especially when the Moon is in the barren signs of Aries, Leo, Virgo, Gemini, Aquarius, and Sagittarius.

The Moon in the Signs

Moon in Aries

Barren, dry, fiery, and masculine sign used for destroying noxious weeds.

Moon in Taurus

Productive, moist, earthy, and feminine sign used for planting many crops when hardiness is important, particularly root crops. Also used for lettuce, cabbage, and similar leafy vegetables.

Moon in Gemini

Barren and dry, airy and masculine sign used for destroying noxious growths, weeds, and pests, and for cultivation.

Moon in Cancer

Fruitful, moist, feminine sign used extensively for planting and irrigation.

Moon in Leo

Barren, dry, fiery, masculine sign used only for killing weeds or cultivation.

Moon in Virgo

Barren, moist, earthy, and feminine sign used for cultivation and destroying weeds and pests.

Moon in Libra

Semi-fruitful, moist, and airy, this sign is used for planting many crops, and producing good pulp growth and roots. A very good sign for flowers and vines. Also used for seeding hay, corn fodder, and the like.

Moon in Scorpio

Very fruitful and moist, watery and feminine. Nearly as productive as Cancer; used for the same purposes. Especially good for vine growth and sturdiness.

Moon in Sagittarius

Barren and dry, fiery and masculine. Used for planting onions, seeding hay, and for cultivation.

Moon in Capricorn

Productive and dry, earthy and feminine. Used for planting potatoes and other tubers.

Moon in Aquarius

Barren, dry, airy, and masculine sign used for cultivation and destroying noxious growths and pests.

Moon in Pisces

Very fruitful, moist, watery, and feminine sign especially good for root growth.

A Guide to Planting

Using Phase & Sign Rulerships

Plant	Phase/Quarter	Sign
Annuals	1st or 2nd	
Apple tree	2nd or 3rd	Cancer, Pisces, Taurus, Virgo
Artichoke	1st	Cancer, Pisces
Asparagus	1st	Cancer, Scorpio, Pisces
Aster	1st or 2nd	Virgo, Libra
Barley	1st or 2nd	Cancer, Pisces, Libra, Capricorn, Virgo
Beans (bush & pole)	2nd	Cancer, Taurus, Pisces, Libra
Beans (kidney, white, & navy)	1st or 2nd	Cancer, Pisces
Beech tree	2nd or 3rd	Virgo, Taurus
Beet	3rd	Cancer, Capricorn, Pisces, Libra
Biennials	3rd or 4th	
Broccoli	1st	Cancer, Pisces, Libra, Scorpio
Brussels sprout	1st	Cancer, Scorpio, Pisces, Libra
Buckwheat	1st or 2nd	Capricorn
Bulbs	3rd	Cancer, Scorpio, Pisces
Bulbs for seed	2nd or 3rd	
Cabbage	1st	Cancer, Scorpio, Pisces, Libra, Taurus

Plant	Phase/Quarter	Sign
Cactus		Taurus, Capricorn
Canes (raspberry, blackberry, and gooseberry)	2nd	Cancer, Scorpio, Pisces
Cantaloupe	1st or 2nd	Cancer, Scorpio, Pisces, Libra, Taurus
Carrot	3rd	Taurus, Cancer, Scorpio, Pisces, Libra
Cauliflower	1st	Cancer, Scorpio, Pisces, Libra
Celeriac	3rd	Cancer, Scorpio, Pisces
Celery	1st	Cancer, Scorpio, Pisces
Cereals	1st or 2nd	Cancer, Scorpio, Pisces, Libra
Chard	1st or 2nd	Cancer, Scorpio, Pisces
Chicory	2nd, 3rd	Cancer, Scorpio, Pisces
Chrysanthemum	1st or 2nd	Virgo
Clover	1st or 2nd	Cancer, Scorpio, Pisces
Corn	1st	Cancer, Scorpio, Pisces
Corn for fodder	1st or 2nd	Libra
Coryopsis	2nd or 3rd	Libra
Cosmo	2nd or 3rd	Libra
Cress	1st	Cancer, Scorpio, Pisces
Crocus	1st or 2nd	Virgo
Cucumber	1st	Cancer, Scorpio, Pisces

Plant	Phase/Quarter	Sign
Daffodil	1st or 2nd	Libra, Virgo
Dahlia	1st or 2nd	Libra, Virgo
Deciduous trees	2nd or 3rd	Cancer, Scorpio, Pisces, Virgo, Taurus
Eggplant	2nd	Cancer, Scorpio, Pisces, Libra
Endive	1st	Cancer, Scorpio, Pisces, Libra
Flowers	1st	Libra, Cancer, Pisces, Virgo, Scorpio, Taurus
Garlic	3rd	Libra, Taurus, Pisces
Gladiola	1st or 2nd	Libra, Virgo
Gourd	1st or 2nd	Cancer, Scorpio, Pisces, Libra
Grape	2nd or 3rd	Cancer, Scorpio, Pisces, Virgo
Hay	1st or 2nd	Cancer, Scorpio, Pisces, Libra, Taurus
Herbs	1st or 2nd	Cancer, Scorpio, Pisces
Honeysuckle	1st or 2nd	Scorpio, Virgo
Hops	1st or 2nd	Scorpio, Libra
Horseradish	1st or 2nd	Cancer, Scorpio, Pisces
Houseplants	1st	Libra, Cancer, Scorpio, Pisces
Hyacinth	3rd	Cancer, Scorpio, Pisces
Iris	1st or 2nd	Cancer, Virgo
Kohlrabi	1st or 2nd	Cancer, Scorpio, Pisces, Libra

Plant	Phase/Quarter	Sign
Leek	1st or 2nd	Cancer, Pisces
Lettuce	1st	Cancer, Scorpio, Pisces, Libra, Taurus
Lily	1st or 2nd	Cancer, Scorpio, Pisces
Maple tree	2nd or 3rd	Virgo, Taurus, Cancer, Pisces
Melon	2nd	Cancer, Scorpio, Pisces
Moon vine	1st or 2nd	Virgo
Morning glory	1st or 2nd	Cancer, Scorpio, Pisces, Virgo
Oak tree	2nd or 3rd	Virgo, Taurus, Cancer, Pisces
Oats	1st or 2nd	Cancer, Scorpio, Pisces, Libra
Okra	1st	Cancer, Scorpio, Pisces, Libra
Onion seed	2nd	Scorpio, Cancer, Sagittarius
Onion set	3rd or 4th	Libra, Taurus, Pisces, Cancer
Pansy	1st or 2nd	Cancer, Scorpio, Pisces
Parsley	1st	Cancer, Scorpio, Pisces, Libra
Parsnip	3rd	Taurus, Capricorn, Cancer, Scorpio, Capricorn
Peach tree	2nd or 3rd	Taurus, Libra, Virgo, Cancer
Peanut	3rd	Cancer, Scorpio, Pisces
Pear tree	2nd or 3rd	Taurus, Libra, Virgo, Cancer
Pea	2nd	Cancer, Scorpio, Pisces, Libra

Plant	Phase/Quarter	Sign
Peony	1st or 2nd	Virgo
Pepper	2nd	Cancer, Pisces, Scorpio
Perennials	3rd	
Petunia	1st or 2nd	Libra, Virgo
Plum tree	2nd or 3rd	Taurus, Virgo, Cancer, Pisces
Poppy	1st or 2nd	Virgo
Portulaca	1st or 2nd	Virgo
Potato	3rd	Cancer, Scorpio, Taurus, Libra, Capricorn
Privet	1st or 2nd	Taurus, Libra
Pumpkin	2nd	Cancer, Scorpio, Pisces, Libra
Quince	1st or 2nd	Capricorn
Radish	3rd	Cancer, Libra, Taurus, Pisces, Capricorn
Rhubarb	3rd	Cancer, Pisces
Rice	1st or 2nd	Scorpio
Rose	1st or 2nd	Cancer, Virgo
Rutabaga	3rd	Cancer, Scorpio, Pisces, Taurus
Saffron	1st or 2nd	Cancer, Scorpio, Pisces
Sage	3rd	Cancer, Scorpio, Pisces
Salsify	1st or 2nd	Cancer, Scorpio, Pisces

Plant	Phase/Quarter	Sign
Shallot	2nd	Scorpio
Spinach	1st	Cancer, Scorpio, Pisces
Squash	2nd	Cancer, Scorpio, Pisces, Libra
Strawberry	3rd	Cancer, Scorpio, Pisces
String bean	1st or 2nd	Taurus
Sunflower	1st or 2nd	Libra, Cancer
Sweet pea	1st or 2nd	
Tomato	2nd	Cancer, Scorpio, Pisces, Capricorn
Shade trees	3rd	Taurus, Capricorn
Ornamental trees	2nd	Libra, Taurus
Trumpet vine	1st or 2nd	Cancer, Scorpio, Pisces
Tubers for seed	3rd	Cancer, Scorpio, Pisces, Libra
Tulip	1st or 2nd	Libra, Virgo
Turnip	3rd	Cancer, Scorpio, Pisces, Taurus, Capricorn, Libra
Valerian	1st or 2nd	Virgo, Gemini
Watermelon	1st or 2nd	Cancer, Scorpio, Pisces, Libra
Wheat	1st or 2nd	Cancer, Scorpio, Pisces, Libra

The Thrifty Gardener

by Maggie Anderson

Gardening has benefits that are seldom assigned monetary value because they are priceless. Good health and an increased awareness of nature's cycles are only two of the advantages that gardeners enjoy when digging in God's green earth. Other gains come later: sound sleep; the perfect, red ripe tomato picked from a kitchen garden; the ongoing beauty of a dried flower arrangement that extends the memory of summer until well after the first snowfall.

No price can be put on these special joys. However, some approaches to gardening are more costly than others. Whether you grow vegetables, flowers, or herbs, there are ways to garden with little cost. It involves being resourceful, recycling, and perhaps the cooperation of family, friends, and neighbors. Money may not grow on trees, but having even a little more to plant in the old savings account each week is a good thing.

Finding Free Information

If you are a newcomer to gardening, you can acquire the knowledge you need at your local library. It's a popular topic and you'll find many good gardening books and magazines in the stacks. Be sure to reserve the ones most in demand before the spring planting season!

A second source for information is your state extension service, which is sponsored by the state agricultural colleges. They have many free and low-cost publications and they are pleased to share their expertise with the public. Many also give workshops and classes on gardening. Some promote Master Gardener programs that maintain gardening hot lines. Call them when you want to know, for example, how to get rid of creeping charlie or what those funny looking brown spots are on your green pole beans.

Perennials Are Forever

There is an obvious financial advantage to planting perennial flowers and vegetables—the one-time expense for seeds, plants, bulbs, or cuttings. The less obvious advantage is time savings— you won't have to plant them again the next year. An old adage about perennials states: The first year they sleep, the second year they creep, and the third year they leap! Within three years, perennials will multiply beyond your expectations. They can be divided and replanted in other corners of your garden, shared with friends and neighbors, or sold at a spring plant sale as a way to recoup your original cost.

Although perennial seeds are cheaper than the plants, some are difficult to germinate. When comparing the costs between these seeds and plant sets, include the price of your seed-starting medium, grow pots, and the energy used by grow lights. If your green thumb does not extend to germinating perennial seed, buy plants directly from a nursery.

Gardeners are eternal optimists and we're sometimes inspired to plant more than necessary. Consider whether you have room in your garden for the fifty-plus perennial catnip plants that are possible from one seed packet. If you only have one cat or little planting space, perhaps it would be best to purchase only one or two plants.

Annuals for Cheapskates

Perennials alone cannot meet the seed and plant needs of most gardeners. What are window boxes for, after all, if not colorful trails of petunias in July? What vegetable gardener worth his or her spade would forego growing at least one tomato plant? These and thousands of other desirable flowers and vegetables are annuals. They can be started from seed or purchased from a nursery as seedlings, ready to grow.

There are three main advantages for starting open-pollinated annual seeds rather than hybrids: (1) you'll have more plant varieties to choose from, (2) seeds from the mature plants can be saved to plant next year, and (3) the saved seeds will produce strong plants that have been adapted to your unique garden environment.

Since seed saving is almost a lost art, I recommend that you read at least one good reference book on this subject. It will help you avoid moldy seeds and other disappointments. The Seed Savers Exchange publishes a massive annual catalog featuring rare varieties of heritage seeds and plants that are available through their members. Seed Savers also sells some heritage seeds directly.

Vegetable gardeners who are new to seed preservation should begin this project slowly. Continue to plant hybrid variety tomatoes, beans, and other veggies that are blight, rust, and wilt resistant alongside your heritage plants. This insures that your freezer will be full next winter even if summer growing conditions are not perfect. Also try new heritage varieties each year and save seeds from the ones that do well. Build your supply of seeds with care, putting a premium on good taste and disease resistance.

Free is Better

Being a curious lot, few gardeners will be satisfied to grow exactly the same plants each year. We want to experiment with new varieties of both hybrid and open-pollinated plants each growing season. Fortunately, there are many ways to acquire free seeds and plants.

If your hometown has a parks department, a quick phone call to them in the fall could reap many free annual and perennial flower seeds. If you live in northern climates, request to pick seeds from public gardens right before the first killing frost. If you're further south, the parks departments normally have a schedule for switching out public flower displays. Make a similar request to pick seeds before their discarded plants are sent to the city compost heap.

Consider organizing a spring seed and plant exchange with friends and neighbors. It's a great way to gather new and unexpected varieties for your garden, as well as build community. No matter what the stated focus, most clubs and organizations have members that are gardeners. A seed and plant exchange could become a welcome part of your annual spring and fall activities.

Plant and Habitat Rescues

This next method of acquiring freebies is not for timid gardeners. A friend of mine is a confirmed dumpster diver. She rescues discarded plants, trees, and shrubs from dumpsters in back of large discount stores and nurseries. Once she transplants them onto her property and gives them TLC, they respond by gifting her with blossoms and fragrance, apples and cabbages, and great joy. If you decide to give dumpster diving a try, call city hall first to make sure that your city or township does not have an ordinance against it.

Another gardening friend tracks new construction in his county and rescues wildflowers, shrubs, and trees that would otherwise be bulldozed. They are his for the asking but he must make arrangements to get them before the heavy equipment starts rolling. Check out the development sites of residential and commercial building and the paths of new roadways in your community. If you decide to save the lives of sumacs or wild daisies, talk to the contractor for permission first. Your city or county engineer should have the contact name and number.

Many states provide very inexpensive trees and shrubs for mass plantings. It's a wonderful resource for people that want windbreaks or wildlife habitats on their rural properties. Call your state's Department of Natural Resources for information and a catalog. Before you order, make sure you have the stamina to dig in 100 plum trees or 200 hazelnut bushes. This can be fun and you'll definitely save money compared to what you'd spend at a nursery, unless it includes the cost of trips to a chiropractor.

Buying From Commercial Nurseries

Once you order even one mini-pack of marigold seeds, nurseries will put your name on their "A" list and seed catalogs will appear in your mailbox like magic every January. Leafing through them is one of winter's pleasures that most gardeners look forward to. However, these catalogs hold great temptations for even the most frugal individuals.

When you purchase flower or vegetable seeds, check the number contained in each packet. If your garden is small, don't waste money buying more seeds than you need each year, especially if they are hybrids. Although surplus seeds can be saved for another season, at least 10 percent will loose their ability to germinate.

Those of you with large gardens will find it cost effective to buy seed in bulk from local hardware stores, nurseries, or specialty catalogs. A few phone calls will help you identify where to purchase a pound of snap pea seeds or two pounds of sweet corn seeds. Also, make an online search for sources of bulk wildflower seeds and other specialty plants.

Start Seeds the Old Fashioned Way

Your can mix your own growing medium and make grow-pots inexpensively. Obtain the recipe for seed-starting soil online or from a gardening book. Make mini-pots from three-inch strips of newspaper. Wrap these around a small drinking glass several times, then tape the side and remove from the glass. Fold the bottom of the little tube in and tape it at the bottom. Set the paper pots in any kind of plastic or metal pan, add water, plant your seeds, and then cover lightly with plastic.

Seeds sprout best when kept in a dark warm place. Facilitate the warming process by putting containers on a heating pad set on "low." As sprouts appear, move your plants off the heating pad to a window with direct sunlight. If that's not possible, purchase or borrow a special grow light from a nursery or discount store. Insert one or more in gooseneck or hanging lamps and give your little seedlings at least eight hours of light each day.

Extend the Season with Thrifty Greenhouses

Since you put time, money, and effort into your vegetable garden, it's not only wise but also thrifty to extend it past the normal growing season. Fresh spinach from your own garden patch tastes even better in November, when it's expensive in the supermarket. In my neighborhood, the gardener with the first ripe tomato of the year and the last bunch of fresh kale is the source of great envy.

Mini-greenhouses can be built inexpensively from PVC pipe, three-mil plastic, and landscape pins. Cut the pipe into lengths that will make hoops with headroom over your plants: three- to four-foot sections are perfect for most greens, brassicas (cabbage, broccoli, kale, and pak choi), and other early vegetables. Push the pipe ends securely into the ground, forming a hoop over your planting area.

Cover this with plastic held down with the pins. Fill three or four plastic gallon jugs with water and set them between the rows. The water will collect the heat of the Sun during the day and release it slowly at night. This inexpensive greenhouse will protect your plants very early in the spring and through periods of light frosty weather in late autumn.

For an early start next spring, the seeds of hardy vegetables (spinach, chard, corn salad, kale, and peas) can be sown directly into the ground in this greenhouse before the ground freezes. Take a peak in early March and you'll find the sprouts are up. Use a similar system for hardy flowers and herbs. Once your plants are growing, don't forget to water your plants and, when the weather allows, open the ends of the greenhouse for air circulation. Continue to water protected plants in the autumn.

Digging in and Mulching

You can double dig raised beds until the thistles cry "uncle!" but, if you don't have the right mix of ingredients, your garden won't make the cover of *House & Garden*. Soil mix and composting is beyond the scope of this article but not difficult to master. Information on these subjects is readily available from the resources listed above. Make good, well-balanced soil one of your first gardening priorities.

Once your soil is just right, maintain it year to year from your own (free) compost pile. A few phone calls to saw mills and quarries should turn up sawdust and sand, if needed. Scan classified ads in your local paper for the "Lawn and Garden" column. You'll find black dirt there that can be delivered by the truckload. This is cheaper than buying it in forty-pound bags. However, be sure to find out where the dirt comes from: if it's a farm field that is being developed, the dirt may contain herbicides and pesticides that you don't want in your soil if you're going organic.

Also search for sources of bales of hay for mulching and rotted manure for fertilizer. If you have a larger garden, unpackaged bulk quantities are cheaper than those that come in small plastic bags. You'll save money on composted manure if you make friends with someone that has a horse or cow. (Gardening is a labor of love.)

Many cities and counties make free mulch available to members of their communities. This mulch consists of trees and shrubs that were cut down for various reasons. You can locate this free mulch by calling city hall or the county.

One note of caution: trees are removed for many reasons, and one reason is that they were diseased. Use this mulch to keep down weeds on walkways and on your flower beds only. Do not spread it under trees, shrubs, or vegetable gardens. Newspaper or black plastic topped with hay or grass clippings is better.

Tool Time

Buy the best tools your budget allows. You'll save money in the long run because they will last longer. Look for tools that feel solid and have handles that are firmly attached. Clean, oil, sharpen, and store these out of the elements and they'll last for years. Avoid collecting more tools than you need. If you want to plant only a few flowers, this can be done with a shovel and a few small hand tools. The ones available at the discount stores are not as pretty as those at upscale specialty shops, but most will do the job.

Fine used garden tools can sometimes be found at garage and estate sales, consignment stores, the Salvation Army, and Goodwill stores. Some public libraries and garden clubs have lending tool libraries. Check around and see if it's possible to borrow tools from a friend or family member before you buy them.

As your garden expands, you'll want a wider variety of equipment. Comparison shop before you buy, and consider the prices of everything from garden tillers to fence post diggers. Remember that large equipment, like a garden tiller, can be rented, thus saving money and avoiding storage problems.

Containers and Greenhouses

Not all pots are equal but most can make wonderful containers for flowers, herbs, and some vegetables. Big or small, round or square, containers with enough depth for roots to grow can hold flowers, herbs, and many vegetables. A garden is the perfect place for your inner decorator to run free and the only limit is your imagination.

Garage and tag sales are the best resources for containers and decorative items. Metal bed headboards or ladders can be used as trellises for morning glories or cucumbers. Recycled bird cages will hold cascading petunias or a pot of rosemary or thyme. I once saw

an attractive garden display that featured a collection of old metal teapots with colorful lavender sprouting from their tops.

However, there are limits to what types of materials can be put in your garden. Decorative wooden items must be made of treated wood. Non-treated wood will eventually rot and attract termites! Metal, stone, and concrete are best for containers and decorations.

Keep a one-year running log of your gardening expenses, and at the end of the season, add up your expenses. Perhaps you will have saved enough to take a trip to a great botanical or exhibition garden, where you can discover even more ways to be a thrifty and productive gardener!

Maggie Anderson makes her home in Mount Vernon, Iowa, where she maintains a full-time astrological practice and teaches astrology. Maggie specializes in "all affairs of the heart," which allows her to utilize her experience as a family therapist when counseling clients. You can see more of her writings on her Web site: www.astromaggie.com.

Lunar Gardens and Plants

by Janice Sharkey

If you've walked near a garden at night and breathed the scents of nighttime flowers or observed the luminous glow of silvery leaves, you know why Moon-ruled plants are special. Maybe we can only truly experience lunar plants at night, possibly at moonrise, when the Moon's own reflectiveness is mirrored on their leaves.

Why should some plants choose to flower at night, being lured by moonlight rather than the rays of the Sun? At night plant life and the garden are shrouded in mystery, and yet at this time we have a heightened sense of life with the Moon highlighting foliage, and its rhythmic push and pull on the water table. At night the garden becomes a meeting point, a fusing between Earth and the cosmos with the luminary Moon taking a starring role.

Astrologers in medieval times established that each planetary energy nfluenced life on Earth in subtle ways. Their maxim—as above, so below—defines the philosophical doctrine of affinity that is accepted and applied by astrolgers yet today. As above, so below establishes that everything on Earth, including a plant, has its own planetary influence. The ancient astrologer Culpepper observed a plant's medicinal use and assigned planetary-ruler-ship of individual plants based on the nature it shared with a planet. For example, many Moon-ruled plants have medicinal properties thought to heal Moon-ruler diseases such as edema, epilepsy, insomnia, and stomach disorders. Plants ruled by the Moon, such as papaya, often have soft leaves that contain a lot of moisture,which can be infused into a tea and used to soothe the stomach and aid digestion.

Mother Moon

Myths surrounding the Moon suggest that she signifies the many aspects of femininity. She's seen as the young maiden, the nur-turning mother, and as a cool seductress, for example. In both myth and astrology she is associated with natural childbirth, is is thought to encourage natural, instinctive behavior. She fertilizes by water, and the Moon's gravitational pull on the Earth's surface is linked to the tides. Its phases coincide with many biological rhythms in plant, animal, and human life.

Many Moon-ruled plants (moonstone, succulents, and Moon-flower, for example) exude a milky sap, which is not unlike mother's milk. The moonseed plant *Menispermum* produces a crescent-shaped seed that is reminiscent of the Moon. The moonflower, if placed near to a melon plant, is said to help ger-minate it—and both are ruled by the Moon. The leaves of moon-wort (better known as Lunaria) become transparent and the seed pods show through. The glint of silvery leaves makes moonwort ideal for flower arrangements.

The Water of Life

The theme of water runs through most lunar plants from the very first drop of moisture needed for germination to the mouth watering succulence of a cantaloupe melon. Dew, the liquid formed from the air over night, is a Moon-ruled. Some plants, like water lilies, need to be floating in water. Others, like the iris, need their feet wet. Plants that have a high water content, like cabbage, lettuce, melon, pumpkins, squashes, cucumber, and cresses come under the liquid element of the crab for obvious reasons.

Another moisture loving plant that is happy at the water's edge and can take windy weather is salix, otherwise known as willow. Culpepper writes that just about every part of this versatile tree has healing properties. Its sweeping leaves can overhang a riverbank and create wonderful reflections—an often forgotten element in garden design—on the water.

Palm trees come under the auspices of the sign of Cancer possibly because of the coconut milk or due to its sheltering habit of fan-shaped leaves and the white flowers some palms produce. (The Washintonia robusta thread palm is a good option.) The silvery foliage of many coastal plants have small thin hairs, which give the leaf its silvery and also offers some protection from the drying effects of salt, Sun, and wind. The hairs trap salt particles and keep them off the surface of the leaf.

Due to this Moon's moisture retentive qualities, planting under a Cancer Moon increases the chances of succulence in plants. Cancer is also the best sign for sowing and for germination. As a lunar gardener I have found Cancer the most productive sign because it rules the growth in green foliage, stalk, leaf, and vine.

Colors of the Moon

Silver typifies the color of Moon plants. All tints of white to gray, silver, and even pale green are symbolic of Cancer colors. The white rose in its simplistic cool beauty belongs in this garden. *Papaver orientialis* with its luscious rough leaves (the luminous

white blooms of Perry's White variety is a must for the summer border). Plants like senecio or lamb's lug, with their silvery-grey foliage, make excellent border dividers. Bellow horned poppies with their blue-green leaves and bright yellow blooms can be found growing wild on sand or shingle. Many more plants can be included under the theme of a Moon garden by their floral or foliage color and their luminosity and reflective ability. Plants with white, grey, or yellow shades—such as the huge luminous trumpet blooms of the datura, evening primrose, and silvery artemisia are good options. From the silvery glint of a crescent Moon to all shades of the sea itself—Moon colors exude watery liquid life.

Night Scents

In the garden many plants come to life not only in flower but in scent. Moonflower (*Ipomoea alba*), is so named because it opens its blossom and releases its fragrance as a natural defense against pests in the evening. Night-scented plants are Moon-ruled. It isn't just for our benefit that some plants perfume the night air, they do so for practical reasons. Possibly plants that are fertilized by insects, like moths and fireflies, have flowers and foliage that give off scent because they have to attract insects via their aroma rather than sight. Certain plants come under attack at night, and to combat this some plants emit a scented chemical that attracts other insects that will eat the predators. Other night aromatic plants are wintergreen, wallflowers, and some varieties of roses.

Making Your Own Moon Garden

Cancer, like water, is a very reflective sign, and a reoccurring theme of the Moon and Cancer is to look back sentimentally to the past—especially to childhood. So in any lunar garden water must be a feature somewhere, if only an tub with a few water plants in it. You can create a small water planter with Moon plants such as iris laevigata, a water lily, or maybe add some cotton grass, which will give you cottonwool-like seed heads in summer, by planting in a half barrel or watertight tub.

Any reflective material adds to the Moon theme in a garden design. You can use mirror, glass, or shiny beads, or try adding a mirror to the back of a water planter to give it that reflective dimension, while it also expands a small garden spaces. Seashells make a natural addition to the water garden even when there isn't any water. A gravel garden with pocket plantings of grasses and a scattering of seashells gives the illusion of ocean tides.

Glass used in the garden will ideally be recycled. Recycled glass comes in various shades and can be used to brighten up pathways and reflect moonlight. Last summer I made a Moon water planter from glass. I chose sandblasted blue flash glass with the four phases of the Moon etched out. A backing piece of glass was attached to the front decorative glass leaving an inner cavity for water to ebb and retreat, thereby mirroring the Moon's magnetic pull on the water table. A timer was connected to a solar pump to enable it

to switch on and off. A solar pump was used to store up the Sun's energy and release the power when needed so it is energy efficient, too. I chose white stary-shaped fragrant blooms of *nymphaea odorata minor*, a water lily, which would appear magical in both the Sun and in moonlight.

As above so below—cosmic energy is all around us. As Moon gardeners we can open our eyes to the infinite possibilities of what is above us and tap into that creative energy whether it be when to prick out that seedling or what to plant in a planter. In a wider sense and in our own miniscule way, the cosmos affects us just as much as we affect it.

Janice Sharkey is a dedicated astrological gardener and she practices both lunar and organic gardening. She studied and gained a certificate from the London Faculty of Astrological Studies. She designs gardens to reflect a client's individual birth chart. She lives in the United Kingdom with her husband William and two kids, David and Rose. She can be reached by e-mail at astrologygarden@aol.com.

Relationships Down on the Farm

by Maggie Anderson

The image most city people have of farm families comes directly from central casting in Hollywood: parents as wise and understanding as Ma and Pa Walton, and young folk as sexy and romantic as the vibrant farm hands in "Oklahoma!" Our ideal country grandma tends her garden and bakes cherry pies while grandpa sits in his rocker and spins tall tales for the young 'uns.

Hollywood's fantasy farm families help reinforce some of our most strongly held American values: independence, self-sufficiency, and strong family values. Teamwork is important to us also. While the Waltons met life challenges head on and with determination, occasionally they needed help from their neighbors.

It takes individual pluck to cope with bad weather, crop failures, sick cows, babies with croup, and financial downturns, but it takes a big group of friends and neighbors to raise a barn.

Generosity is also featured as an American value in films about rural life. No matter how little they have in material goods, farm families share their time and resources with others. Even city slickers without an ounce of common sense can be transplanted to the countryside and survive, thanks to their kindly neighbors. The clueless inhabitants of *Green Acres*, fresh from the city, are rescued from one close encounter with disaster after another, thanks to the friendly locals.

Hollywood depicts the relationships of farm couples as warm and nurturing. Individuals play traditional roles within their marriages, divorce is rare or nonexistent, and intergenerational harmony is a given. Family members are a dependable resource for one another so elders are respected and parents raise their children with gentle discipline. Occasionally, grandma and grandpa can be cranky and the youngsters might challenge authority, but they do it in most adorable ways.

Most successful television series and motion pictures featuring rural characters were period pieces set in the mid-1800s through the 1960s. As modern life styles became more frenetic, we embraced these stories with nostalgia. Sadly, only the Amish and rural Mennonites have been able to maintain the rural traditions of our forebears. This modern world has intruded on farm life in ways that were unimaginable in centuries past.

If a television series about current life and relationships on an American farm were to be launched now, a sitcom would not be appropriate. Rural reality today has too heavy a feel to it for the plot to generate much humor. A drama or perhaps even a reality show might be best. I recall that Paris Hilton and her sidekick lived on a working farm for a few days in 2004. Hollywood could be getting ready to start filming *The Hunters of Berrymay* any day now!

Who is the 2006 TV Farm Family?

So what might the cast of characters for a 2006 rural television series be like? Let's name our fictional but typical farm couple Duane and Peggy Hunter. They have a teenaged son, Josh, and twelve-year-old daughter, Emma. (Rural families have become smaller since the birth control pill was introduced in the 1960s.) Their large, two-story farmhouse is in the Midwest, on a picturesque 140 acres that has been in Duane's family for over 100 years. There is a 1930s-style red barn, an inflated plastic machine shed, and a corn silo on the property. Emma's horse, Red Rider, lives in the barn with many cats and two border collies for company.

As a small farmer in the age of globalization, Duane finds it a challenge to compete with large foreign and domestic agribusiness. He often talks about selling the farm but believes he has no skills that would be marketable in the city. Besides, he can't imagine his life away from the farm. Like many farmers, Duane has had several bouts with skin cancer and is worried about his health.

Peggy's life differs little from that of other modern working mothers, except that she has a longer commute. She enjoys her job as a dispatcher for a big trucking company because it gives her certain freedoms that she would not have as a farm wife. Peggy's job provides her family with health insurance that they could not afford otherwise. However, the job also combines the worst of two worlds: a seventy-mile round trip to work along with the lack of local community resources.

Peggy has little time for herself or for social activities. By the time she gets home each night, she's one tired farm wife and mother. She shops for food at the large discount store near her work, and Josh and Emma cook the evening meal. Peggy and Duane's relationship suffers because they have so little time together. He seldom voices his jealousy of the men Peggy works with, but Duane remains suspicious of her time with them.

Josh, a gangly teenager, will soon be sixteen and he looks forward to getting his own car. Because of declining population and school consolidations, he and Emma have a twenty-five-mile round trip to their classes on the school bus each day. Neither Josh nor Emma is involved in after-school activities because they have no way to get home if not on the bus. Josh wants a car so he can get a part-time job to support his favorite hobbies: computers and archery. He and his dad hunt deer in the autumn with their homemade bows and arrows.

Stealing a character that worked in *Little House on the Prairie*, we'll introduce Emma, the little heroine of the series. Every family needs one eternal optimist and she's it in the Hunter family. Emma has a vivid imagination and is highly creative. In addition to her obvious artistic talent, she has great social and domestic skills. When not with Red Rider galloping around the farm, she likes to decorate. Emma's mission is to make farm life festive. No holiday goes uncelebrated.

Duane inherited the farm from his parents, Howard and Hazel. They were "snowbirds" until Hazel's memory began to fail. Grandpa Hunter can tell good alligator stories because of their winters in the Florida Everglades. Hazel is in the Alzheimers unit of a nursing home in the next county east of Berrymay, and someone in the family visits her every Sunday. Grandpa Hunter misses his wife but three nearby widows make sure he doesn't get too lonely. Duane and Peggy often joke about grandpa's fan club.

Peggy's parents, Earl and Marlene, divorced in 1987 after the hardware store they owned in town went bankrupt. Earl moved to a condo in Arizona and Marlene still lives nearby. She works part time as a cook in the nursing home where Duane's mother is a patient. Peggy's relationship with her dad is strained. He's virtually a stranger to his grandchildren and makes little effort to contact them at holidays.

The Hunters' rural roots run deep. It's a close family that is very attached to the land. They are as self-sufficient, resourceful, and generous as any nuclear family can be in the twenty-first century. Unfortunately, the community support system that was there for their ancestors is disappearing fast.

Commercial activity has all but disappeared in Berrymay, the closest town to the farm. There's a post office on Main Street, a small convenience store down on the highway, and one Methodist church. The Hunters miss the old café, now boarded up, where a group of neighboring farmers used to gather each day to swap news and dine out with their families on Saturday nights. Many of their old friends quit farming altogether and have moved away. The nearest supermarket and retail stores are fifteen miles distant, and they must drive twenty-five miles to see a doctor, dentist, or other health-care professional.

A few families living close to the Hunters have expanded by buying out their neighbors. Clarence Family Farms, Inc. owns 6,000 acres of prime farmland. In order to avoid taxes, dozens of old homesteads and outbuilding have been torn down. Duane can drive straight east from his property for many miles without seeing another farmhouse.

The neighbors that live north, south, and west of the Hunters are an interesting mix. The children are grown and gone. They run the cooperative grain elevator in the next town. Duane rents the Farley farmland each spring. Melanie and Ned Price, who are writers and photographers, escaped from Chicago several years ago for the peace and quiet of country life. Pastor Graham and his wife Kim have five children. Kim homeschools the children and he divides his time between the Methodist Church in Berrymay and another town to the west.

The Hunters also have several older neighbors that will retire from farming soon, and rumors have circulated about what will happen to their farms. Duane's own farm operations are not profitable. He cannot afford to expand his farm but he's constantly concerned about how his neighbor's land will be used.

Hollywood producers! Here's a few plot lines to use in the first year's episodes of *The Hunters of Berrymay*.

Episode 1: "Carnival in Brazil Day"

Duane and his father discuss farm finances and the reality of the global commodities markets. Dad Hunter suggests that they consider buying land in Brazil where they can get cheap labor and grow corn and beans. Josh and Emma overhear this conversation and are excited about the possibilities. Josh orders Portuguese language tapes on eBay. Missy cuts frozen waffles in the shape of Brazil and toasts them for breakfast the next day. Peggy notices the Brazil theme and is furious about being left out of the conversation. Duane sleeps on the sofa that night.

Episode 2: "Pig Freedom Day"

One of the Hunters' neighbors sells their land to an agribusiness concern that has plans to build a hog confinement lot for 55,000 hogs. This will jeopardize the Hunters' air and water quality and ruin the value of their land. The family organizes a protest. Josh sets up a Web site for the project. The Prices design informational flyers about the hog confinement lot. Josh and Emma distribute them from farmhouse to farmhouse and throughout Berrymay. Then Duane, Peggy, and their neighbors speak before the county board of supervisors, and the county passes an ordinance against confinement lots of this size. Missy declares the day a "pork free day," and that evening the family watches *Babe* on their PPV satellite dish.

Episode 3: "Three Grandmas Day"

Peggy's father makes a surprise visit from Arizona with his new wife, Mazie. Emma has never seen Grandpa Earl: she wonders why her mother and Grandma Marlene never talk about him. Mazie has never been on a working farm before and she is disappointed not to find cows, chickens, or a garden. Duane takes Maizie on a tractor ride. The whole family conspires to keep the news of her visit from Peggy's mother, but Marlene stops by the farm. Tensions are high between the women. Peggy's loyalties are divided. Emma saves the day by thanking Grandpa Earl for bringing her a new Grandma to replace the one in the nursing home that can't come to see her anymore. She convinces the two women to help her bake cookies to take to Grandma Hazel in the home.

Episode 3: "Independence Day"

While tearing down an old chicken coop, Josh discovers a metal box containing the original 1865 land grant and deed for the farm, along with pictures of the first settlers. This inspires the family to find a way to keep the farm, even if it involves a drastic change of lifestyle. Emma posts pictures of their ancestors throughout the house and declares the day "Hunter heritage day." Grandpa Hunter comes to Sunday dinner. The kids make a pitch for raising llamas and miniature ponies. Grandpa declares: "You can't make money on anything that eats." Peggy wants to start a greenhouse business. Josh talks about selling something on eBay. The family is divided and can't agree on their future direction.

Episode 4: "Senorita's Festival Day"

The weather becomes hostile while Peggy is at work. She leaves work early because it's Josh's birthday and while driving through heavy rain she spots tornados. She and other travelers take refuge at a rest stop. When the storm subsides, Peggy returns home with two young Hispanic women and their children who were abandoned by their driver at the rest stop. They are illegal aliens, speak no English, and are very frightened. Duane calls Pastor Graham because his church is a "sanctuary" church. The Graham family speaks Spanish and they come to act as interpreters. The Hispanic women have relatives in Chicago but it takes a few days to contact them. In the meantime, Emma and the visitors cook Mexican food and invite the Grahams and other neighbors to a farewell dinner. The next day, the Prices drive the visitors to Chicago.

Episode 5: "Our Hero's Day"

Josh gets his driver's license. Without getting permission, he takes his dad's pickup for a spin around on nearby gravel roads. Esther Farley runs out to the road and flags him down. While clearing damaged trees from their property after the storm, a tree has fallen on Ned Farley. Josh brings a chain saw from the truck and cuts away enough of the tree to pull Ned free. He is conscious but seems to have a broken shoulder and head injuries. They decide not to wait for an ambulance and get Ned in the truck instead. Josh speeds 90 mph to the nearest hospital. A highway patrol officer tries to pull him over but Ned goes into shock so Josh doesn't stop. Ned survives his injuries and Josh makes the 6:00 PM news, although he gets a speeding ticket and is grounded for two weeks when he gets home. Emma makes big hero sandwiches for supper.

Episode 6: "Money From Heaven Day"

The Hunters research, explore, and then discard various ways to generate income from their farm. They visit successful community subscription gardens, rural nurseries, orchards, and pumpkin farms with petting zoos. However, the Hunter farm is in a lightly populated county so these are not viable options. Peggy's mother, Grandma Marlene, makes a shocking revelation and a surprising offer: she's been day trading stocks online and has accumulated a small fortune. She will make interest-free loans to bankroll whatever project the family decides on. In addition, she'll give smaller sums to Josh and Emma to test their own entrepreneurial skills. Emma makes popcorn and insists that the family play Monopoly after supper.

Episode 7: "Goals and Goats Day"

Duane and Peggy decide on a two-pronged approach to financial survival on the farm. Duane will continue to plant corn and

beans, but without herbicides and pesticides until the land can be declared organic. Then they'll grow herbs on contract for a large herb company. They will also clear the twenty acres of rolling hills, plant grapes, and eventually start their own winery. Duane talks with their county extension agent and learns about resources at the state agricultural college. With his windfall, Josh will make and sell custom bow and arrows online. Emma convinces her parents to let her purchase a pair of miniature goats to breed and sell. Peggy quits her job. Grandpa Hunter takes everyone to a nice restaurant one-and-a-half hours away for dinner, and shows the family his round-trip ticket to Brazil.

Does the Hunter family live happily ever after down on the farm? Well, maybe or maybe not. It's clear that the national and international events will continue to intrude on the lives of American farm families. The stress of these changes will create a direct impact on family relationships. Today's farm families are much different than they were in 1906. They now resemble urban dwellers more than they do their rural ancestors.

However, if you're feeling distressed about the state of twenty-first century living, watch a few reruns of *The Real McCoys* and *Little House on the Prairie*. You can store away an image of Pa driving the hay wagon behind a slow-moving team of horses on a crisp autumn morning. This will come in handy next time you're stuck in heavy traffic on the interstate: take a few deep breaths and voilá! In your imagination, you'll be able to time travel back to the good old days—and feel your blood pressure lowering.

Note From the Editor: An e-mail from Maggie

I asked Maggie Anderson what people who want to stay on the farm are doing in a difficult economy. Here is her response:

Diversify—go organic, specialize in other niche markets that appeal to townies. That only works if the farm is close to a county with a good-sized population. Around here that takes many forms: community subscription gardens, pumpkin farms with one big marketing effort in the fall featuring corn mazes, cider making, and petting zoos. There's a little co-op that makes and markets its own organic tofu; another raises heritage mini-popcorn that is now carried in several supermarket chains throughout Iowa. I do know a family that planted twenty acres in wine grapes this year. Iowa used to have a thriving wine industry, but that was before the 1940s.

I have relatives in Lowden, Iowa, about forty miles east of here. The town and others around it are literally ghost towns, with the main street all boarded up. This is literally the case with most small towns between where I live and the Mississippi River. My cousin recently had to drive forty miles (each way) to a WalMart in Tipton to get film for her camera in preparation for her granddaughter's first birthday. When she got home, the battery was dead in the camera, so she drove back to WalMart. That's 160 miles in one day for something that most of us assume can be bought locally. There's just no retail activity nearby at all. God only knows how these people will survive when the price of gas goes up.

Maggie, August 2004

2006 Gardening Dates

Dates	Qtr.	Sign	Activity
Jan 3, 7:43 am- Jan 5, 9:44 am	1st	Pisces	Plant grains, leafy annuals. Fertilize (chemical). Graft or bud plants. Irrigate. Trim to increase growth.
Jan 7, 2:09 pm- Jan 9, 8:58 pm	2nd	Taurus	Plant annuals for hardiness. Trim to increase growth.
Jan 12, 5:50 am- Jan 14, 4:48 am	2nd	Cancer	GarnPlant grains, leafy annuals. Fertilize (chemical). Graft or bud plants. Irrigate. Trim to increase growth.
Jan 14, 4:48 am- Jan 14, 4:31 pm	3rd	Cancer	Plant biennials, perennials, bulbs, and roots. Prune. Irrigate. Fertilize (organic).
Jan 14, 4:31 pm- Jan 17, 4:49 am	3rd	Leo	Cultivate. Destroy weeds and pests. Harvest fruits and root crops for food. Trim to retard growth.
Jan 17, 4:49 am- Jan 19, 5:49 pm	3rd	Virgo	Cultivate, especially medicinal plants. Destroy weeds and pests. Trim to retard growth.
Jan 22, 5:28 am- Jan 22, 10:14 am	3rd	Scorpio	Plant biennials, perennials, bulbs, and roots. Prune. Irrigate. Fertilize (organic).
Jan 22, 10:14 am- Jan 24, 1:38 pm	4th	Scorpio	Plant biennials, perennials, bulbs, and roots. Prune. Irrigate. Fertilize (organic).
Jan 24, 1:38 pm- Jan 26, 5:31 pm	4th	Sagittarius	Cultivate. Destroy weeds and pests. Harvest fruits and root crops for food. Trim to retard growth.
Jan 26, 5:31 pm- Jan 28, 6:09 pm	4th	Capricorn	Plant potatoes and tubers. Trim to retard growth.
Jan 28, 6:09 pm- Jan 29, 9:15 am	4th	Aquarius	Cultivate. Destroy weeds and pests. Harvest fruits and root crops for food. Trim to retard growth.
Jan 30, 5:32 pm- Feb 1, 5:46 pm	1st	Pisces	Plant grains, leafy annuals. Fertilize (chemical). Graft or bud plants. Irrigate. Trim to increase growth.
Feb 3, 8:31 pm- Feb 5, 1:29 am	1st	Taurus	Plant annuals for hardiness. Trim to increase growth.
Feb 5, 1:29 am- Feb 6, 2:32 am	2nd	Taurus	Plant annuals for hardiness. Trim to increase growth.
Feb 8, 11:33 am- Feb 10, 10:44 pm	2nd	Cancer	Plant grains, leafy annuals. Fertilize (chemical). Graft or bud plants. Irrigate. Trim to increase growth.
Feb 12, 11:44 pm- Feb 13, 11:13 am	3rd	Leo	Cultivate. Destroy weeds and pests. Harvest fruits and root crops for food. Trim to retard growth.
Feb 13, 11:13 am- Feb 16, 12:09 am	3rd	Virgo	Cultivate, especially medicinal plants. Destroy weeds and pests. Trim to retard growth.
Feb 18, 12:11 pm- Feb 20, 9:38 pm	3rd	Scorpio	Plant biennials, perennials, bulbs, and roots. Prune. Irrigate. Fertilize (organic).
Feb 20, 9:38 pm- Feb 21, 2:17 am	3rd	Sagittarius	Cultivate. Destroy weeds and pests. Harvest fruits and root crops for food. Trim to retard growth.

Dates	Qtr.	Sign	Activity
Feb 21, 2:17 am– Feb 23, 3:16 am	4th	Sagittarius	Cultivate. Destroy weeds and pests. Harvest fruits and root crops for food. Trim to retard growth.
Feb 23, 3:16 am– Feb 25, 5:14 am	4th	Capricorn	Plant potatoes and tubers. Trim to retard growth.
Feb 25, 5:14 am– Feb 27, 4:56 am	4th	Aquarius	Cultivate. Destroy weeds and pests. Harvest fruits and root crops for food. Trim to retard growth.
Feb 27, 4:56 am– Feb 27, 7:31 pm	4th	Pisces	Plant biennials, perennials, bulbs, and roots. Prune. Irrigate. Fertilize (organic).
Feb 27, 7:31 pm– Mar 1, 4:18 am	1st	Pisces	Plant grains, leafy annuals. Fertilize (chemical). Graft or bud plants. Irrigate. Trim to increase growth.
Mar 3, 5:22 am– Mar 5, 9:37 am	1st	Taurus	Plant annuals for hardiness. Trim to increase growth.
Mar 7, 5:38 pm– Mar 10, 4:42 am	2nd	Cancer	Plant grains, leafy annuals. Fertilize (chemical). Graft or bud plants. Irrigate. Trim to increase growth.
Mar 14, 6:35 pm– Mar 15, 6:12 am	3rd	Virgo	Cultivate, especially medicinal plants. Destroy weeds and pests. Trim to retard growth.
Mar 17, 5:59 pm– Mar 20, 3:43 am	3rd	Scorpio	Plant biennials, perennials, bulbs, and roots. Prune. Irrigate. Fertilize (organic).
Mar 20, 3:43 am– Mar 22, 10:36 am	3rd	Sagittarius	Cultivate. Destroy weeds and pests. Harvest fruits and root crops for food. Trim to retard growth.
Mar 22, 10:36 am– Mar 22, 2:10 pm	3rd	Capricorn	Plant potatoes and tubers. Trim to retard growth.
Mar 22, 2:10 pm– Mar 24, 2:21 pm	4th	Capricorn	Plant potatoes and tubers. Trim to retard growth.
Mar 24, 2:21 pm– Mar 26, 3:33 pm	4th	Aquarius	Cultivate. Destroy weeds and pests. Harvest fruits and root crops for food. Trim to retard growth.
Mar 26, 3:33 pm– Mar 28, 3:31 pm	4th	Pisces	Plant biennials, perennials, bulbs, and roots. Prune. Irrigate. Fertilize (organic).
Mar 28, 3:31 pm– Mar 29, 5:15 am	4th	Aries	Cultivate. Destroy weeds and pests. Harvest fruits and root crops for food. Trim to retard growth.
Mar 30, 4:00 pm– Apr 1, 6:49 pm	1st	Taurus	Plant annuals for hardiness. Trim to increase growth.
Apr 4, 2:15 am– Apr 5, 8:01 am	1st	Cancer	Plant grains, leafy annuals. Fertilize (chemical). Graft or bud plants. Irrigate. Trim to increase growth.
Apr 5, 8:01 am– Apr 6, 12:25 am	2nd	Cancer	Plant grains, leafy annuals. Fertilize (chemical). Graft or bud plants. Irrigate. Trim to increase growth.
Apr 11, 1:46 pm– Apr 13, 12:40 pm	2nd	Libra	Plant annuals for fragrance and beauty. Trim to increase growth.
Apr 14, 1:08 am– Apr 16, 10:19 am	3rd	Scorpio	Plant biennials, perennials, bulbs, and roots. Prune. Irrigate. Fertilize (organic).

Dates	Qtr.	Sign	Activty
Apr 16, 10:19 am- Apr 18, 5:13 pm	3rd	Sagittarius	Cultivate. Destroy weeds and pests. Harvest fruits and root crops for food. Trim to retard growth.
Apr 18, 5:13 pm- Apr 20, 9:56 pm	3rd	Capricorn	Plant potatoes and tubers. Trim to retard growth.
Apr 20, 9:56 pm- Apr 20, 11:28 pm	3rd	Aquarius	Cultivate. Destroy weeds and pests. Harvest fruits and root crops for food. Trim to retard growth.
Apr 20, 11:28 pm- Apr 23, 12:43 am	4th	Aquarius	Cultivate. Destroy weeds and pests. Harvest fruits and root crops for food. Trim to retard growth.
Apr 23, 12:43 am- Apr 25, 2:12 am	4th	Pisces	Plant biennials, perennials, bulbs, and roots. Prune. Irrigate. Fertilize (organic).
Apr 25, 2:12 am- Apr 27, 3:27 am	4th	Aries	Cultivate. Destroy weeds and pests. Harvest fruits and root crops for food. Trim to retard growth.
Apr 27, 3:27 am- Apr 27, 3:44 pm	4th	Taurus	Plant potatoes and tubers. Trim to retard growth.
Apr 27, 3:44 pm- Apr 29, 5:58 am	1st	Taurus	Plant annuals for hardiness. Trim to increase growth.
May 1, 11:17 am- May 3, 8:18 pm	1st	Cancer	Plant grains, leafy annuals. Fertilize (chemical). Graft or bud plants. Irrigate. Trim to increase growth.
May 8, 9:10 pm- May 11, 8:24 am	2nd	Libra	Plant annuals for fragrance and beauty. Trim to increase growth.
May 11, 8:24 am- May 13, 2:51 am	2nd	Scorpio	Plant grains, leafy annuals. Fertilize (chemical). Graft or bud plants. Irrigate. Trim to increase growth.
May 13, 2:51 am- May 13, 4:56 pm	3rd	Scorpio	Plant biennials, perennials, bulbs, and roots. Prune. Irrigate. Fertilize (organic).
May 13, 4:56 pm- May 15, 10:59 pm	3rd	Sagittarius	Cultivate. Destroy weeds and pests. Harvest fruits and root crops for food. Trim to retard growth.
May 15, 10:59 pm- May 18, 3:19 am	3rd	Capricorn	Plant potatoes and tubers. Trim to retard growth.
May 18, 3:19 am- May 20, 5:20 am	3rd	Aquarius	Cultivate. Destroy weeds and pests. Harvest fruits and root crops for food. Trim to retard growth.
May 20, 5:20 am- May 20, 6:39 am	4th	Aquarius	Cultivate. Destroy weeds and pests. Harvest fruits and root crops for food. Trim to retard growth.
May 20, 6:39 am- May 22, 9:24 am	4th	Pisces	Plant biennials, perennials, bulbs, and roots. Prune. Irrigate. Fertilize (organic).
May 22, 9:24 am- May 24, 12:00 am	4th	Aries	Cultivate. Destroy weeds and pests. Harvest fruits and root crops for food. Trim to retard growth.
May 24, 12:00 am- May 26, 3:19 pm	4th	Taurus	Plant potatoes and tubers. Trim to retard growth.
May 26, 3:19 pm- May 27, 1:25 am	4th	Gemini	Cultivate. Destroy weeds and pests. Harvest fruits and root crops for food. Trim to retard growth.

Dates	Qtr.	Sign	Activity
May 28, 8:33 pm– May 31, 4:51 am	1st	Cancer	Plant grains, leafy annuals. Fertilize (chemical). Graft or bud plants. Irrigate. Trim to increase growth.
Jun 5, 5:08 am– Jun 7, 4:41 pm	2nd	Libra	Plant annuals for fragrance and beauty. Trim to increase growth.
Jun 7, 4:41 pm– Jun 10, 1:05 am	2nd	Scorpio	Plant grains, leafy annuals. Fertilize (chemical). Graft or bud plants. Irrigate. Trim to increase growth.
Jun 11, 2:03 pm– Jun 12, 6:19 am	3rd	Sagittarius	Cultivate. Destroy weeds and pests. Harvest fruits and root crops for food. Trim to retard growth.
Jun 12, 6:19 am– Jun 14, 9:32 am	3rd	Capricorn	Plant potatoes and tubers. Trim to retard growth.
Jun 14, 9:32 am– Jun 16, 12:05 am	3rd	Aquarius	Cultivate. Destroy weeds and pests. Harvest fruits and root crops for food. Trim to retard growth.
Jun 16, 12:05 am– Jun 18, 10:08 am	3rd	Pisces	Plant biennials, perennials, bulbs, and roots. Prune. Irrigate. Fertilize (organic).
Jun 18, 10:08 am– Jun 18, 2:54 pm	4th	Pisces	Plant biennials, perennials, bulbs, and roots. Prune. Irrigate. Fertilize (organic).
Jun 18, 2:54 pm– Jun 20, 6:23 pm	4th	ARI	Cultivate. Destroy weeds and pests. Harvest fruits and root crops for food. Trim to retard growth.
Jun 20, 6:23 pm– Jun 22, 10:49 pm	4th	Taurus	Plant potatoes and tubers. Trim to retard growth.
Jun 22, 10:49 pm– Jun 25, 4:48 am	4th	Gemini	Cultivate. Destroy weeds and pests. Harvest fruits and root crops for food. Trim to retard growth.
Jun 25, 4:48 am– Jun 25, 12:05 pm	4th	Cancer	Plant biennials, perennials, bulbs, and roots. Prune. Irrigate. Fertilize (organic).
Jun 25, 12:05 pm– Jun 27, 12:09 pm	1st	Cancer	Plant grains, leafy annuals. Fertilize (chemical). Graft or bud plants. Irrigate. Trim to increase growth.
Jul 2, 1:06 pm– Jul 3, 12:37 pm	1st	Libra	Plant annuals for fragrance and beauty. Trim to increase growth.
Jul 3, 12:37 pm– Jul 5, 1:13 am	2nd	Libra	Plant annuals for fragrance and beauty. Trim to increase growth.
Jul 5, 1:13 am– Jul 7, 10:13 am	2nd	Scorpio	Plant grains, leafy annuals. Fertilize (chemical). Graft or bud plants. Irrigate. Trim to increase growth.
Jul 9, 3:25 pm– Jul 10, 11:02 pm	2nd	Capricorn	Graft or bud plants. Trim to increase growth.
Jul 10, 11:02 pm– Jul 11, 5:46 pm	3rd	Capricorn	Plant potatoes and tubers. Trim to retard growth.
Jul 11, 5:46 pm– Jul 13, 6:59 pm	3rd	Aquarius	Cultivate. Destroy weeds and pests. Harvest fruits and root crops for food. Trim to retard growth.
Jul 13, 6:59 pm– Jul 15, 8:39 pm	3rd	Pisces	Plant biennials, perennials, bulbs, and roots. Prune. Irrigate. Fertilize (organic).

Dates	Qtr.	Sign	Activity
Jul 15, 8:39 pm- Jul 17, 3:12 pm	3rd	Aries	Cultivate. Destroy weeds and pests. Harvest fruits and root crops for food. Trim to retard growth.
Jul 17, 3:12 pm- Jul 17, 11:44 pm	4th	Aries	Cultivate. Destroy weeds and pests. Harvest fruits and root crops for food. Trim to retard growth.
Jul 17, 11:44 pm- Jul 20, 4:38 am	4th	Taurus	Plant potatoes and tubers. Trim to retard growth.
Jul 20, 4:38 am- Jul 22, 11:28 am	4th	Gemini	Cultivate. Destroy weeds and pests. Harvest fruits and root crops for food. Trim to retard growth.
Jul 22, 11:28 am- Jul 24, 8:24 pm	4th	Cancer	Plant biennials, perennials, bulbs, and roots. Prune. Irrigate. Fertilize (organic).
Jul 24, 8:24 pm- Jul 24, 12:31 pm	4th	Leo	Cultivate. Destroy weeds and pests. Harvest fruits and root crops for food. Trim to retard growth.
Jul 29, 8:27 pm- Aug 1, 9:08 am	1st	Libra	Plant annuals for fragrance and beauty. Trim to increase growth.
Aug 1, 9:08 am- Aug 2, 4:46 am	1st	Scorpio	Plant grains, leafy annuals. Fertilize (chemical). Graft or bud plants. Irrigate. Trim to increase growth.
Aug 2, 4:46 am- Aug 3, 7:13 pm	2nd	Scorpio	Plant grains, leafy annuals. Fertilize (chemical). Graft or bud plants. Irrigate. Trim to increase growth.
Aug 6, 1:19 am- Aug 8, 3:47 am	2nd	Capricorn	Graft or bud plants. Trim to increase growth.
Aug 9, 6:54 am- Aug 10, 4:10 am	3rd	Aquarius	Cultivate. Destroy weeds and pests. Harvest fruits and root crops for food. Trim to retard growth.
Aug 10, 4:10 am- Aug 12, 4:22 am	3rd	Pisces	Plant biennials, perennials, bulbs, and roots. Prune. Irrigate. Fertilize (organic).
Aug 12, 4:22 am- Aug 14, 6:00 am	3rd	Aries	Cultivate. Destroy weeds and pests. Harvest fruits and root crops for food. Trim to retard growth.
Aug 14, 6:00 am- Aug 15, 9:51 pm	3rd	Taurus	Plant potatoes and tubers. Trim to retard growth.
Aug 15, 9:51 pm- Aug 16, 10:07 am	4th	Taurus	Plant potatoes and tubers. Trim to retard growth.
Aug 16, 10:07 am- Aug 18, 5:03 pm	4th	Gemini	Cultivate. Destroy weeds and pests. Harvest fruits and root crops for food. Trim to retard growth.
Aug 18, 5:03 pm- Aug 21, 2:33 am	4th	Cancer	Plant biennials, perennials, bulbs, and roots. Prune. Irrigate. Fertilize (organic).
Aug 21, 2:33 am- Aug 23, 2:08 pm	4th	Leo	Cultivate. Destroy weeds and pests. Harvest fruits and root crops for food. Trim to retard growth.
Aug 23, 2:08 pm- Aug 23, 3:10 pm	4th	Virgo	Cultivate, especially medicinal plants. Destroy weeds and pests. Trim to retard growth.
Aug 26, 3:01 am- Aug 28, 3:56 pm	1st	Libra	Plant annuals for fragrance and beauty. Trim to increase growth.

Dates	Qtr.	Sign	Activity
Aug 28, 3:56 pm– Aug 31, 3:00 am	1st	Scorpio	Plant grains, leafy annuals. Fertilize (chemical). Graft or bud plants. Irrigate. Trim to increase growth.
Sep 2, 10:34 am– Sep 4, 2:15 pm	2nd	Capricorn	Graft or bud plants. Trim to increase growth.
Sep 6, 2:56 pm– Sep 7, 2:42 pm	2nd	Pisces	Plant grains, leafy annuals. Fertilize (chemical). Graft or bud plants. Irrigate. Trim to increase growth.
Sep 7, 2:42 pm– Sep 8, 2:23 pm	3rd	Pisces	Plant biennials, perennials, bulbs, and roots. Prune. Irrigate. Fertilize (organic).
Sep 8, 2:23 pm– Sep 10, 2:30 pm	3rd	Aries	Cultivate. Destroy weeds and pests. Harvest fruits and root crops for food. Trim to retard growth.
Sep 10, 2:30 pm– Sep 12, 4:59 pm	3rd	Taurus	Plant potatoes and tubers. Trim to retard growth.
Sep 12, 4:59 pm– Sep 14, 7:15 am	3rd	Gemini	Cultivate. Destroy weeds and pests. Harvest fruits and root crops for food. Trim to retard growth.
Sep 14, 7:15 am– Sep 14, 8:53 pm	4th	Gemini	Cultivate. Destroy weeds and pests. Harvest fruits and root crops for food. Trim to retard growth.
Sep 14, 10:53 pm– Sep 17, 8:15 am	4th	Cancer	Plant biennials, perennials, bulbs, and roots. Prune. Irrigate. Fertilize (organic).
Sep 17, 8:15 am– Sep 19, 8:07 pm	4th	Leo	Cultivate. Destroy weeds and pests. Harvest fruits and root crops for food. Trim to retard growth.
Sep 19, 8:07 pm– Sep 22, 7:45 am	4th	Virgo	Cultivate, especially medicinal plants. Destroy weeds and pests. Trim to retard growth.
Sep 22, 9:06 am– Sep 24, 9:54 pm	1st	Libra	Plant annuals for fragrance and beauty. Trim to increase growth.
Sep 24, 9:54 pm– Sep 27, 9:16 am	1st	Scorpio	Plant grains, leafy annuals. Fertilize (chemical). Graft or bud plants. Irrigate. Trim to increase growth.
Sep 29, 6:01 pm– Sep 30, 7:04 am	1st	Capricorn	Graft or bud plants. Trim to increase growth.
Sep 30, 7:04 am– Oct 1, 11:24 pm	2nd	Capricorn	Graft or bud plants. Trim to increase growth.
Oct 4, 1:33 am– Oct 6, 1:32 am	2nd	Pisces	Plant grains, leafy annuals. Fertilize (chemical). Graft or bud plants. Irrigate. Trim to increase growth.
Oct 6, 11:13 pm– Oct 8, 1:04 am	3rd	Aries	Cultivate. Destroy weeds and pests. Harvest fruits and root crops for food. Trim to retard growth.
Oct 8, 1:04 am– Oct 10, 2:06 am	3rd	Taurus	Plant potatoes and tubers. Trim to retard growth.
Oct 10, 2:06 am– Oct 12, 6:21 am	3rd	Gemini	Cultivate. Destroy weeds and pests. Harvest fruits and root crops for food. Trim to retard growth.
Oct 12, 6:21 am– Oct 13, 8:25 pm	3rd	Cancer	Plant biennials, perennials, bulbs, and roots. Prune. Irrigate. Fertilize (organic).

Dates	Qtr.	Sign	Activity
Oct 13, 8:25 pm- Oct 14, 2:38 pm	4th	Cancer	Plant biennials, perennials, bulbs, and roots. Prune. Irrigate. Fertilize (organic).
Oct 14, 2:38 pm- Oct 17, 2:15 am	4th	Leo	Cultivate. Destroy weeds and pests. Harvest fruits and root crops for food. Trim to retard growth.
Oct 17, 2:15 am- Oct 19, 3:19 pm	4th	Virgo	Cultivate, especially medicinal plants. Destroy weeds and pests. Trim to retard growth.
Oct 22, 1:14 am- Oct 22, 3:54 am	1st	Libra	Plant annuals for fragrance and beauty. Trim to increase growth.
Oct 22, 3:54 am- Oct 24, 2:53 pm	1st	Scorpio	Plant grains, leafy annuals. Fertilize (chemical). Graft or bud plants. Irrigate. Trim to increase growth.
Oct 26, 11:47 pm- Oct 29, 5:17 am	1st	Capricorn	Graft or bud plants. Trim to increase growth.
Oct 31, 9:10 am- Nov 2, 10:46 am	2nd	Pisces	Plant grains, leafy annuals. Fertilize (chemical). Graft or bud plants. Irrigate. Trim to increase growth.
Nov 4, 11:05 am- Nov 5, 7:58 am	2nd	Taurus	Plant annuals for hardiness. Trim to increase growth.
Nov 5, 7:58 am- Nov 6, 11:46 am	3rd	Taurus	Plant potatoes and tubers. Trim to retard growth.
Nov 6, 11:46 am- Nov 8, 2:46 pm	3rd	Gemini	Cultivate. Destroy weeds and pests. Harvest fruits and root crops for food. Trim to retard growth.
Nov 8, 2:46 pm- Nov 10, 9:34 pm	3rd	Cancer	Plant biennials, perennials, bulbs, and roots. Prune. Irrigate. Fertilize (organic).
Nov 10, 9:34 pm- Nov 12, 12:45 pm	3rd	Leo	Cultivate. Destroy weeds and pests. Harvest fruits and root crops for food. Trim to retard growth.
Nov 12, 12:45 pm- Nov 13, 8:18 am	4th	Leo	Cultivate. Destroy weeds and pests. Harvest fruits and root crops for food. Trim to retard growth.
Nov 13, 8:18 am- Nov 15, 9:14 pm	4th	Virgo	Cultivate, especially medicinal plants. Destroy weeds and pests. Trim to retard growth.
Nov 18, 9:46 am- Nov 20, 5:18 pm	4th	Scorpio	Plant biennials, perennials, bulbs, and roots. Prune. Irrigate. Fertilize (organic).
Nov 20, 5:18 pm- Nov 20, 8:15 pm	1st	Scorpio	Plant grains, leafy annuals. Fertilize (chemical). Graft or bud plants. Irrigate. Trim to increase growth.
Nov 23, 4:25 am- Nov 25, 10:41 am	1st	Capricorn	Graft or bud plants. Trim to increase growth.
Nov 27, 3:20 pm- Nov 28, 1:29 am	1st	Pisces	Plant grains, leafy annuals. Fertilize (chemical). Graft or bud plants. Irrigate. Trim to increase growth.
Nov 28, 1:29 am- Nov 29, 6:30 pm	2nd	Pisces	Plant grains, leafy annuals. Fertilize (chemical). Graft or bud plants. Irrigate. Trim to increase growth.
Dec 1, 8:26 pm- Dec 3, 10:05 pm	2nd	Taurus	Plant annuals for hardiness. Trim to increase growth.

Dates	Qtr.	Sign	Activity
Dec 4, 7:25 pm– Dec 6, 1:00 am	3rd	Gemini	Cultivate. Destroy weeds and pests. Harvest fruits and root crops for food. Trim to retard growth.
Dec 6, 1:00 am– Dec 8, 6:52 am	3rd	Cancer	Plant biennials, perennials, bulbs, and roots. Prune. Irrigate. Fertilize (organic).
Dec 8, 6:52 am– Dec 10, 4:31 pm	3rd	Leo	Cultivate. Destroy weeds and pests. Harvest fruits and root crops for food. Trim to retard growth.
Dec 10, 4:31 pm– Dec 12, 9:32 am	3rd	Virgo	Cultivate, especially medicinal plants. Destroy weeds and pests. Trim to retard growth.
Dec 12, 9:32 am– Dec 13, 5:00 am	4th	Virgo	Cultivate, especially medicinal plants. Destroy weeds and pests. Trim to retard growth.
Dec 15, 5:42 pm– Dec 18, 4:10 pm	4th	Scorpio	Plant biennials, perennials, bulbs, and roots. Prune. Irrigate. Fertilize (organic).
Dec 18, 4:10 am– Dec 20, 9:01 am	4th	Sagittarius	Cultivate. Destroy weeds and pests. Harvest fruits and root crops for food. Trim to retard growth.
Dec 20, 11:39 am– Dec 22, 4:49 pm	1st	Capricorn	Graft or bud plants. Trim to increase growth.
Dec 24, 8:43 pm– Dec 27, 12:04 am	1st	Pisces	Plant grains, leafy annuals. Fertilize (chemical). Graft or bud plants. Irrigate. Trim to increase growth.
Dec 29, 3:08 am– Dec 31, 6:16 am	2nd	Taurus	Plant annuals for hardiness. Trim to increase growth.

2006 Dates to Destroy Weeds and Pests

Date	Time	Date	Time	Sign	Qtr.
Jan. 14	4:31 pm	Jan. 17	4:49 am	Leo	3rd
Jan. 17	4:49 am	Jan. 19	5:49 pm	Virgo	3rd
Jan. 24	1:38 pm	Jan. 26	5:31 pm	Sagittarius	4th
Jan. 28	6:09 pm	Jan. 29	9:15 am	Aquarius	4th
Feb. 12	11:44 pm	Feb. 13	11:13 am	Leo	3rd
Feb. 13	11:13 am	Feb. 16	12:09 am	Virgo	3rd
Feb. 20	9:38 pm	Feb. 21	2:17 am	Sagittarius	3rd
Feb. 21	2:17 am	Feb. 23	3:16 am	Sagittarius	4th
Feb. 25	5:14 am	Feb. 27	4:56 am	Aquarius	4th
Mar. 14	6:35 pm	Mar. 15	6:12 am	Virgo	3rd
Mar. 20	3:43 am	Mar. 22	10:36 am	Sagittarius	3rd
Mar. 24	2:21 pm	Mar. 26	3:33 pm	Aquarius	4th
Mar. 28	3:31 pm	Mar. 29	5:15 am	Aries	4th
Apr. 16	9:19 am	Apr. 18	4:13 pm	Sagittarius	3rd
Apr. 20	8:56 pm	Apr. 20	10:28 pm	Aquarius	3rd
Apr. 20	10:28 pm	Apr. 22	11:43 pm	Aquarius	4th
Apr. 25	1:12 am	Apr. 27	2:27 am	Aries	4th
May 13	3:56 pm	May 15	9:59 pm	Sagittarius	3rd
May 18	2:19 am	May 20	4:20 am	Aquarius	3rd
May 20	4:20 am	May 20	5:39 am	Aquarius	4th
May 22	8:24 am	May 24	11:00 am	Aries	4th
May 26	2:19 pm	May 27	12:25 am	Gemini	4th
Jun. 11	1:03 pm	Jun. 12	5:19 am	Sagittarius	3rd
Jun. 14	8:32 am	Jun. 16	11:05 am	Aquarius	3rd
Jun. 18	1:54 pm	Jun. 20	5:23 pm	Aries	4th
Jun. 22	9:49 pm	Jun. 25	3:48 am	Gemini	4th
Jul. 11	4:46 pm	Jul. 13	5:59 pm	Aquarius	3rd

Date	Time	Date	Time	Sign	Qtr,
Jul. 15	7:39 pm	Jul. 17	2:12 pm	Aries	3rd
Jul. 17	2:12 pm	Jul. 17	10:44 pm	Aries	4th
Jul. 20	3:38 am	Jul. 22	10:28 am	Gemini	4th
Jul. 24	7:24 pm	Jul. 24	11:31 pm	Leo	4th
Aug. 9	5:54 am	Aug. 10	3:10 am	Aquarius	3rd
Aug. 12	3:22 am	Aug. 14	5:00 am	Aries	3rd
Aug. 16	9:07 am	Aug. 18	4:03 pm	Gemini	4th
Aug. 21	1:33 am	Aug. 23	1:08 pm	Leo	4th
Aug. 23	1:08 pm	Aug. 23	2:10 pm	Virgo	4th
Sep. 8	1:23 pm	Sep. 10	1:30 pm	Aries	3rd
Sep. 12	3:59 pm	Sep. 14	6:15 am	Gemini	3rd
Sep. 14	6:15 am	Sep. 14	9:53 pm	Gemini	4th
Sep. 17	7:15 am	Sep. 19	7:07 pm	Leo	4th
Sep. 19	7:07 pm	Sep. 22	6:45 am	Virgo	4th
Oct. 6	10:13 pm	Oct. 8	12:04 am	Aries	3rd
Oct. 10	1:06 am	Oct. 12	5:21 am	Gemini	3rd
Oct. 14	1:38 pm	Oct. 17	1:15 am	Leo	4th
Oct. 17	1:15 am	Oct. 19	2:19 pm	Virgo	4th
Nov. 6	11:46 am	Nov. 8	2:46 pm	Gemini	3rd
Nov. 10	9:34 pm	Nov. 12	12:45 pm	Leo	3rd
Nov. 12	12:45 pm	Nov. 13	8:18 am	Leo	4th
Nov. 13	8:18 am	Nov. 15	9:14 pm	Virgo	4th
Dec. 4	7:25 pm	Dec. 6	1:00 am	Gemini	3rd
Dec. 8	6:52 am	Dec. 10	4:31 pm	Leo	3rd
Dec. 10	4:31 pm	Dec. 12	9:32 am	Virgo	3rd
Dec. 12	9:32 am	Dec. 13	5:00 am	Virgo	4th
Dec. 18	4:10 am	Dec. 20	9:01 am	Sagittarius	4th

2006 Egg-setting Dates

Dates to be Born	Sign	Qtr.	Set Eggs
Jan. 30 5:32 pm-Feb. 1 5:46 pm	Pisces	1st	Jan. 10
Feb. 27 4:56 am-Mar. 1 4:18 am	Pisces	1st	Feb. 6
Mar. 7 5:38 pm-Mar. 10 4:42 am	Cancer	2nd	Feb. 14
Apr. 27 3:27 am-Apr. 29 5:58 am	Taurus	1st	Apr. 7
May 11 8:24 am-May 13 4:56 pm	Scorpio	2nd	Apr. 20
Jun. 7 4:41 pm-Jun. 10 1:05 pm	Scorpio	2nd	May 17
Jun. 25 4:48 am-Jun. 27 1:09 pm	Cancer	1st	Jun. 6
Jul. 5 1:13 am-Jul. 7 10:13 am	Scorpio	2nd	Jun. 14
Aug. 1 9:06 am-Aug. 3 7:13 pm	Scorpio	1st	Jul. 11
Aug. 28 3:56 pm-Aug. 31 3:00 am	Scorpio	1st	Aug. 7
Sep. 6 2:56 pm-Sep. 8 2:23 pm	Pisces	2nd	Aug. 16
Sep. 24 9:54 pm-Sep. 27 9:16 am	Scorpio	1st	Sep. 4
Oct. 4 1:33 am-Oct. 6 1:32 am	Pisces	2nd	Sep. 13
Sep. 22 3:54 am-Sep. 24 2:53 pm	Scorpio	1st	Sep. 1
Nov. 4 11:06 am-Nov. 6 11:46 am	Taurus	2nd	Oct. 14
Nov. 27 3:20 pm-Nov. 29 6:30 pm	Pisces	2nd	Nov. 6
Dec. 1 8:26 pm-Dec. 3 10:05 pm	Taurus	2nd	Nov. 10
Dec. 29 3:08 am-Dec. 31 6:16 am	Taurus	2nd	Dec. 10

Companion-planting Guide
Plant Helpers and Hinderers

Plant	Helped By	Hindered By
Asparagus	Tomato, parsley, basil	
Bean	Carrot, cucumber, cabbage, beet, corn	Onion, gladiola
Bush bean	Cucumber, cabbage, strawberry	Fennel, onion
Beet	Onion, cabbage, lettuce	Pale bean
Cabbage	Beet, potato, onion, celery	Strawberry, tomato
Carrot	Pea, lettuce, chive, radish, leek, onion	Dill
Celery	Leek, bush bean	
Chive	Bean	
Corn	Potato, bean, pea, melon, squash, pumpkin, cucumber	
Cucumber	Bean, cabbage, radish, sunflower, lettuce	Potato, herbs
Eggplant	Bean	
Lettuce	Strawberry, carrot	
Melon	Morning glory	
Onion, leek	Beet, chamomile, carrot, lettuce	Pea, bean
Garlic	Summer savory	
Pea	Radish, carrot, corn, cucumber, bean, turnip	Onion
Potato	Bean, corn, pea, cabbage, hemp, cucumber	Sunflower

Plant	Helped By	Hindered By
Radish	Pea, lettuce, nasturtium, cucumbers	Hyssop
Spinach	Strawberry	
Squash, Pumpkin	Nasturtium, corn	Potatoes
Tomatoes	Asparagus, parsley, chives, onions, carrot, marigold, nasturtium	Dill, cabbage, fennel
Turnip	Pea, bean	

Plant Companions and Uses

Plant	Companions and Uses
Anise	Coriander
Basil	Tomato; dislikes rue; repels flies and mosquitoes
Borage	Tomato, squash
Buttercup	Clover; hinders delphinium, peony, monkshood, columbine
Chamomile	Helps peppermint, wheat, onions, and cabbage; large amounts destructive
Catnip	Repels flea beetles
Chervil	Radish
Chives	Carrot; prone to apple scab and powdery mildew
Coriander	Hinders seed formation in fennel
Cosmos	Repels corn earworms
Dill	Cabbage; hinders carrot and tomato
Fennel	Disliked by all garden plants
Garlic	Aids vetch and roses; hinders peas and beans
Hemp	Beneficial as a neighbor to most plants
Horseradish	Repels potato bugs

Plant	Companions and Uses
Horsetail	Makes fungicide spray
Hyssop	Attracts cabbage fly away from cabbages; harmful to radishes
Lovage	Improves hardiness and flavor of neighbor plants
Marigold	Pest repellent; use against Mexican bean beetles and nematodes
Mint	Repels ants, flea beetles, and cabbage worm butterflies
Morning glory	Corn; helps melon germination
Nasturtium	Cabbage, cucumbers; deters aphids, squash bugs, and pumpkin beetles
Nettle	Increases oil content in neighbors
Parsley	Tomatoes, asparagus
Purslane	Good ground cover
Rosemary	Repels cabbage moths, bean beetles, and carrot flies
Sage	Repels cabbage moths and carrot flies
Savory	Deters bean beetles
Sunflower	Hinders potatoes; improves soil
Tansy	Deters Japanese beetles, striped cucumber beetles, and squash bugs
Thyme	Repels cabbage worms
Yarrow	Increases essential oils of neighbors

2006 Weather Forecasts

by Kris Brandt Riske

Astrometeorology—astrological weather forecasting—reveals seasonal and weekly weather trends based on the cardinal ingresses (Summer and Winter Solstices, and Spring and Autumn Equinoxes) and the four monthly lunar phases. The planetary alignments and the longitudes and latitudes they influence have the strongest effect, but the zodiacal signs are also involved in creating weather conditions.

The components of a thunderstorm, for example, are heat, wind, and electricity. A Mars-Jupiter configuration generates the necessary heat and Mercury adds wind and electricity. A severe thunderstorm, and those that produce tornados, usually involve

Mercury, Mars, Uranus, or Neptune. The zodiacal signs add their energy to the planetary mix to increase or decrease the chance of weather phenomena and their severity.

In general, the fire signs (Aries, Leo, Sagittarius) indicate heat and dryness, both of which peak when Mars, the planet with a similar nature, is in these signs. Water signs (Cancer, Scorpio, Pisces) are conducive to precipitation, and air signs (Gemini, Libra, Aquarius) to cool temperatures and wind. Earth signs (Taurus, Virgo, Capricorn) vary from wet to dry, heat to cold. The signs and their prevailing weather conditions are listed here:

Aries: Heat, dry, wind
Taurus: Moderate temperatures, precipitation
Gemini: Cool temperatures, wind, dry
Cancer: Cold, steady precipitation
Leo: Heat, dry, lightning
Virgo: Cold, dry, windy
Libra: Cool, windy, fair
Scorpio: Extreme temperatures, abundant precipitation
Sagittarius: Warm, fair, moderate wind
Capricorn: Cold, wet, damp
Aquarius: Cold, dry, high pressure, lightning
Pisces: Wet, cool, low pressure

Take note of the Moon's sign at each lunar phase. It reveals the prevailing weather conditions for the next six to seven days. The same is true of Mercury and Venus. These two influential weather planets transit the entire zodiac each year, unless retrograde patterns add their influence.

Planetary Influences

People relied on astrology to forecast weather for thousands of years. They were able to predict drought, floods, and temperature variations through interpreting planetary alignments. In recent years there has been a renewed interest in astrometeorology, the ancient branch of astrology that focuses on weather forecasting. Unlike meteorology, which at best can forecast weather trends a week in advance, astrometeorology is limitless. A weather forecast can be composed for any date—tomorrow, next week, or a thousand years in the future. Astrometeorology reveals seasonal and weekly weather trends based on the cardinal ingresses (Summer and Winter Solstices, and Spring and Fall Equinoxes) and the four lunar phases that occur monthly in combination with the transiting planets. According to astrometeorology, each planet governs certain weather phenomena. When certain planets are aligned with other planets, weather—precipitation, cloudy or clear skies, tornados, hurricanes, and other conditions—are generated.

Sun and Moon

The Sun governs the constitution of the weather and, like the Moon, it serves as a trigger for other planetary configurations that result in weather events. When the Sun is prominent in a cardinal ingress or lunar phase chart, the area is often warm and sunny. The Moon can bring or withhold moisture, depending upon its sign placement.

Mercury

Mercury is also a triggering planet, but its main influence is wind direction and velocity. In its stationary periods, Mercury reflects high winds, and its influence is always prominent in major weather events, such as hurricanes and tornados, when it tends to lower the temperature.

Venus

Venus governs moisture, clouds, and humidity. It brings warming trends that produce sunny, pleasant weather if in positive aspect to other planets. In some signs—Libra, Virgo, Gemini, Sagittarius—Venus is drier. It is at its wettest when placed in Cancer, Scorpio, Pisces, or Taurus.

Mars

Mars is associated with heat, drought, and wind, and can raise the temperature to record-setting levels when in a fire sign (Aries, Leo, Sagittarius). Mars also provides the spark that generates thunderstorms and is prominent in tornado and hurricane configurations.

Jupiter

Jupiter, a fair-weather planet, tends toward higher temperatures when in Aries, Leo, or Sagittarius. It is associated with high-pressure systems and is a contributing factor at times to dryness. Storms are often amplified by Jupiter.

Saturn

Saturn is associated with low-pressure systems, cloudy to overcast skies, and excessive precipitation. Temperatures drop when Saturn is involved. Major winter storms always have a strong Saturn influence, as do storms that produce a slow, steady downpour for hours or days.

Uranus

Like Jupiter, Uranus indicates high-pressure systems. It reflects descending cold air and, when prominent, is responsible for a jet stream that extends far south. Uranus can bring drought in winter, and it is involved in thunderstorms, tornados, and hurricanes.

Neptune

Neptune is the wettest planet. It signals low-pressure systems and is dominant when hurricanes are in the forecast. When Neptune is strongly placed, flood danger is high. It's often associated with winter thaws. Temperatures, humidity, and cloudiness increase where Neptune influences weather.

Pluto

Pluto is associated with weather extremes, as well as unseasonably warm temperatures and drought. It reflects the high winds involved in major hurricanes, storms, and tornados.

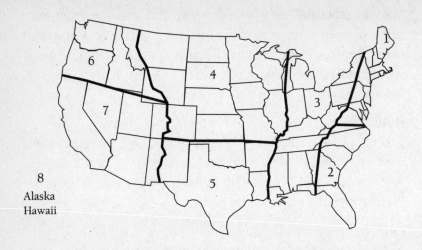

Seasonal Weather Forecast

Winter 2006

Zone 1: The zone is cold, with high winds, cloudy skies, and some major storms that deliver abundant precipitation.

Zone 2: Conditions are mostly seasonal south, with periods of chilly weather. Northern areas are cold and windy. Precipitation is average to above average.

Zone 3: Western and central areas see some major storms, with significant precipitation, as well as periods of dryness. Weather is more seasonal east, and cold and windy northeast, with average precipitation.

Zone 4: Western and central areas see high winds and major storms delivering abundant precipitation, as well as periods of dryness. Weather is cold, with average precipitation east; and cold east, with major storms and some dryness.

Zone 5: Major storms with significant precipitation west, which is windy and cold and, at times, dry. Central areas are cloudy with major storms carrying abundant precipitation. Weather to the east is cold, with average to below-average precipitation.

324

Zone 6: Temperatures are very cold west, where stormy, cloudy, windy weather prevails. Conditions in central locations are more seasonal, with wind, storms, and some dryness. Temperatures east are seasonal to below average, with precipitation average to below average.

Zone 7: Weather is windy west, cold north, with major storms; more seasonal south. Central areas are seasonal with average precipitation; and eastern locations are warmer and drier.

Zone 8: Alaska—Stormy, cold, cloudy, windy weather prevails central; eastern areas are seasonal, with average precipitation; western locations are drier. Hawaii—Precipitation is average to above average and temperatures are seasonal to cool.

Spring 2006

Zone 1: The zone is cold and windy, with precipitation average to below average.

Zone 2: Warm, humid weather triggers storms having hail and tornado potential south; to the north, conditions are colder and cloudier with some significant precipitation.

Zone 3: Western areas are cloudy and damp with some abundant precipitation; and central locations are cloudy with average precipitation. Eastern areas are cool with average to below-average precipitation; storms have tornado potential.

Zone 4: Areas to the west are windy with some abundant precipitation and cloudy skies; west central areas are windy and cold, with below-average precipitation. Weather to the east is seasonal, with significant precipitation in some areas.

Zone 5: Western areas are cloudy and seasonal, with some storms that produce abundant downfall. In central locations, temperatures are seasonal to above average with below-average precipitation. Seasonal temperatures and average to below-average precipitation prevail to the east.

Zone 6: Weather is seasonal west; cloudy and cooler central; cold east, with more storms than other zonal locations.

Zone 7: Western and central areas are cloudy and cool with average precipitation; to the east, conditions are drier with above average temperatures.

Zone 8: Alaska—Major storms central and east; western areas are seasonal with average precipitation. Hawaii—Temperatures are seasonal to above, somewhat windy, with normal to below-average precipitation.

Summer 2006

Zone 1: Weather is seasonal, with average to above-average precipitation.

Zone 2: Precipitation is average to below, and temperatures are seasonal.

Zone 3: The zone sees thunderstorms, some severe, average precipitation, and seasonal to above-average temperatures. Areas to the northeast are drier.

Zone 4: Western and west central areas see abundant precipitation; conditions are drier and seasonal east.

Zone 5: Western areas are seasonal with some abundant precipitation; central locations are hot with significant precipitation, high winds and storms. To the east, weather is seasonal and precipitation average to below average.

Zone 6: Weather west and central is seasonal and windy, with average precipitation, while eastern areas are drier, windy, and seasonal.

Zone 7: Much of the zone is seasonal with average to below-average precipitation. Desert areas are hot and dry, and northern coastal areas wet.

Zone 8: Alaska—Temperatures and precipitation are seasonal to below. Hawaii—Temperatures are seasonal; warmer east, with periods of dryness.

Autumn 2006

Zone 1: Zonal temperatures are seasonal to below average and precipitation is average to above average.

Zone 2: Precipitation is average to above-average and abundant in some areas, and temperatures are seasonal to below, especially north.

Zone 3: Zonal temperatures are seasonal with precipitation average to above-average and significant downfall in some areas.

Zone 4: Precipitation is average to above-average and temperatures are seasonal.

Zone 5: Seasonal temperatures prevail, and much of the zone sees abundant precipitation.

Zone 6: Cloudy, wet weather prevails across the zone, with temperatures seasonal to below average.

Zone 7: Precipitation across the zone is average, but heavier west, and temperatures are seasonal to below average.

Zone 8: Alaska—Temperatures are seasonal and precipitation is average to above, with major storms. Hawaii—The zone is seasonal with average precipitation.

Lunar Weather Forecast

New Moon, December 31, 2005

Zone 1: Precipitation across the zone, with some significant downfall to the south. Wind prevails, and temperatures are seasonal to below average.

Zone 2: Temperatures are cooler to the south, while northern areas are more seasonal. Cloudy skies signal precipitation across much of the zone.

Zone 3: Conditions are seasonal west and central under fair to partly cloudy skies. Temperatures dip to the east under cloudy skies that bring precipitation.

Zone 4: Western areas are stormy with precipitation. Central portions of the zone are fair to partly cloudy with a lower range of temperatures and a chance for precipitation. The east is mostly dry and seasonal.

Zone 5: Fair skies and temperatures ranging from seasonal to above-average prevail in western and central areas, while the east sees variable cloudiness and cooler weather.

Zone 6: Stormy, cold weather, with high winds visiting eastern areas. Western portions see cool and windy weather; central areas are seasonal with precipitation.

Zone 7: Cloudy, wet weather in southern coastal areas moves inland, bringing significant precipitation to the mountains and eastern portions of the zone. Northern coastal and central areas can expect precipitation with seasonal to cool temperatures.

Zone 8: Alaska—Western and central areas are cold, windy, and stormy, with significant precipitation. Fair to partly cloudy skies and temperatures ranging from seasonal to below average prevail to the east. Hawaii—Much of the zone is windy, wet, and cool as a front moves through the state.

First Quarter Moon, January 6, 2006

Zone 1: Windy, cold, and overcast north, with abundant downfall in some areas. Southern portions of the zone are seasonal with variable cloudiness.

Zone 2: Wind and cloudy skies prevail across the zone, with temperatures ranging from seasonal to below. Northern areas see the most precipitation.

Zone 3: Precipitation in western areas, with variable cloudiness; mostly fair in central portions of the zone. Eastern areas are windy and cloudy with precipitation.

Zone 4: Increasing clouds signal precipitation as a front moves in to the west. Conditions in central areas are fair and warmer, with colder weather and precipitation later in the week. Eastern portions are seasonal to below average with precipitation.

Zone 5: Western and central areas are windy, with mostly fair skies and seasonal conditions. Clouds increase to the east and temperatures drop as precipitation develops to the east.

Zone 6: Western weather is windy and fair to partly cloudy, with seasonal temperatures. Central areas are windy with clearing skies, and eastern portions of the zone see increasing clouds, precipitation and colder, windier conditions.

Zone 7: Wind, cloudy skies and precipitation, some abundant, accompany a front that moves through much of the zone, bringing colder temperatures.

Zone 8: Alaska—Western areas are fair to partly cloudy and windy, with increasing cloudiness and precipitation. Central areas also see precipitation and cloudy skies, and conditions are fair to partly cloudy and cold after a front moves out of the area. Hawaii—Weather is fair to partly cloudy, with scattered precipitation and temperatures ranging from seasonal to above average.

Full Moon, January 14, 2006

Zone 1: The zone is overcast and cold, with precipitation and heavier downfall to the north.

Zone 2: Much of the zone is seasonal, with a chance for precipitation. Temperatures drop to the south, with some areas recieving abundant precipication—flood potential exists.

Zone 3: Western areas are cold with precipitation. To the east, conditions are more seasonal, but with abundant precipitation, thawing, and flood potential.

Zone 4: Western areas see precipitation later in the week as a front moves into the zone. Conditions are colder in central areas with precipitation, and to the east, skies are overcast with heavy downfall.

Zone 5: Cold temperatures and precipitation in western and central areas. Conditions to the east are more seasonal and windy, with scattered precipitation and falling temperatures.

Zone 6: Abundant precipitation in western areas of the zone, along with thawing, increase the flood potential. Central and eastern portions of the zone are mostly fair, with temperatures seasonal to below average.

Zone 7: Some western portions of the zone see abundant precipitation as a front moves through and into central areas, especially the mountains. Eastern areas have a chance for precipitation, and temperatures throughout the zone are seasonal to below average.

Zone 8: Alaska—Cold temperatures prevail across the state, and western areas are mostly fair. Heavy downfall and high winds in central areas signal stormy conditions, which move east as the front advances.

Third Quarter Moon, January 22, 2006

Zone 1: Conditions are windy, with increasing clouds and precipitation south. Northern areas are fair to partly cloudy and cold.

Zone 2: Skies are fair to partly cloudy, with increasing clouds and precipitation, especially north. Wind prevails throughout the zone.

Zone 3: Overcast skies yield significant precipitation as a front moves across much of the zone, which is cloudy and cold.

Zone 4: Variable cloudiness and cold temperatures prevail to the west. The rest of the zone is windy with precipitation, which is heaviest to the east.

Zone 5: Wind and cold temperatures prevail in central and western areas, with a chance for precipitation west. Eastern portions of the zone are windy, but temperatures are more seasonal and precipitation is abundant in some locations.

Zone 6: Heavy precipitation west increases flood potential. In central and eastern areas, conditions are seasonal, with scattered precipitation east and variable cloudiness.

Zone 7: Northern coastal areas see significant precipitation. Other areas are fair to partly cloudy, with warmer temperatures in the desert, and cooler conditions in areas to the north and east with cloudiness.

Zone 8: Alaska—Eastern areas are fair to partly cloudy and seasonal. Precipitation, some abundant, falls in western and central areas of the zone. Hawaii—Conditions are fair and seasonal west and central, with precipitation and cloudiness to the east preceding clear skies.

New Moon, January 29, 2006

Zone 1: Windy, wet, and cold conditions in southern areas move to the north, where heaviest downfall occurs.

Zone 2: Cloudy skies and below-average seasonal temperatures prevail across the zone, much of which sees precipitation.

Zone 3: Windy and cloudy conditions with precipitation to the west advance into central areas of the zone, bringing abundant moisture. Eastern portions are windy, cold, and cloudy, becoming fair as weather moves east.

Zone 4: Skies are partly cloudy to cloudy west, where it's windy with precipitation and seasonal temperatures. Lower temperatures, wind, and precipitation prevail central and east, with heaviest downfall to the north and east.

Zone 5: Western and central areas see scattered precipitation under partly cloudy to cloudy skies. Wind, precipitation, and colder temperatures prevail to the east with more cloudiness.

Zone 6: A front bringing precipitation—some abundant—colder temperatures, and fog to western areas moves east, triggering heavy downfall in central portions of the zone. Eastern areas are mostly fair and seasonal.

Zone 7: Western portions of the zone are cloudy with heavy precipitation and flood potential south; northern areas are colder and windier. Stormy conditions and abundant precipitation in central areas of the zone could develop into a blizzard. Conditions east are mostly fair with temperatures ranging from seasonal to above average.

Zone 8: Alaska—Cold and cloudy weather, precipitation—some heavy—blankets the zone. Hawaii—The zone is cloudy and cool with scattered precipitation.

First Quarter Moon, February 5, 2006

Zone 1: Conditions are cold north, and more seasonal south under cloudy skies.

Zone 2: Skies are variably cloudy throughout the zone, producing precipitation in many areas. Temperatures range from seasonal to below average, and northern areas are windy.

Zone 3: High winds accompany cold, cloudy, wet weather across the zone. Some areas see abundant downfall, freezing rain, or hail.

Zone 4: Western and central areas are fair to partly cloudy, and eastern locations see abundant precipitation under overcast skies. Temperatures across the zone are seasonal to below average.

Zone 5: Weather is cloudy, windy, wet and cool across the zone, and eastern areas are very windy with significant precipitation, including flood potential.

Zone 6: Coastal areas see fog and significant precipitation, which moves inland, bringing high winds, cold temperatures and precipitation to central areas. Conditions east are mostly fair and windy with temperatures seasonal to below average.

Zone 7: Western areas see precipitation, and central and eastern portions of the zone are mostly fair, windy and cold.

Zone 8: Alaska—Western and central areas are windy, cold, and cloudy with scattered precipitation; and eastern locations are overcast with heavy downfall. Fog in coastal areas. Hawaii—The zone is partly cloudy to cloudy with precipitation, some locally heavy, and temperatures ranging from seasonal to above average.

Full Moon, February 12, 2006

Zone 1: Cloudy skies, seasonal temperatures and precipitation prevail throughout the zone, with abundant downfall south.

Zone 2: The zone is cloudy and cold with precipitation, which is abundant in northern coastal areas with flood potential.

Zone 3: Temperatures range from seasonal to below average across the zone, which is fair to the west, and overcast and wet central and east, where downfall is significant.

Zone 4: Western and central areas see precipitation, some abundant, especially in the mountains and foothills. Temperatures are seasonal to below average across the zone; eastern locations are fair and windy, with a chance for precipitation later in the week.

Zone 5: Downfall is abundant in some western areas, where temperatures are seasonal. Central and eastern locations are colder with precipitation and wind.

Zone 6: Western areas of the zone are fair to partly cloudy with a chance for precipitation. Cloudy skies prevail central and east, along with wind, stormy conditions, and temperatures seasonal to below average.

Zone 7: Central and eastern areas are stormy, with some areas seeing abundant precipitation prior to clearing and colder temperatures. Western locations are partly cloudy to cloudy with scattered precipitation.

Zone 8: Alaska—Weather is fair and seasonal west and east, with precipitation, wind and cloudy skies in central areas. Hawaii—Conditions are fair and windy west with temperatures seasonal to above average. To the east, precipitation precedes clearing and fair skies.

Third Quarter Moon, February 21, 2006

Zone 1: Southern areas are cloudy and windy with precipitation. Northern areas are cold and mostly fair with a chance for precipitation.

Zone 2: Conditions are mostly fair, windy, and seasonal south; and cloudy, windy, and cold with precipitation to the north.

Zone 3: A weather front brings overcast skies, abundant precipitation, and wind to western and central areas of the zone. Northeastern areas are cloudy.

Zone 4: Cloudy, windy weather with precipitation prevails west and in the west central Plains. Eastern Plains are mostly dry, with a chance for precipitation north. Eastern areas of the zone see significant downfall under windy, overcast skies. Temperatures are very cold central and east.

Zone 5: Overcast skies, high winds and precipitation prevail west and central, along with icy temperatures. Conditions are seasonal to the east with a chance for precipitation south.

Zone 6: Temperatures are seasonal to below average west and central, where cloudy skies yield abundant precipitation in some areas. Eastern locations are fair and cold.

Zone 7: Windy, wet, and cloudy weather in western areas, especially to the south, moves inland. Eastern portions of the zone are mostly fair and dry, with colder temperatures and a chance for precipitation north.

Zone 8: Alaska—Most of the zone sees precipitation, especially eastern areas. Temperatures are seasonal west, and cooler central and east. Hawaii—Precipitation in western areas moves into central portions of the state by week's end. Other areas are mostly fair, and zonal temperatures are seasonal to below average.

New Moon, February 27, 2006

Zone 1: Precipitation throughout the zone is heaviest to the very windy north.

Zone 2: Temperatures seasonal to below average accompany stormy conditions, including high winds, throughout the zone.

Zone 3: Variable cloudiness and seasonal temperatures prevail to the west. Eastern areas are windy, cold, and cloudy with precipitation. The northeast is stormy.

Zone 4: Cloudy, wet weather to the west extends into the Plains, where weather is cold and stormy. Eastern areas are cloudy and seasonal.

Zone 5: Precipitation prevails throughout the zone, with central and eastern areas seeing storms with high winds.

Zone 6: Conditions are cold, windy, and stormy west. Central areas are seasonal with fair to partly cloudy skies. Eastern locations are cloudy and cold with precipitation.

Zone 7: Weather is fair to partly cloudy west, with a chance for precipitation north. Central locations are fair, and variable cloudiness and precipitation prevails to the east.

Zone 8: Alaska—Cloudy skies and precipitation across much of the zone is accompanied by temperatures seasonal to below average. Hawaii—Mostly fair and dry conditions prevail.

First Quarter Moon, March 6, 2006

Zone 1: The zone is overcast and windy, with significant precipitation. Northern areas are very cold with high winds.

Zone 2: Southern areas see significant downfall and tornado potential, and northern areas are overcast with abundant precipitation. Temperatures are seasonal to below average.

Zone 3: Western and central locations are fair to partly cloudy. To the east, overcast skies yield abundant precipitation and cold temperatures.

Zone 4: The northwest sees abundant precipitation, as do the foothills. Central areas are cloudy, cold and windy with a chance for precipitation, and fair to partly cloudy skies and cold temperatures prevail to the east.

Zone 5: Temperatures are seasonal to below average, with variable cloudiness throughout the zone.

Zone 6: A weather front brings precipitation to western areas and windy, stormy conditions to central portions of the zone. Eastern areas are cold and fair to partly cloudy.

Zone 7: Western and central areas see cloudy skies and precipitation, some significant, especially in the mountains. Eastern areas of the zone are very windy and fair to partly cloudy.

Zone 8: Alaska—A storm front moves through western and central areas of the zone with high winds and cold temperatures. Conditions are seasonal and windy east with precipitation. Hawaii—Central and western areas are overcast with precipitation and seasonal temperatures. Eastern locations are fair to partly cloudy.

Full Moon, March 14, 2006

Zone 1: Overcast skies yield abundant precipitation throughout the zone.

Zone 2: Southern areas see overcast skies and abundant precipitation, which moves north later in the week.

Zone 3: Stormy weather with tornado potential prevails throughout much of the zone, along with heavy downfall and high winds.

Zone 4: Western and central areas are cloudy with scattered precipitation. Eastern areas are stormy with tornado potential and some significant downfall.

Zone 5: Much of the zone is cloudy with scattered precipitation. Eastern areas are stormy, with tornado potential, and then much colder.

Zone 6: Overcast skies signal heavy precipitation west and central with flood potential. Seasonal conditions and fair to partly cloudy skies prevail to the east.

Zone 7: Precipitation in northern coastal locations moves inland, and other areas of the zone are seasonal and fair to partly cloudy.

Zone 8: Alaska—Central and western areas are windy and cold with precipitation, and eastern skies are mostly fair and cold. Hawaii—Scattered showers with wind and variable cloudiness prevail.

Spring 2006

Zone 1: The zone is cold and windy, with precipitation average to below average.

Zone 2: Warm, humid weather triggers storms with hail and tornado potential south. To the north, conditions are colder and cloudier with some significant precipitation.

Zone 3: Western areas are cloudy and damp with some abundant precipitation, and central locations are cloudy with average precipitation. Eastern areas are cool. Storms there have tornado potential and average to below-average precipitation.

Zone 4: Areas to the west are windy with some abundant precipitation and cloudy skies. West central areas are windy and cold with below-average precipitation. Weather to the east is seasonal with significant precipitation in some areas.

Zone 5: Western areas are cloudy and seasonal with some storms that produce abundant downfall. In central locations, temperatures are seasonal to above-average with below-average precipitation. Seasonal temperatures and average to below-average precipitation prevail to the east.

Zone 6: Weather is seasonal west, cloudy, and cooler central. It's cold east with more storms than in other zonal locations.

Zone 7: Western and central areas are cloudy and cool with average precipitation, and to the east, conditions are drier with above-average temperatures.

Zone 8: Alaska—Major storms central and east. Western areas are seasonal with average precipitation. Hawaii—Temperatures are seasonal to above average, with wind and normal to below-average precipitation.

Third Quarter Moon, March 22, 2006

Zone 1: Much of the zone sees stormy weather, including overcast skies, cold temperatures, and high winds. Precipitation is abundant to the south.

Zone 2: Overcast and stormy with heavy precipitation north, and thunderstorms with tornado potential to the south. Temperatures are seasonal to below average.

Zone 3: Western and central areas are partly cloudy to cloudy with precipitation later in the week. Eastern areas are stormy with tornado potential and then much cooler.

Zone 4: Cloudy skies east and west signal abundant precipitation, and central areas are stormy with tornado potential.

Zone 5: Temperatures throughout the zone are seasonal to below. Abundant precipitation falls to the west, central areas are mostly fair, and thunderstorms to the east could trigger tornados.

Zone 6: Conditions are stormy and cold west and central with some areas receiving significant precipitation. Weather to the east is fair and windy.

Zone 7: A front brings stormy, windy, and cold weather to west and central areas of the zone, with significant downfall in the mountains. To the east, weather is fair to partly cloudy, and warm and dry in the desert.

Zone 8: Alaska—Wet weather central and east could trigger flooding, and some areas see fog. To the west, weather is stormy with high winds. Hawaii—The state is mostly fair to partly cloudy, warm, and seasonal.

New Moon, March 29, 2006

Zone 1: Weather is cold, wet, and windy to the south, and scattered precipitation and seasonal temperatures prevail to the north.

Zone 2: Thunderstorms in southern areas of the zone have the potential for abundant precipitation and tornados, and northern locations are stormy and cold.

Zone 3: Western and central areas are fair and very windy. Cloudy skies, colder temperatures, and precipitation prevail to the east, where significant downfall and tornado potential occurs in some areas.

Zone 4: Some western areas see precipitation, and central portions of the zone are fair to partly cloudy. Precipitation to the east is followed by colder temperatures as skies clear.

Zone 5: Weather is fair to partly cloudy throughout the zone, with temperatures seasonal to below. Western areas see precipitation later in the week.

Zone 6: Central and western areas are mostly fair to partly cloudy, with some unseasonably cold temperatures. Eastern locations see significant precipitation followed by clearing and cold.

Zone 7: Much of the zone is windy with precipitation, some abundant with flood potential, and temperatures range from seasonal to below average.

Zone 8: Alaska—Cloudy skies signal heavy precipitation central and east. Western areas are mostly fair, and fog is possible in coastal areas. Hawaii—Eastern areas are cloudy, with precipitation, some abundant. Central and western locations are fair and warm.

First Quarter Moon, April 5, 2006

Zone 1: Southern areas see scattered precipitation, variable cloudiness, and chilly temperatures, while conditions to the north are seasonal and overcast with precipitation.

Zone 2: Weather to the south is fair, seasonal, windy, and humid. Northern areas are mostly fair, windy and cold.

Zone 3: Western areas are cold as a front moves through the area, leaving fair skies and warming temperatures. Precipitation develops to the east, and the northeast is mostly fair and windy.

Zone 4: Central areas become cloudy as a storm with high winds moves in from the west, bringing precipitation later in the week. Eastern locations are fair to partly cloudy and cold.

Zone 5: Skies are fair to partly cloudy throughout the zone, with scattered precipitation central later in the week.

Zone 6: Weather is fair to partly cloudy west and central with temperatures seasonal to below average. Eastern locations see abundant precipitation followed by clearing and colder temperatures.

Zone 7: Conditions are cold and windy west, with heaviest precipitation centered north and inland under overcast skies. Desert areas are warm and dry.

Zone 8: Alaska—Overcast skies, high winds and precipitation move across the zone, and some areas see abundant moisture. Hawaii—Central and eastern areas see thunderstorms with high winds. Weather is fair and windy west, with scattered precipitation later in the week.

Full Moon, April 13, 2006

Zone 1: Fair and seasonal to the south. Northern areas are windy with variable cloudiness and scattered precipitation.

Zone 2: Southern areas see scattered precipitation, and northern locations are mostly fair with a chance for precipitation.

Zone 3: Thunderstorms with tornado potential develop in western and central areas. The east sees fair to partly cloudy skies with scattered precipitation later in the week.

Zone 4: Precipitation, some abundant, develops to the west later in the week, followed by colder temperatures as the front moves into west central areas. Eastern areas are cloudy with precipitation much of the week, and central and eastern locations could see thunderstorms with tornado potential.

Zone 5: Western areas are fair and seasonal with precipitation later in the week. Central and eastern locations see scattered thunderstorms, wind and tornado potential.

Zone 6: Temperatures are seasonal to below average throughout the zone, and west and central areas are windy and fair to partly cloudy. Cloudy skies yield precipitation to the east.

Zone 7: Eastern and central areas are windy, cold and fair to partly cloudy. Eastern mountains see precipitation with a chance for moisture in the desert, where clouds are variable.

Zone 8: Alaska—Central areas are fair to partly cloudy early in the week, with significant precipitation, colder temperatures, and overcast skies developing. Conditions are fair and seasonal west, and eastern areas see increasing clouds and wind, cold temperatures, and precipitation. Hawaii—Conditions are fair to partly cloudy with scattered showers and temperatures seasonal to below average.

Third Quarter Moon, April 20, 2006

Zone 1: Conditions are windy and cloudy, with thunderstorms and abundant precipitation south. Temperatures decline north as a front brings precipitation.

Zone 2: Southern areas are fair to partly cloudy and windy with scattered thunderstorms. Locations north see abundant precipitation. Tornado potential exists across the zone.

Zone 3: Cloudy weather prevails west and central with wind and precipitation later in the week. Thunderstorms to the east could produce tornados.

Zone 4: Thunderstorms in the Plains have tornado potential, followed by cooler temperatures. Eastern areas are fair to partly cloudy with temperatures seasonal to below average, with a chance for precipitation.

Zone 5: Western and central locations are fair to partly cloudy and windy, while areas to the east see thunderstorms and tornado potential.

Zone 6: Weather is fair to partly cloudy west, and windy with precipitation central and east as cloudiness increases. Temperatures are seasonal to below average.

Zone 7: Windy conditions in southern coastal areas accompany precipitation, some abundant, that moves inland. Northern coastal areas see variable cloudiness with precipitation. Eastern desert areas are warm, windy, and dry, with a chance for precipitation north.

Zone 8: Alaska—Central and eastern areas are fair and cool. Western locations are windy with precipitation. Hawaii—The state sees variable clouds with precipitation and wind, and temperatures range from seasonal to below average.

New Moon, April 27, 2006

Zone 1: Northern locations are overcast with significant downfall. Conditions to the south are windy, humid, and cloudy with precipitation.

Zone 2: Thunderstorms with tornado potential pop up throughout much of the zone as humidity rises.

Zone 3: Western areas are mostly fair and central locations have a chance for showers with increasing cloudiness. Temperatures fall to the east after thunderstorms with high winds and tornado potential.

Zone 4: Conditions are fair and windy west, and central locations see scattered showers and thunderstorms. Cloudy skies and cooler temperatures east bring a chance for showers.

Zone 5: Heat, humidity, and fair to partly cloudy skies prevail to the west, while central and eastern areas, also humid, see showers.

Zone 6: Western locations are fair, cool, and dry. Central and eastern areas see precipitation and then cooler temperatures.

Zone 7: Overcast skies, cool temperatures, and precipitation prevail in central areas with high winds. Eastern areas are fair to partly cloudy with hot weather in the desert and windy conditions and scattered showers north.

Zone 8: Alaska—Central areas are fair to partly cloudy prior to increasing cloudiness and wind with precipitation. The zone is fair east and west. Hawaii—Showers, seasonal temperatures, and cloudy skies prevail across much of the zone.

First Quarter Moon, May 5, 2006

Zone 1: Humid and cloudy conditions yield significant precipitation to the south, while northern areas are mostly fair and windy with a chance for precipitation.

Zone 2: Conditions are hot and humid throughout the zone. Southern areas are mostly fair with scattered thunderstorms, with showers to the north.

Zone 3: Cloudy skies yield moisture west and central. Skies are fair to partly cloudy to the east with rising temperatures and scattered showers and thunderstorms that produce significant downfall in some areas.

Zone 4: Weather is fair and dry west, and fair to partly cloudy central and east with a chance for precipitation later in the week, especially in eastern areas. Temperatures are seasonal to below average.

Zone 5: Conditions are mostly fair and humid with a chance for precipitation west and thunderstorms east.

Zone 6: Western areas are fair, windy and cool. Central locations are overcast with abundant precipitation that advances into eastern areas.

Zone 7: Northern coastal areas see abundant downfall that moves inland, where cool and cloudy conditions develop. Southern coastal areas are cloudy with showers, and the desert is hot and dry with a chance for precipitation east.

Zone 8: Alaska—Western areas see abundant precipitation later in the week. Central and eastern areas are mostly fair, cool, and windy, with a chance for precipitation. Hawaii—Much of the state is fair to partly cloudy and windy with a chance of showers later in the week. Conditions are cloudy west, with precipitation.

Full Moon, May 13, 2006

Zone 1: Seasonal temperatures, varied cloudiness, and scattered showers prevail throughout the zone, with more humidity south.

Zone 2: The zone is fair to partly cloudy and mostly dry and windy, with scattered thunderstorms north.

Zone 3: Heat, humidity and fair to partly cloudy skies prevail, with more cloudiness to the east, which sees scattered thunderstorms.

Zone 4: Cloudy skies west signal showers; the Plains see scattered thunderstorms. Areas to the east are mostly dry, windy, and fair to partly cloudy. Temperatures are seasonal to above average.

Zone 5: The zone is hot, humid and dry with a chance for showers.

Zone 6: Cloudy, cool weather with precipitation prevails west and central. Areas to the east are fair and windy with a chance for showers.

Zone 7: Most of the zone is fair to partly cloudy, and desert areas are hot and windy. Northern coastal locations are overcast with precipitation.

Zone 8: Alaska—Eastern areas are seasonal with precipitation, and central and western locations are windy, fair, and cool. Hawaii—The state is windy and fair with showers west.

Third Quarter Moon, May 20, 2006

Zone 1: Temperatures are seasonal to below average with varied cloudiness, wind, and a chance for showers later in the week.

Zone 2: Areas to the south see thunderstorms, and northern locations are fair to partly cloudy and windy.

Zone 3: Western areas are fair, central locations see thunderstorms. Areas to the east are fair to partly cloudy with a chance for showers.

Zone 4: Variable cloudiness prevails west and central. Eastern areas are fair, humid, and windy under clearing skies.

Zone 5: The zone is fair to partly cloudy with temperatures seasonal to below average.

Zone 6: Temperatures dip west following showers, which move into central areas, where significant downfall occurs. Eastern locations are fair and windy.

Zone 7: Variable cloudiness west and central accompanies scattered showers and thunderstorms. Eastern areas are fair and dry, and temperatures are seasonal to above average.

Zone 8: Alaska—Skies are fair to partly cloudy throughout the zone with a chance for precipitation central. Temperatures are seasonal to above. Hawaii—Western and central areas are fair and seasonal. Variable clouds east signal a chance for showers.

New Moon, May 27, 2006

Zone 1: Hot, humid weather triggers thunderstorms to the south. Northern areas are humid and windy with showers.

Zone 2: The zone is hot and humid with variable cloudiness and scattered precipitation south. Thunderstorms are more severe north with tornado potential.

Zone 3: Variable cloudiness, heat, and humidity signal scattered thunderstorms throughout the zone, with tornado potential east, where storms are more severe.

Zone 4: Much of the zone sees hot, humid weather with scattered thunderstorms and showers, and some areas receive significant downfall and severe storms with tornado potential.

Zone 5: The zone is mostly fair, hot, and humid, with scattered showers and thunderstorms east.

Zone 6: Coastal areas are mostly fair. Thunderstorms, some severe, and showers prevail central and east, which is overcast. Temperatures are seasonal to below average.

Zone 7: The zone is mostly fair and windy, with scattered thunderstorms east.

Zone 8: Alaska—Conditions are cold, dry and fair west, fair to partly central with a chance of showers, and fair east. Hawaii—Windy with variable cloudiness and scattered showers.

First Quarter Moon, June 3, 2006

Zone 1: Hot and humid with thunderstorms, some severe.

Zone 2: Variable cloudiness and scattered showers prevail.

Zone 3: Hot and humid with scattered thunderstorms.

Zone 4: Significant downfall occurs in western areas and the western Plains, and central and eastern areas are fair to partly cloudy with scattered showers and thunderstorms, humidity and temperatures seasonal to above average.

Zone 5: Increasing clouds to the west precede significant precipitation in some areas. Central and eastern locations are fair to partly cloudy, hot and humid with scattered thunderstorms.

Zone 6: Conditions are fair and seasonal west, central locations are windy with thunderstorms, and overcast skies and significant downfall prevails to the east.

Zone 7: Severe thunderstorms in the mountains produce significant precipitation in some areas. Overcast with precipitation east, and fair to partly cloudy west.

Zone 8: Alaska—Central areas are very windy with scattered precipitation, western locations are fair to partly cloudy, and conditions are fair and windy east. Hawaii—Humidity and variable cloudiness with scattered showers prevail in Hawaii, where temperatures are seasonal to above average.

Full Moon, June 11, 2006

Zone 1: The zone is cloudy with showers, thunderstorms and significant downfall in some areas.

Zone 2: The zone sees scattered showers and thunderstorms, with more precipitation and wind to the north.

Zone 3: The zone is hot and humid with showers and thunderstorms, some severe. Some areas in the central and eastern portion of the zone see significant downfall.

Zone 4: Hot and humidity trigger scattered showers and thunderstorms across much of the zone, which is humid and windy.

Zone 5: The zone is hot, humid, and mostly fair with scattered thunderstorms, some of which are severe.

Zone 6: Abundant precipitation west increases flood potential. Central and eastern areas are fair and windy with temperatures seasonal to above average.

Zone 7: The zone is mostly fair and windy, with scattered thunderstorms east.

Zone 8: Alaska—temperatures are seasonal and skies fair to partly cloudy east and west, with wind and scattered precipitation central. Hawaii—conditions are windy and fair to partly cloudy with a chance for showers.

Summer 2006

Zone 1: Weather is seasonal, with average to above-average precipitation.

Zone 2: Precipitation is average to below average, and temperatures are seasonal.

Zone 3: The zone sees thunderstorms, some severe, average precipitation and seasonal to above-average temperatures. Areas to the northeast are drier.

Zone 4: Western and west central areas see abundant precipitation, and conditions are drier and seasonal east.

Zone 5: Western areas are seasonal with some abundant precipitation. Central locations are hot with significant precipitation, high winds, and storms. To the east, weather is seasonal and precipitation average to below average.

Zone 6: Weather west and central is seasonal and windy with average precipitation. Eastern areas are drier, windy, and seasonal.

Zone 7: Seasonal with average to below-average precipitation throughout much of the zone. Desert areas are hot and dry, and northern coastal areas wet.

Zone 8: Alaska—Temperatures and precipitation in Alaska are seasonal to below average. Hawaii—Temperatures are seasonal and warmer east. The zone has periods of dryness.

Third Quarter Moon, June 18, 2006

Zone 1: Weather is fair to partly cloudy and humid with scattered precipitation and significant downfall in some areas to the north.

Zone 2: The zone is hot, humid, and windy. Thunderstorms, some severe, have tornado potential.

Zone 3: Fair west; stormy in the central and east areas, with abundant precipitation, high winds, and tornado potential.

Zone 4: Clouds replace fair weather west, bringing scattered showers and thunderstorms. Central and eastern areas are fair to partly cloudy with scattered showers.

Zone 5: Fair to partly cloudy skies, with scattered precipitation central and east. Temperatures ranging from seasonal to above average.

Zone 6: Stormy west with high winds, and clouds increase in central areas, bringing showers. Eastern locations see scattered thunderstorms. Temperatures are seasonal to below average.

Zone 7: Stormy weather prevails in north coastal areas and inland, and the remainder of the zone is fair with scattered thunderstorms east. Temperatures are seasonal to below average.

Zone 8: Alaska—Conditions are stormy in central and eastern portions of the zone, some of which receive abundant downfall. Eastern areas are fair and seasonal. Hawaii—Cloudy skies yield precipitation, some significant, to the east, and other areas are fair to partly cloudy, hot, and humid.

New Moon, June 25, 2006

Zone 1: The zone is hot and humid with variable cloudiness and scattered thunderstorms, some severe.

Zone 2: Zonal temperatures are seasonal with scattered thunderstorms south. Expect fair and humid weather in the north.

Zone 3: Western areas are cloudy with scattered precipitation, central areas see thunderstorms, and fair skies prevail to the east. Temperatures are seasonal.

Zone 4: Western locations are fair and windy, and increasing clouds central and east bring showers. Temperatures are seasonal.

Zone 5: Fair to partly cloudy skies prevail west and central with a chance for showers. Eastern areas see showers.

Zone 6: Conditions are fair to partly cloudy and seasonal west. Cloudy, windy weather with thunderstorms in central areas moves east, where some downfall is abundant.

Zone 7: Western skies are variably cloudy with precipitation and wind, which moves into central areas of the zone. The desert is hot and humid with scattered thunderstorms east.

Zone 8: Alaska—Central and western areas are windy and cool with precipitation, and eastern locations are fair and seasonal. Hawaii—The state is windy with scattered showers.

First Quarter Moon, July 3, 2006

Zone 1: Heat triggers scattered showers and thunderstorms throughout the zone, which is fair to partly cloudy.

Zone 2: Conditions are fair to partly cloudy south with seasonal temperatures, wind and scattered showers. Northern areas are hot and humid with scattered thunderstorms.

Zone 3: Hot and humid weather west and central triggers thunderstorms. Eastern areas are fair to partly cloudy with thunderstorms, some severe with tornado potential.

Zone 4: Conditions are hot, humid, and windy across the zone with showers and thunderstorms.

Zone 5: Hot, humid weather triggers showers and thunderstorms.

Zone 6: Weather is warm with fog and scattered showers west. Central and eastern areas are windy and mostly fair with seasonal temperatures.

Zone 7: Much of the zone is fair and windy, with temperatures seasonal to above average. Northern coastal areas see precipitation and fog.

Zone 8: Alaska—Scattered precipitation and fog prevail throughout the zone with variable cloudiness and temperatures seasonal to above average. Hawaii—Hawaii is hot and humid with variable cloudiness and scattered showers.

Full Moon, July 10, 2006

Zone 1: Heat and humidity trigger showers and thunderstorms across the zone.

Zone 2: Temperatures are seasonal with variable clouds and scattered showers and thunderstorms.

Zone 3: Temperatures range from seasonal to above-average across the zone, which is fair to partly cloudy with scattered showers and thunderstorms east.

Zone 4: Western and central areas are windy with thunderstorms, and eastern areas are mostly fair and windy with a chance for precipitation. Temperatures are seasonal to above.

Zone 5: Humidity and heat trigger scattered thunderstorms across much of the zone.

Zone 6: Wind and showers prevail west and central, where abundant downfall occurs under overcast skies. Eastern areas are partly cloudy to cloudy.

Zone 7: Cloudy skies signal precipitation west and central, and the desert is hot and humid with variable cloudiness north and a chance for showers.

Zone 8: Alaska—Conditions are fair east, with variable cloudiness, wind, and precipitation west and central. Temperatures range from seasonal to above average. Hawaii—Windy with fair to partly cloudy skies, seasonal temperatures, with showers west and central.

Third Quarter Moon, July 17, 2006

Zone 1: Heat and humidity trigger thunderstorms south. Northern areas see showers and rising temperatures.

Zone 2: Thunderstorms, some severe, accompany hot, windy, and humid weather. Some areas see significant moisture.

Zone 3: Cloudy skies, humidity, and precipitation, some abundant, prevail west and central. Eastern areas are windy, hot, and humid with thunderstorms.

Zone 4: Western areas see showers and thunderstorms, and central locations are dry and hot. Eastern areas are fair to partly cloudy with scattered precipitation.

Zone 5: Showers and thunderstorms prevail west and central, and eastern areas are fair with higher temperatures.

Zone 6: The zone is windy with scattered precipitation under fair to partly cloudy skies.

Zone 7: Conditions are fair to partly cloudy west and central, with scattered showers. Eastern areas are mostly fair with showers in the mountains.

Zone 8: Alaska—Fair skies prevail to the east, and central and eastern areas see variable cloudiness and precipitation, some abundant. Hawaii—Weather is fair to partly cloudy with scattered showers and seasonal temperatures.

New Moon, July 25, 2006

Zone 1: Conditions across the zone are windy with a chance for precipitation and temperatures seasonal to above average.

Zone 2: Hot, humid, and windy with scattered thunderstorms.

Zone 3: Variable cloudy, hot, and humid, with precipitation west and central. Windy and fair with a chance for precipitation east.

Zone 4: Thunderstorms, some severe, with abundant precipitation, are triggered by hot and humid weather across much of the zone. Western areas are mostly dry with a chance for showers, and eastern areas are more seasonal.

Zone 5: Eastern areas are cloudy with precipitation, and heat and humidity bring scattered thunderstorms to central areas. Western areas are windy with a chance for precipitation. Temperatures across the zone are seasonal to above average.

Zone 6: The zone is fair to partly cloudy and breezy with seasonal temperatures.

Zone 7: Mostly dry with temperatures seasonal to above. Western and eastern areas have a chance for precipitation.

Zone 8: Alaska—Weather is fair and seasonal west and central, with cloudiness east. Hawaii—Scattered showers accompany mostly fair skies and seasonal temperatures.

First Quarter Moon, August 2, 2006

Zone 1: Southern areas are fair to partly cloudy, with more cloudiness and precipitation north. Temperatures are seasonal to above average.

Zone 2: Areas to the south are cloudy and humid with precipitation. Northern locations are fair, hot, and humid.

Zone 3: Western areas see scattered showers and thunderstorms. Central and northeastern portions of the zone are fair to partly cloudy. Precipitation in central areas, with east under overcast skies. Temperatures are seasonal to above average.

Zone 4: Temperatures are seasonal to above average, with scattered showers and thunderstorms across the zone with tornado potential in some areas.

Zone 5: Western areas are hot with thunderstorms. Temperatures rise in the central Plains, with scattered showers and thunderstorms later in the week. Eastern locations are fair to partly cloudy, with scattered showers and thunderstorms.

Zone 6: Overcast skies signal abundant precipitation west and central, where downfall is less. Mostly fair weather prevails to the east.

Zone 7: Northern coastal areas are cloudy with significant precipitation. Skies are fair to partly cloudy to the south. Central and eastern areas see variable cloudiness with precipitation in the mountains. Temperatures are seasonal.

Zone 8: Alaska—Precipitation in central areas, with variable cloudiness east, and fair skies west, where temperatures are higher. Hawaii—Showers across the state with rising temperatures.

Full Moon, August 9, 2006

Zone 1: Cloudy, windy weather with abundant precipitation prevails across the zone, including hurricane potential.

Zone 2: Significant precipitation, overcast skies and a strong low pressure increase hurricane potential.

Zone 3: Areas to the west are fair and dry, central locations are hot with scattered thunderstorms, and overcast skies and abundant precipitation increase flood and hurricane potential.

Zone 4: Eastern areas are fair and dry, and the west sees fair to partly cloudy skies. Central locations are stormy with severe thunderstorms with tornado potential.

Zone 5: Dry and fair to partly cloudy west, and central and eastern areas see showers and thunderstorms with tornado potential.

Zone 6: Conditions are fair to partly cloudy and seasonal west, with more cloudiness and precipitation central. Temperatures rise to the east, which is fair and dry.

Zone 7: Western areas are cloudy with precipitation, some abundant, which moves into central locations. Scattered thunderstorms, seasonal temperatures, and fair to partly cloudy skies prevail to the east.

Zone 8: Alaska—Fair to partly cloudy skies prevail in central locations, while eastern and western areas are stormy with abundant precipitation. Hawaii—Weather is fair to partly cloudy with scattered showers central and east, and stormy west.

Third Quarter Moon, August 15, 2006

Zone 1: The zone is variably cloudy and humid with precipitation and thunderstorms, some severe.

Zone 2: Cloudy skies, humidity, abundant precipitation in some areas. Thunderstorms with tornado potential and high winds north prevail across the zone.

Zone 3: Precipitation across the zone is heaviest east, where skies are overcast and thunderstorms have tornado potential.

Zone 4: Weather is fair and windy west. Variably cloudy in central areas, where thunderstorms have tornado potential. Expect fair to partly cloudy skies east with scattered showers.

Zone 5: Western areas are fair and windy. Heat and humidity central and east trigger thunderstorms, some severe with tornado potential and abundant downfall.

Zone 6: Western areas are windy with abundant precipitation, while central and eastern locations are fair to partly cloudy with scattered precipitation central later in the week.

Zone 7: North coastal areas see precipitation, some abundant, and other areas are fair to partly cloudy and seasonal.

Zone 8: Alaska—Much of the state sees precipitation, some abundant to the east, variable cloudiness and seasonal temperatures. Hawaii—Skies are fair to partly cloudy with scattered precipitation, humidity, and rising temperatures.

New Moon, August 23, 2006

Zone 1: Hurricane potential, cloudy skies, and significant precipitation south. Northern areas see scattered thunderstorms and high winds. Temperatures range from seasonal to below average.

Zone 2: A hurricane is possible with thunderstorms, cloudy skies, high winds and abundant precipitation across the zone.

Zone 3: Much of the zone is hot and dry with scattered thunderstorms. Precipitation, some abundant, centers over the east.

Zone 4: Conditions are fair and seasonal west and in the western Plains, with thunderstorms, some severe with high winds, in central and eastern areas.

Zone 5: The zone is mostly fair, dry and windy, with a chance for scattered showers and thunderstorms.

Zone 6: Overcast skies west and central yield precipitation and high winds, and eastern areas are fair and windy.

Zone 7: Abundant precipitation west is heaviest south under cloudy skies with flood potential before moving into central areas. Eastern locations are fair and windy.

Zone 8: Alaska—The zone is variably cloudy with scattered precipitation west and central, and fair east. Hawaii—Fair and seasonal with a chance for showers.

First Quarter Moon, August 31, 2006

Zone 1: Zone is stormy with high winds and hurricane potential.

Zone 2: Weather is mostly fair with scattered showers south. Northern areas are stormy with high winds and tornado and hurricane potential.

Zone 3: Precipitation prevails, with thunderstorms and showers west and central, and stormy conditions east with severe thunderstorms, high winds, and tornado and hurricane potential.

Zone 4: Cloudy skies throughout the zone signal abundant precipitation in some areas along with high winds.

Zone 5: Thunderstorms, high winds, and overcast skies prevail throughout the zone and temperatures are seasonal to below.

Zone 6: Fair to partly cloudy west. Scattered showers and stormy central, becoming cloudy east as a front advances into the area.

Zone 7: Weather is windy and stormy west and central, and fair with rising temperatures east with scattered thunderstorms.

Zone 8: Alaska—Western and eastern areas are windy and stormy, while central areas are fair; expect stormy and colder conditions later in the week. Hawaii—Fair to partly cloudy and seasonal with a chance for precipitation.

Full Moon, September 7, 2006

Zone 1: The zone is variably cloudy with more cloudiness north, scattered precipitation and cooler temperatures.

Zone 2: Weather is fair to partly cloudy north and cool, with thunderstorms with tornado potential south.

Zone 3: Much of the zone sees thunderstorms, some severe with tornado potential. Northeast is fair to partly cloudy and cool.

Zone 4: Areas to the west are fair and cool with precipitation later in the week, and central and eastern locations see scattered thunderstorms and cool temperatures.

Zone 5: Western areas are fair and dry with precipitation later in the week. Strong thunderstorms are triggered in central locations, and eastern areas are fair to partly cloudy and windy with scattered thunderstorms.

Zone 6: Areas to the west are cloudy with showers, and central locations are fair to partly cloudy and windy with scattered thunderstorms. More precipitation occurs east, where it's windy, with showers and thunderstorms.

Zone 7: Southern coastal and inland areas are fair with scattered showers. Northern coastal locations are windy with precipitation. Increasing clouds signal precipitation in the mountains and east.

Zone 8: Alaska—Much of Alaska is fair to partly cloudy with scattered precipitation and seasonal to above average temperatures. Hawaii—Windy, fair to partly cloudy and seasonal, with scattered showers.

Third Quarter Moon, September 15, 2006

Zone 1: Areas to the south are fair and windy. Northern locations are stormy, with wind and abundant precipitation.

Zone 2: Southern locations are cloudy and windy with precipitation. Skies are mostly fair north.

Zone 3: West and central areas are cloudy and windy with precipitation, and eastern locations are fair and windy. Temperatures are seasonal to below average.

Zone 4: Weather is fair to partly cloudy and seasonal west, with precipitation and cooler temperatures central and east.

Zone 5: The zone is breezy and fair west. Cooler east with precipitation. Temperatures rise in central areas, where there are scattered thunderstorms.

Zone 6: Eastern and central locations are cloudy with thunderstorms; and some areas see abundant precipitation. To the west, conditions are fair and seasonal.

Zone 7: Western areas are overcast and stormy and some receive abundant precipitation. Other areas are mostly fair with scattered thunderstorms, some severe. Skies are cloudy to the east.

Zone 8: Alaska—Stormy west; windy central, with scattered precipitation; and fair and seasonal east. Hawaii—Rising temperatures, wind, thunderstorms, and variable cloudiness prevail.

Autumn 2006

Zone 1: Zonal temperatures are seasonal to below average and precipitation is average to above average.

Zone 2: Precipitation is average to above average and abundant in some areas, and temperatures are seasonal to below average, especially north.

Zone 3: Zonal temperatures are seasonal with precipitation average to above average and significant downfall in some areas.

Zone 4: Precipitation average to above average. Temperatures are seasonal.

Zone 5: Seasonal temperatures prevail, and much of the zone sees abundant precipitation.

Zone 6: Cloudy, wet weather prevails across the zone, with temperatures seasonal to below average.

Zone 7: Precipitation across the zone is average, but heavier west, and temperatures are seasonal to below average.

Zone 8: Alaska—Temperatures are seasonal and precipitation average to above average, with major storms. Hawaii—The zone is seasonal with average precipitation.

New Moon, September 22, 2006

Zone 1: Weather across the zone is fair to partly cloudy with scattered precipitation.

Zone 2: The zone is fair to partly cloudy with scattered precipitation and temperatures seasonal to below average. Northern areas are windy.

Zone 3: Western locations are windy with precipitation later in the week. Central and eastern areas are variably cloudy and windy with precipitation.

Zone 4: Precipitation across the zone varies from scattered to heavy and temperatures are seasonal to below average.

Zone 5: Cloudy skies signal precipitation, some abundant, in central and eastern areas, and western locations have a chance for precipitation. Temperatures are seasonal to below average.

Zone 6: The zone is windy with temperatures seasonal to below average. Weather is fair and seasonal west, with precipitation later in the week. Central and eastern areas are fair and seasonal.

Zone 7: Most of the zone is dry and windy, with scattered precipitation north, and heat in the desert and areas east.

Zone 8: Alaska—Temperatures are seasonal, with cloudiness and precipitation across the zone. Hawaii—Seasonal to cool, with partly cloudy to cloudy skies and precipitation.

First Quarter Moon, September 30, 2006

Zone 1: Precipitation across the zone is heaviest north, along with cloudiness and wind.

Zone 2: Cloudiness prevails throughout the zone, along with precipitation, some abundant to the south. Temperatures are seasonal to below average.

Zone 3: Temperatures are seasonal to below average with precipitation, some abundant, across the zone.

Zone 4: Areas to the west are dry. The eastern Plains and east are seasonal with a chance for precipitation.

Zone 5: Weather is windy, fair, and dry west, with variable cloudiness and scattered precipitation east and central.

Zone 6: Overcast skies west yield abundant precipitation, and central areas are fair to partly cloudy and windy with a chance for precipitation. Fair skies prevail to the east. Temperatures are seasonal to below average.

Zone 7: Much of the zone is fair, dry, windy, and seasonal. Northern coastal and inland areas are cloudy with precipitation.

Zone 8: Alaska—Windy and wet, with the heaviest downfall creating flood potential in the west. Eastern areas are cooler, and fog occurs in coastal areas. Hawaii—Fair to partly cloudy, with scattered showers and rising temperatures west.

Full Moon, October 6, 2006

Zone 1: Weather is fair, seasonal and windy south with a chance for precipitation. Cloudy and windy north with precipitation.

Zone 2: Fair skies and cool temperatures prevail to the north. Southern areas have a chance for showers.

Zone 3: Eastern areas are cold with precipitation. Central and western areas see scattered thunderstorms.

Zone 4: Western areas see scattered precipitation, the northwest is fair and cloudy, and eastern and central areas are cloudy, some with abundant precipitation.

Zone 5: Variable cloudiness across the zone yields precipitation, and eastern and central areas are cooler.

Zone 6: The zone is fair to partly cloudy and cool with a chance for precipitation east.

Zone 7: Fair west, cooler north, windy with scattered precipitation central; and fair, dry, windy, and seasonal east.

Zone 8: Alaska—Precipitation falls east after fair skies turn cloudy. Central and western areas are seasonal, windy, and fair to partly cloudy. Coastal areas are foggy. Hawaii—Windy with scattered showers, with warmer temperatures, more humid showers west.

Third Quarter Moon, October 13, 2006

Zone 1: Areas to the south are windy with scattered precipitation. To the north, wind and abundant precipitation prevail. Temperatures are seasonal.

Zone 2: The zone is fair and seasonal.

Zone 3: Weather is fair east. Windy west, with precipitation and cool temperatures.

Zone 4: Cloudy, windy, cool, wet weather across the zone yield heavy downfalls in some locations.

Zone 5: Temperatures are seasonal to below average across the zone and conditions are cloudy, wet and windy.

Zone 6: Abundant precipitation falls in some areas across a cloudy, windy, and wet zone.

Zone 7: Western areas are windy with colder temperatures north and significant precipitation in some locations, which moves into central and eastern areas of the zone.

Zone 8: Alaska—Cold with precipitation east. Central and western areas are overcast with heavy downfall. Hawaii—Cloudy, windy, and cool, with abundant precipitation.

New Moon, October 22, 2006

Zone 1: Southern areas are fair, windy, and seasonal, and northern locations are cold.

Zone 2: Thunderstorms, some severe with tornado potential, are triggered in southern locations. Northern areas are fair with increasing clouds and precipitation.

Zone 3: Western and central areas are variably cloudy with scattered precipitation. Severe thunderstorms with tornado potential and abundant downfall prevail to the south. The northeast is fair with precipitation later in the week.

Zone 4: Conditions are windy with precipitation, some abundant, west and central. Fair to partly cloudy skies east with scattered precipitation.

Zone 5: Eastern areas are fair. Central and western locations are cloudy with precipitation.

Zone 6: Western areas are cold and wet, with central locations more seasonal. Eastern areas are variably cloudy with precipitation.

Zone 7: Wind, cloudy skies and precipitation to the west, with colder temperatures north that move into central areas of the zone. Eastern locations are fair to partly cloudy and windy with a chance for precipitation.

Zone 8: Alaska—Seasonal temperatures throughout the zone accompany precipitation, cloudy skies, and fog in all but western areas. Hawaii—Weather is fair and seasonal west and central, with precipitation east.

First Quarter Moon, October 29, 2006

Zone 1: The zone is cold and fair to partly cloudy north, with scattered precipitation south.

Zone 2: Skies are cloudy throughout the zone with precipitation, abundant in some areas to the south, and windy.

Zone 3: Western and central areas are fair to partly cloudy and windy with scattered precipitation and temperatures seasonal to above average. Eastern locations are cool and cloudy with abundant precipitation in some areas.

Zone 4: Conditions are fair to partly cloudy west, and cold northwest and fair. Central and eastern areas are windy and cloudy with precipitation, some abundant.

Zone 5: Western areas are fair to partly cloudy and warm, with abundant precipitation central and east, along with cloudy skies and high winds.

Zone 6: The zone is fair and seasonal west and central, and windy and cold east.

Zone 7: Mostly fair except for northern coastal areas, which are windy with precipitation. Temperatures are seasonal to above average.

Zone 8: Alaska—Fair to partly cloudy skies and cold prevail west and central. East is cloudy with precipitation. Hawaii—Fair to partly cloudy with temperatures seasonal to below average.

Full Moon, November 5, 2006

Zone 1: Cold, cloudy, and windy with precipitation.

Zone 2: Windy and fair south. Fair to partly cloudy and cold north.

Zone 3: Blizzard conditions are possible west, where overcast skies yield abundant precipitation. Central and eastern areas are fair to partly cloudy with temperatures seasonal to below average.

Zone 4: Western areas are windy and cold, and central portions of the zone are overcast with abundant precipitation and blizzard potential. Eastern areas are cloudy with precipitation.

Zone 5: Central and east are stormy with blizzard potential, including high winds, overcast skies, and abundant precipitation. Western areas are windy and cloudy with precipitation.

Zone 6: Cloudy with precipitation west and central, and fair skies prevail to the east. Temperatures are seasonal to below average.

Zone 7: Much of the zone is fair and seasonal with temperatures ranging from seasonal to below average, and northern coastal areas are cloudy with precipitation.

Zone 8: Alaska—Western areas are fair. Central and eastern portions of the zone are very windy with abundant precipitation. Hawaii—Windy and cloudy with precipitation.

Third Quarter Moon, November 12, 2006

Zone 1: The zone is variably cloudy with scattered precipitation and temperatures seasonal to below average.

Zone 2: Northern areas are seasonal and fair to partly cloudy with scattered precipitation. Overcast skies yield abundant moisture and cool temperatures to the south.

Zone 3: Overcast in west and central areas, with significant downfall. Fair to partly cloudy and windy east, with temperatures seasonal to below average.

Zone 4: Conditions are fair west. Windy with variably cloudiness with precipitation central. Abundant downfall east.

Zone 5: Fair skies west. Eastern and central areas are windy and stormy with tornado potential and abundant precipitation.

Zone 6: Weather across the zone is fair to partly cloudy, with colder temperatures central and east.

Zone 7: Clouds and precipitation west move inland to central portions of the zone. It's cool east, with precipitation north.

Zone 8: Alaska—Central and eastern areas are very cold with precipitation, and fair and seasonal conditions prevail to the west. Hawaii—Fair, breezy, and seasonal.

New Moon, November 20, 2006

Zone 1: Stormy and overcast with significant downfall.

Zone 2: Areas to the south are windy with precipitation, and northern locations are fair with precipitation later in the week. Temperatures range from seasonal to below average.

Zone 3: Fair skies to the west become cloudy, producing significant moisture. Central and eastern areas are fair, cool, and windy with precipitation east later in the week.

Zone 4: Weather is fair to partly cloudy west with scattered precipitation. Colder and cloudy with significant downfall central. Fair and seasonal east.

Zone 5: Windy and cloudy with precipitation, which is more abundant central and east, along with colder temperatures.

Zone 6: Cloudy skies and precipitation across the zone produce abundant downfall central and east, and temperatures are seasonal to below average.

Zone 7: Cloudy and windy with precipitation, which is abundant in the mountains. Eastern areas are colder.

Zone 8: Alaska—Fair east, with precipitation west and central. Hawaii—Temperatures range from seasonal to above average under mostly fair skies, with precipitation east.

First Quarter Moon, November 28, 2006

Zone 1: Damp, cloudy, and windy, with precipitation and seasonal temperatures.

Zone 2: Cloudy skies and wind produce precipitation, which is more intense to the north. Temperatures are seasonal to below average.

Zone 3: Precipitation throughout the zone is abundant in some locations. Eastern areas are stormy with high winds. Temperatures are seasonal to below average.

Zone 4: Western areas are fair with temperatures seasonal to below average, and cold, windy, cloudy weather, while precipitation prevails east and central.

Zone 5: Fair west and central, where temperatures dip; cold east with precipitation.

Zone 6: Western and central areas are cold and windy with precipitation, and the east is overcast and stormy with abundant downfall.

Zone 7: High winds, cloudy skies, and cold temperatures accompany precipitation, some abundant, throughout the zone.

Zone 8: Alaska—Much of Alaska is cold, cloudy, and wet; and some areas see abundant downfall. Eastern areas are fair. Hawaii—Cloudy and cool with precipitation.

Full Moon, December 4, 2006

Zone 1: Weather is fair and seasonal south, and cloudy, cold and stormy north.

Zone 2: Southern areas are windy and cloudy with precipitation, and weather to the north is seasonal and fair.

Zone 3: Cloudy skies and precipitation in western areas move across the zone. Temperatures are seasonal.

Zone 4: Conditions are fair west, and cloudy with precipitation central and east. Temperatures are seasonal.

Zone 5: The zone is very cold with precipitation central and east, and fair skies west.

Zone 6: Weather is cloudy and cool west before becoming fair and warmer. Central areas see scattered precipitation with fair to partly cloudy skies, and eastern areas are stormy with overcast skies and abundant precipitation.

Zone 7: Skies are fair to partly cloudy with scattered precipitation south, and cooler and cloudier weather north with precipitation. Central areas are partly cloudy and seasonal, and eastern areas are windy and cloudy with precipitation.

Zone 8: Alaska—Skies clear after stormy weather with abundant downfall in central areas moves east. Eastern areas are windy with precipitation. Hawaii—Cloudy and windy with showers west and central, and fair, warm and breezy east.

Third Quarter Moon, December 12, 2006

Zone 1: The zone is overcast with abundant precipitation.

Zone 2: Conditions are cool and windy south with precipitation, and cloudy north with precipitation, some abundant.

Zone 3: Weather is fair and seasonal west, cloudy and windy central with scattered precipitation, and cold and windy east with abundant precipitation northeast.

Zone 4: Areas to the west are fair to partly cloudy with scattered precipitation, and mostly fair east with temperatures seasonal to above average. Central areas are cloudy and cold with precipitation.

Zone 5: Western areas are fair, seasonal and warm, central locations see precipitation, and cloudy, cold, windy weather with precipitation prevails to the east.

Zone 6: Western areas are windy, cloudy and cold, and central and eastern portions of the zone are stormy, cold and windy with abundant precipitation.

Zone 7: Northern coastal areas are partly cloudy and windy, as precipitation centers to the south and inland; abundant downfall in the mountains. Eastern areas are cloudy and windy with precipitation later in the week.

Zone 8: Alaska—The zone is cloudy and windy with precipitation. Hawaii—Seasonal and cloudy with showers, some locally heavy with flood potential.

New Moon, December 20, 2006

Zone 1: The zone is seasonal with precipitation.

Zone 2: Variable cloudiness, scattered clouds and cool temperatures prevail to the south, and northern areas are windy and cold with abundant downfall.

Zone 3: Weather is windy and fair west and central, and colder east with precipitation, some abundant.

Zone 4: Western skies are fair to partly cloudy and breezy with scattered precipitation. Central locations are stormy, and eastern areas are windy and fair to partly cloudy.

Zone 5: Conditions are fair and warm west and variably cloudy and cooler central and east with scattered precipitation.

Zone 6: Weather is fair to partly cloudy west, windy central with scattered precipitation, and cold and windy with precipitation east.

Zone 7: Western and central areas are mostly fair and windy with temperatures ranging from seasonal to below average. Eastern locations are windy with precipitation, stormy in the mountains and then colder.

Zone 8: Alaska—Abundant precipitation falls from overcast skies in central areas. Weather is fair and seasonal west and east. Hawaii—Western and central areas are warm, humid, cloudy and breezy with precipitation. Eastern areas are cooler and overcast with significant downfall.

First Quarter Moon, December 27, 2006

Zone 1: Scattered precipitation accompanies fair to partly cloudy weather south, and northern areas are windy and cold with precipitation later in the week.

Zone 2: Southern areas of the zone are cloudy and windy with precipitation, and fair skies and seasonal temperatures prevail to the north.

Zone 3: Cloudy weather west yields precipitation, some abundant with flood potential. Central areas are colder and overcast, and to the east, skies are windy and fair.

Zone 4: Fair weather prevails west and central, where temperatures are seasonal to below average. Eastern areas are cloudy with precipitation, some abundant, and potential for thawing and flooding.

Zone 5: Weather is fair west, cooler central, and cloudy east, with precipitation and flood potential.

Zone 6: Eastern and central areas are cloudy, windy, and cool with precipitation, and fair and windy skies with seasonal temperatures prevail to the west.

Zone 7: Skies are fair to partly cloudy and windy north with a chance for precipitation, while southern coastal and inland areas see precipitation. Weather to the east is fair, cool and windy.

Zone 8: Alaska—Central areas are very cold, windy, and dry. Eestern areas are fair; stormy east. Hawaii—Cool, windy, and fair.

New Moon, December 31, 2005

Zone 1: Precipitation across the zone, with some significant downfall to the south. Wind prevails, and temperatures are seasonal to below average.

Zone 2: Temperatures are cooler to the south, while northern areas are more seasonal. Cloudy skies signal precipitation across much of the zone.

Zone 3: Conditions are seasonal east and central under fair to partly cloudy skies. Temperatures dip to the east under cloudy skies that bring precipitation.

Zone 4: Western areas are stormy with precipitation. Central portions of the zone are fair to partly cloudy with a lower range of temperatures and a chance for precipitation. The east is mostly dry and seasonal.

Zone 5: Fair skies and temperatures ranging from seasonal to above average prevail in western and central areas, while the east sees variable cloudiness and cooler weather.

Zone 6: Stormy and cold with high winds in eastern areas. Western portions see cool and windy, and central areas are seasonal with precipitation.

Zone 7: Cloudy and wet in southern coastal areas, moving inland and bringing significant precipitation to the mountains and eastern portions of the zone. Northern coastal and central areas can expect precipitation with seasonal to cool temperatures.

Zone 8: Alaska—Western and central areas are cold, windy, and stormy, with significant precipitation. Fair to partly cloudy skies and temperatures ranging from seasonal to below average prevail to the east. Hawaii—Windy, wet, and cool as a front moves through the state.

Kris Brandt Riske holds professional certification from the American Federation of Astrologers (AFA). She's the author of Astrometeorology: Planetary Power in Weather Forecasting, *and of Llewellyn titles* Mapping Your Money *and* Mapping Your Future. *She resides in Arizona.*

Electional Astrology:
The Art of Timing
by Joann Hampar

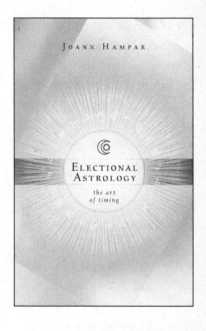

Planning a wedding? Scheduling surgery? Buying a house? How do you choose a date and time that offers the best chance of success? The odds are in your favor when you plan life events using electional astrology—a branch of astrology that helps you align with the power of the universe. Professional astrologer Joann Hampar teaches the principles of electional astrology—explaining the significance of each planet and how to time events according to their cycles. Readers will learn how to analyze the planetary alignments and compile an electional chart that pinpoints the optimal time to buy a diamond ring, adopt a pet, close a business deal, take a trip, move, file an insurance claim, take an exam, schedule a job interview, and just about anything else!

ISBN: 0-7387-0701-5 • 216 pp. • 6 x 9 • U.S. $14.95

The Art of Predictive Astrology:
Forecasting Your Life Events

Carol Rushman

Become an expert at seeing the future in anyone's astrological chart! Insight into the future is a large part of the intrigue and mystery of astrology. *The Art of Predictive Astrology* clearly lays out a step-by-step system that astrologers can use to forecast significant events including love and financial success. When finished with the book, readers will be able to predict cycles and trends for the next several years, and give their clients fifteen important dates for the coming year. An emphasis is on progressions, eclipses, and lunations as important predictive tools.

ISBN: 0-7387-0164-5 • 288 pp.• 6 x 9 • U.S. $14.95

Lunar Returns

by John Townley

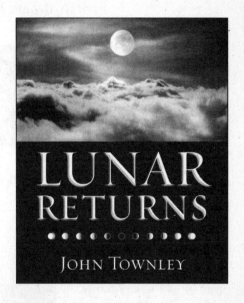

Cast your lunar chart to unravel the surprises and opportunities for the next 27 ½ days. Each month of your life has its own special dynamic—will it come on like a juggernaut, sneak up like a cat, or stride in like a hero? Find the answer when the transiting Moon hits your natal Moon. This is your lunar return—an emotional rebirthing that occurs every twenty-seven-and-a-half days.

The lunar return chart exposes the immediate terrain of your life and can guide your day-to-day decisions. It lives in its own right and in relation to the natal chart, and it responds to transits during the month.

This book explores the interpretation of the lunar return in depth. Learn the five significant factors to be delineated through the lunar return chart, and refer to the extensive cookbook-style reference section of houses, aspects, and transits.

ISBN: 0-7387-0302-8 • 272 pp. • 7 ½ x 9 ⅛ • U.S. 19.95

Mapping Your Money:
Understanding Your Financial Potential

by Kris Brandt Riske

From the rich to the impoverished, money plays an important role in all our lives. Getting a grasp on finances can be as simple as consulting the stars. Whether you're a pinchpenny or a spendthrift, *Mapping Your Money* can help you understand your money mindset and financial outlook.

How can I become more wealthy? Why is my sister so frugal? Is it too late to change my spending habits? These and other financial questions can be answered with this valuable astrological tool. No previous astrological knowledge is needed. A birth date and time is all that's required to astrologically analyze financial traits for yourself and others. Includes a CD-ROM for PC format with Windows 95/98/ME/XP.

ISBN: 0-7387-0672-8 • 240 pp. • 7 ½ x 9 ⅛ • U.S. $19.95

Mapping Your Birthchart:
Understanding Your Needs and Potential
by Stephanie Jean Clement, Ph.D.

You know your "sign," but that's just the tip of the astrological iceberg. You've got a Moon sign, a rising sign, and loads of other factors in your astrological make-up. Together they form the complete picture of you as an individual: your desires, talents, emotions, public persona, and your private needs.

Mapping Your Birthchart removes the mystery from astrology so you can look at any chart and get a basic understanding of the person behind it. Learn the importance of the planets, the different signs of the zodiac, and how they relate to your everyday life. A chapter is devoted to each planet and provides simple explanations of astrological and psychological factors, and includes examples from the charts of well-known people including Tiger Woods, Celine Dion, and George W. Bush.

Includes a CD-ROM that allows you to calculate and interpret your birthchart, and print out astrological reports and charts for yourself, your family, and friends.

ISBN: 0-7387-0202-1 • 240 pp. • 7 ½ x 9 ⅛ • U.S. $19.95

New A to Z Horoscope Maker and Interpreter

by Llewellyn George

New and improved: the #1 astrology text in the world! For ninety-three years, astrologers the world over have trusted the *A to Z* as their primary textbook and reference for all major facets of astrology.

Now this famous classic enters the new millennium with a huge makeover and additions totaling more than 31,000 words. Today's generation of astrologers can benefit from Llewellyn George's timeless interpretations, along with new material by contemporary astrologer and author Stephanie Jean Clement. The expansion includes modern developments in astrology as well as a study guide, making Llewellyn's *New A to Z* the most comprehensive self-study course available. (The classic text revised and expanded by Marylee Bytheriver and Stephanie Jean Clement, Ph.D. includes a free birth chart offer.)

ISBN: 0-7387-0322-2 • 504 pp. • 7½ x 9⅛ • U.S. $19.95

Llewellyn's 2006 Starview Almanac
An Astrological Look at People, Events & Trends

Find out what the planets are saying about our world in Llewellyn's *Starview Almanac*. Renowned astrologers provide reliable insight into politics, entertainment, and the economy. Forecasts and trends relating to current events and issues, such as employment, robotics, rock stars, and the shaky status of Social Security, are discussed in everyday language. Also included are financial and weather forecasts for 2006 and profiles of famous people, such as

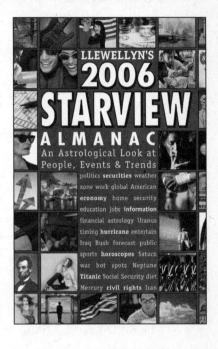

Michael Moore, Martha Stewart, and Arnold Schwarzenegger. Includes calendar with weekly forecasts.

ISBN: 0-7387-0676-0 • 288 pp. • 5 ¼ x 8 • U.S. $8.99

Llewellyn's
2006 Daily Planetary Guide

More than a datebook, the *Daily Planetary Guide* is a powerhouse of planetary insight. It has all the day-to-day astrological information anyone could want between two covers. Knowing when to schedule a long-awaited vacation or ask for that much-deserved raise is made a whole lot easier when you tap into the powerful energies that affect you every day.

This year's edition features Opportunity Periods—times when the positive flow of energy won't be obstructed by transiting planets. From closing a business deal to searching for romance, astrologer Jim Shawvan also explains how to take advantage of these special times. Spiral-bound datebook with ephemerides.

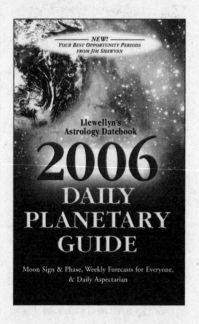

ISBN: 0-7387-0155-6 • 208 pp. • 5¼ x 8 • U.S. $9.99

Llewellyn's 2006 Sun Sign Book

Horoscopes for Everyone!

Why purchase a book about only one zodiac sign when you can get the scoop on every sign in Llewellyn's generous *Sun Sign Book*? Gain amazing insights into yourself and all the important people in your life with upbeat and perceptive horoscopes by astrologer Terry Lamb.

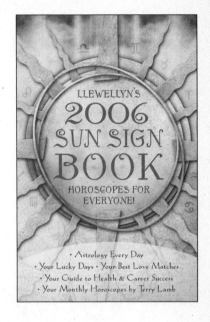

Plus, you'll get articles from our trusted experts, including "Your Soul's Purpose" by Anne Windsor; "Solar Return Highlights" by Dorothy Oja; and "Astrological Qualities" by Sasha Fenton.

ISBN: 0-7387-0149-1 • 384 pp. • 5¼ x 8 • U.S. $7.99

Notes:

Notes:

Notes:

Notes:

Notes: